Human and Natural Resources of India

Human and Natural Resources of India

K. Narindar Jetli

New Century Publications
New Delhi, India

NEW CENTURY PUBLICATIONS
4800/24, Bharat Ram Road,
Ansari Road, Daryaganj,
New Delhi – 110 002 (India)

Tel.: 011-2324 7798, 4358 7398, 6539 6605
Fax: 011-4101 7798
E-mail: indiatax@vsnl.com • info@newcenturypublications.com
www.newcenturypublications.com

Editorial office:
LG–7, Aakarshan Bhawan,
4754-57/23, Ansari Road, Daryaganj,
New Delhi – 110 002

Tel.: 011-4356 0919

First Published: **July 2010**

ISBN: **978-81-7708-236-4**

Published by New Century Publications and printed at Salasar Imaging Systems, New Delhi.

Designs: Patch Creative Unit, New Delhi.

PRINTED IN INDIA

Brief Contents

Detailed Contents

Part III: Natural Resources

About the Book

The resource base of a country consists of (a) human resources, (b) non-renewable resources which are an endowment of nature and whose total size gets depleted with time and (c) renewable resources which can be continuously created and whose base can be expanded through human efforts.

The Planning Commission—set up in March 1950 by a resolution of the Government of India—makes an assessment of the material, capital and human resources of the country, including technical personnel, and investigates the possibilities of augmenting such of these resources as are found to be deficient in relation to the nation's requirements. Further, it formulates a Plan for the most effective and balanced utilisation of the country's resources.

The objective of planning is to raise the standard of living of the people as a whole. The attainment of this objective involves the development on scientific lines of the nation's human and natural resources.

National Development Council (NDC)—set up in August 1952—reviews the working of the National Plan from time to time, considers important questions of social and economic policy affecting national development and recommends measures for the achievement of the aims and targets of the National Plan.

NDC, being the apex body for economic matters, takes all final decisions as regards the size, contents, objectives, and strategies of the Plan. The Planning Commission functions as an advisory body to NDC.

This book provides a vivid account of the various dimensions of human and natural resources of India and the issues associated with their utilization.

Author's Profile

K. Narindar Jetli did his post-graduation from the University of Delhi. He worked for 30 years (1963-1993) with Indian Oil Corporation (IOC), a Fortune 500 company. At IOC, he served as a senior officer and worked in the public relations, operations, sales and marketing departments.

Mr. Jetli is currently General Manager (HRD and Administration) with Jaquar & Co. Ltd. (an ISO 9001:2000 company), New Delhi. He was elected as member of Confederation of Indian Industry (CII), Delhi State Council for 2002-03.

He has also delivered lectures at the Delhi School of Economics, University of Delhi, International School of Business, New Delhi, International School of Business and Media, Kolkata and Pune and Institute of Productivity and Management, Meerut. He is also on the panel for selecting students for admission in these management institutes. He has so far written 3 books, viz. *Industry and Infrastructure Development in India Since 1947*; *India: Manpower, Employment Policy and Labour Welfare, 1947 to 2007* and *India: Economic Reforms and Labour Policy.* He has also contributed numerous articles in journals and newspapers of repute.

Preface

The resource base of a country consists of (a) human resources, (b) non-renewable resources which are an endowment of nature and whose total size gets depleted with time and (c) renewable resources which can be continuously created and whose base can be expanded through human efforts.

Utilisation of Human and Natural Resources in India

Vide entry 20 of List III (Concurrent List) of the Seventh Schedule of the Constitution of India, economic and social planning is a subject in which the Centre as well as the States are interested and have to work in unison. The Centre has certain emergency powers, but normally coordination of policies is effected through mutual consultation. This system of consultation and of formulation of policies on the basis of over-all national requirements is ensured in the interests of planning. Care is taken to see that the plan is implemented throughout the country as a single coordinated whole. The National Development Council is intended to secure this result. It is obvious that without complete coordination of policies and timely, concerted action, there is danger of waste and misdirection of effort, which may have consequences extending far beyond the area of responsibility of any single authority, and this places special responsibilities on the Centre. In short, planning is a matter of common interest to the Central and the State Governments.

Planning Commission: The Planning Commission was set up in March 1950 by a resolution of the Government of India which defined the scope of its work in the following terms:

"The Constitution of India has guaranteed certain Fundamental Rights to the citizens of India and enunciated certain Directive Principles of State Policy, in particular, that the State shall strive to promote the welfare of the people by securing and protecting as effectively as it may a social order in which justice, social, economic and political shall form all the institutions of the national life, and shall direct its policy towards securing, among other things:

(a) that the citizens, men and women equally, have the right to an adequate means of livelihood;

(b) that the ownership and control of the material resources of the community are so distributed as best to subserve the common good; and

(c) that the operation of the economic system does not result in the concentration of wealth and means of production to the common detriment.

Having regard to these rights and in furtherance of these principles as well as of the declared objective of the Government to promote a rapid rise in the standard of living of the people by efficient exploitation of the resources of the country, increasing production and offering opportunities to all for employment in the service of the community,

The Planning Commission will:

(1) make an assessment of the material, capital and human resources of the country, including technical personnel, and investigate the possibilities of augmenting such of these resources as are found to be deficient in relation to the nation's requirements;

(2) formulate a Plan for the most effective and balanced utilisation of the country's resources;

(3) on a determination of priorities, define the stages in which the Plan should be carried out and propose the allocation of resources for the due completion of each stage;

(4) indicate the factors which are tending to retard economic development, and determine the conditions which, in view of the current social and political situation, should be established for the successful execution of the Plan;

(5) determine the nature of the machinery which will be necessary for securing the successful implementation of each stage of the Plan in all its aspects;

(6) appraise from time to time the progress achieved in the execution of each stage of the Plan and recommend the adjustments of policy and measures that such appraisal may show to be necessary; and

(7) make such interim or ancillary recommendations as appear to it to be appropriate either for facilitating the discharge of the duties assigned to it; or, on a consideration of the prevailing economic conditions, current policies, measures and development programmes; or on an examination of such specific problems as may be referred to it for advice by Central or State Governments."

Accordingly, the First Five Year Plan (1951-56) presented an account of the land, water, mineral and energy resources of the country on the basis of information then available. It drew attention to the main problems in each field and set out programmes for further surveys and investigations. It also offered suggestions for strengthening the organisations responsible for these surveys, providing them with personnel and equipment, and expanding programmes of training.

The objective of planning is to raise the standard of living of the people as a whole. The attainment of this objective involves the development on scientific lines of the nation's human and natural resources.

National Development Council (NDC): The NDC was set up in August 1952 with the following objectives.

1. To review the working of the National Plan from time to time.
2. To consider important questions of social and economic policy affecting national development.
3. To recommend measures for the achievement of the aims and targets of the National Plan.

The Planning Commission prepares the blueprint of economic plans in consultation with the States and in accordance with the guidelines provided by the National Development Council (NDC) which consists of the Prime Minister (chairman), Central Cabinet Ministers, Chief

Ministers of the States, and Members of the Planning Commission. After the draft plan is approved by the NDC and finalised by the Central Government, it is implemented, to a substantial extent, through the state machinery. Apparently, successful execution of a plan presupposes co-operation between the Central and the State Governments.

NDC, being the apex body for economic matters, takes all final decisions as regards the size, contents, objectives, and strategies of the Plan. The Planning Commission functions as an advisory body to NDC.

Human Resources

Human resources in terms of demographic trends are important, as also the development of human resources through programmes in education, health, social welfare and science and technology. In the long-run, the improvement in the standard of living of a country depends largely on the nature of technology which it adopts. It is advanced technology which can create sufficient surplus to generate resources for accelerated growth. However, the avoidance of a mismatch between the technology adopted and the institutional structure, including the organisation and distribution system of a country, is very important.

Thus, the technology revolution in India and the associated necessary changes in the social strata and the growth of human capital and communication have to keep pace with each other over this long term horizon.

Natural Resources

Expanded demand for natural resources and materials has led to technological developments which have in part overcome limitations and thus increased the supply of resources. The dynamic forces at work in creating shifts in the demand for and supply of natural resources necessitate their continuous study as well as reformulation of policies relating to them. Natural resources must be looked at in a coordinated manner and their investigation and utilisation planned for long-term needs. The extent to which resources have been studied and possibilities established ahead of needs is an important factor determining the rate at which the economy can grow.

Natural resources give India a large potential for agricultural and industrial production, and their rapid development is an essential condition for the achievement of a self-reliant and self-sustained economy which can provide to the mass of the people continually rising living standards and opportunities for gainful employment.

Natural resources cover a most extensive field and it is not possible to do more than touch upon a few broad features of the subject. A great deal of new information regarding the country's natural resources has become available. The principal organisations engaged in surveys of resources are now equipped with personnel and expertise to expand their activities even more rapidly in the future. States are also more fully seized of their own problems of resource development. Considerable numbers of highly trained scientists and technologists are already engaged in studies relating to resources. There is growing recognition of the need for conservation of natural resources in all fields.

However, in this direction much still remains to be done. A great deal of valuable scientific research is being undertaken for resource location and resource utilisation in the National Laboratories, in the universities and in other research establishments. Technological changes are already transforming the economic life of the country. With economic development, there will also be greater technological progress and many new possibilities will open up.

May 2010
New Delhi

K. Narindar Jetli

Part I: Human Resources: Magnitude, Quality and Deployment

1

Demographic Trends and Policy

After China, India is the most populated country in the world accounting for 16 percent of world population and having only 2.4 percent of total world area.

1.1 Socio-economic Profile of India

India inherited a dismal economy from the British rulers at the time of Independence in 1947. Owing to poor technological and scientific capabilities, industrialisation was limited and lop-sided. Agricultural sector exhibited features of feudal and semi-feudal institutions, resulting into low productivity. Means of transport and communications were underdeveloped, educational and health facilities inadequate and social security measures virtually non-existent. In brief, poverty was rampant and unemployment widespread, both making for low general standard of living. In short, the country was backward in every respect.

Even after more than six decades of developmental efforts, India is a low-income developing economy, facing the twin formidable problems of unemployment and poverty. It suffers from over-population which shows no signs of abating. Its high birth-rate coupled with declining death-rate provides typical example of the *second stage* of the demographic transition theory. The sharp fall in death-rate is attributable mainly to improved health conditions, control of epidemics, better handling of famine conditions and general improvement in the standard of living. As a direct consequence of high birth-rate and low death-rate, India continues to register around 1.5 percent annual growth rate in population. Population explosion has thrown to winds the gains of developmental plans and the policy makers are baffled by the prospects of further increase in population.

The rapid growth of population has resulted in high density of population, leading to pressure on natural resources, particularly land. For example, the land-man ratio in India declined from 0.92 hectare in 1951 to 0.48 hectare in 1981 and further down to 0.33 hectare in the year 2000. [1] Although Indian economy is basically rural in nature, rising trend toward urbanisation is noticeable. This trend has been accompanied by such ill-effects as congestion, pollution, lawlessness and transport and housing difficulties. Resources of the Central and State Governments are under severe strain in view of the ever-increasing need for civic amenities. This has cut into the funds available for developmental projects.

Apart from low level of per capita income, factors affecting physical quality of life index are also reflective of poverty in India.

The country remained trapped in a low level average GDP growth rate of 3-4 percent per annum during 1950-80. It picked up to 5-6 percent during 1980-90 and further up to 7-8 percent since the initiation of economic reforms in 1991. Annual growth rate of per capita income has remained relatively low due to rapid growth of population.

1.2 Pre-Independence Demographic Trends

The first all-India census was completed in 1872. Thereafter decennial censuses have been organised. Demographic trends during pre-Independence period may be divided into two periods: (a) Pre-1921, a period of slow and fluctuating population growth and (b) Post-1921, a period of steady and accelerating growth of population. The year 1921 is therefore, called as *the year of great divide*.

Prior to 1921, the growth of population was not only slow but erratic. In fact, India's population declined during the decade 1911-1921 (Table 1.1). The slow and sporadic growth was the result of abnormal deaths due to famines and epidemics whose incidence was severe in some decades. To start with, there was the great Indian famine of 1867-68. Again, the decade 1891-1901 saw the recurrence of famines in many parts of the country. The effects of famines were reinforced by the outbreak of plague, malaria and *kala azar* in fairly extensive areas. The decade 1901-1910 was comparatively normal. The most outstanding catastrophe of the next decade 1911-1921 was the great influenza epidemic of 1918 which claimed around one million lives.

Table 1.1: Population Growth and Projections, 1901-2011

Period	Population at the end of the period (as on 1st March)		Per thousand population		
	Total (in millions)	Urban population as percent of total population	Birth rate	Death rate	Growth rate
1901-11	252.09	10.29	49.20	42.60	6.60
1911-21	251.32	11.18	48.10	48.60	-0.50
1921-31	278.98	11.99	46.40	36.30	10.10
1931-41	318.66	13.86	45.20	31.20	14.00
1941-51	361.09	17.29	39.90	27.40	12.50
1951-61	439.23	17.97	41.70	22.80	18.90
1961-71	548.16	19.91	41.20	19.00	22.20
1971-81	683.33	23.34	37.20	15.00	22.20
1981-91	844.32	25.72	32.50	11.40	21.10
1991-96	925.13	27.82	27.50	9.40	18.10
1996-01	1006.20	30.50	24.90	8.40	16.50
2001-06	1085.98	33.48	23.00	7.80	15.20
2006-11	1164.25	36.57	20.90	7.10	13.80

Source: Government of India, Planning Commission, *Eighth Five Year Plan* (1992-97), Vol. I, pp. 22-23, Tables 2.1 and 2.2.

After 1921, the country faced no major calamity except for the great Bengal famine of 1943. Extension of irrigation facilities and improvements in transport and communications kept off any widespread famine. Similarly, improvements in public health and sanitation prevented the outbreak of any major epidemic.

Trends in population growth may be better understood by analysing the trends in birth and death-rate during pre and post-1921 period.

Until 1921, death-rate was high and erratic and ranged between 42 and 48 per thousand during 1901-1921. Apart from natural calamities, death-rate was high on account of malnutrition, poor sanitation, and lack of medical facilities.

Birth-rate was also high, hovering around 48 per thousand during 1901-1921. It was high on account of widespread illiteracy, early age of marriage, absence of family planning techniques, and deep-rooted religious and social beliefs about family size and male children. In India, the mean age at marriage has been low as compared to other countries of the world. Moreover, the compulsions of an agrarian economy also promoted large families.

Broadly speaking, the pre-1921 period belonged to the first stage of demographic transition theory. High birth-rate was balanced by high death-rate, and the growth rate of population was marginal.

The post-1921 period witnessed a steady decline in death-rate, largely due to the control of widespread epidemics like plague, smallpox and cholera. Demographers have observed that death-rate can be reduced more easily because it is affected by exogenous factors like control of epidemics, immunisation programmes, better sanitation, and improvements in nutritional levels. Moreover, improvements in transport and communications made food supplies more regular, reducing the chances and severity of famines. Death-rate declined from 48 per thousand for the decade 1911-21, to 36 for 1921-31, to 31 for 1931-41 and further down to 27 for the decade 1941-51. The declining trend has continued since then (Table 1.1).

However, birth-rate continued to remain high till

Independence, hovering around 45 per thousand. Birth-rate is determined by endogenous factors like social and religious beliefs about marriage, family size, male children, and family planning methods. Clearly, it requires a much longer time to change the social attitudes of the people. In other words, birth-rate tends to fall after a time lag. The high birth-rate and the declining death-rate after 1921 caused India's population to grow at an accelerated rate. The *second stage* of demographic transition theory had set in. [2]

In short, demographic trends during colonial period were typical of an underdeveloped agrarian economy. There was neither any thinking nor any programme for family planning, and family welfare. There was hardly any population policy of the British rulers.

1.3 Post-Independence Demographic Trends

India's population has increased rapidly since Independence in 1947. The population increased from 36.1 crore in 1951 to 43.9 crore in 1961, to 54.8 crore in 1971, and to 68.5 crore in 1981. The census of 1991 enumerated the population at 84.4 crore which rose to 102.9 crore in 2001 and is projected at 116.4 crore in the year 2011. Thus, after China it is India that has crossed the 1 billion population mark. According to Economic Survey, 2001-02, "It is now estimated that by 2050, India will most likely overtake China to become the most populous country on the earth with 17.2 percent population living here." [3]

The unabated growth of population is attributable to a sharp decline in death-rate coupled with relatively high birth-rate. The 2001 Census recorded birth-rate and death-rate at 25.8 and 8.5 percent respectively for the year 2001. During 1951-71, birth-rate remained almost unchanged while death-rate declined appreciably (Table 1.1). The death-rate has fallen due to improved health conditions, control of epidemics, better handling of famine conditions, and general improvement in the standard of living. There has been a significant decline in the infant mortality rate since Independence.

However, birth-rate in India is still very high, hovering in the vicinity of 26 per thousand. Many social and economic factors are responsible for high birth-rate. These include universality of marriage, preference for male children, illiteracy, and poverty. The rapid growth of population has seriously hampered developmental efforts.

1.4 Characteristics of India's Population

1.4.1 Age Composition: Age composition of population is important because it indicates the dependency ratio of the population. Dependency ratio is defined as the ratio of children below 15 years to population above 15 years. The age composition also determines the proportion of the labour force (15-60 years) in the total population. Projections of total population and its age structure are given in Table 1.2. Due to expected decline in fertility and mortality, the age structure of the population will change in the future.

Table 1.2: Projections of Age Structure of India's Population

(million)

Year	2006	2011	2016	2021	2026
Total	1112 (100.0)	1193 (100.0)	1269 (100.0)	1340 (100.0)	1400 (100.0)
Below 15 years	357 (32.1)	347 (29.1)	340 (26.8)	337 (25.1)	327 (23.4)
15-64 years	699 (62.9)	780 (65.4)	851 (67.1)	908 (67.8)	957 (68.3)
Above 65 years	56 (5.0)	66 (5.5)	78 (6.1)	95 (7.1)	116 (8.3)

Figures in parentheses are percentages of respective totals.

Source: Government of India, *Economic Survey*, 2006-07, p. 215, Table 10.7 (excerpted).

1.4.2 Sex Ratio: In 1921, the number of females per thousand males was 955. This trend has persisted till today with minor variations. There are many reasons for excess of male over female population. The lack of pre-natal and post-natal care has been the major cause of high death-rate among women in reproductive age. The evil practice of female infanticide in some parts of the country during British rule also contributed to reduced share of female population in total population. The preference for male child persists even to this day and is reflected in better food and other amenities of life provided to boys in preference to girls.

The trend of sex ratio in India has been in favour of masculine population. According to the 1991 census, there were 927 females per thousand males. As per 2001 Census, the sex ratio stood at 933 females per 1,000 males, a marginal improvement over 1991. The persistent tendency towards low sex ratio can be attributed to lack of attention and care given to female children, sex selective female abortions, and the higher death-rate among women in the reproductive age. It is noteworthy that in Western countries, the sex ratio favours the feminine population.

Expressing concern over the decline in the sex ratio, the Ninth Five Year Plan (1997-2002) observed, "One of the features of Indian demographic behaviour which has been the cause for considerable concern has been the more or less steady decline in the sex ratio during the current century from 972 females per thousand males in 1901 to 927 in 1991. The factors responsible for this continued decline are as yet not clearly identified. However, it is well recognised that the adverse sex ratio is a reflection of gender disparity and appropriate steps to correct this trend will need to be taken during the Ninth Plan period." [4]

1.4.3 Life Expectancy: In 1993-94, life expectancy in India at birth was 60.3 years (59.7 for males and 60.9 for females). [5] At the current level (2001), it stands at 65.3 (63.8 for males and 66.9 for females).

The life expectancy has improved after Independence owing to decline in infant mortality, control of epidemics, and general improvement in the standard of living. Life expectancy of both males and females is projected to increase in the coming decades.

1.4.4 Literacy: Literacy is an important factor in judging the quality of population. For the purpose of the census, a person is deemed as literate if he or she can read and write with understanding in any language. A person who can merely read but cannot write is not defined as literate. In 1990-91, the literacy percentage was 52.20 (males 64.10 and females 39.30). [6] The literacy rate recorded an increase of 13.17 percentage points from 1991 to 2001, standing at 65.38 (males 75.85 and females 54.16) as per Census 2001.

Illiteracy is widespread in rural areas as compared to urban areas. Therefore, concerted efforts are needed to direct literacy programmes towards rural areas with particular emphasis on female literacy.

1.4.5 Degree of Urbanisation: Urbanisation is directly associated with economic development. In fact, a shift of population from rural to urban areas is an indicator of economic development. The shift of population to urban areas was slow during British rule, signifying that the process of economic development itself was slow during that period. Urban population which formed 10 percent of total population in 1911, moderately increased to 14 percent in 1941. This was in sharp contrast to the urbanisation trend taking place in Europe.

India ranks poorly among the countries of the world in respect of degree of urbanisation. The share of urban population in total population was 25.7 percent in 1991 which increased to 27.8 percent in 2001, as per Census 2001. With prospect of industrialisation and the consequent migration of rural population to urban areas, the trend toward urbanisation will gain momentum. In this context, the Eighth Five Year Plan (1992-97) observed, "There has been a marked acceleration in urbanisation over the past two decades. If the present trends continue, urban population may account for about one-third of the total population by the turn of the century. Urban infrastructure, even at a minimum level, for this size of population will need considerable resources." [7]

Some States such as Tamil Nadu and Maharashtra are now more than 40 percent urban. There are now 35 cities with a population of above 1 million, as compared with 23 in 1991. As the proportion of the urban population continues to grow, investments in urban infrastructure for the provision of services such as roads, water supply and sewerage, urban transportation and the like will need to be much higher than they have been in the past.

1.4.6 Density of Population: Density of population means the average number of persons living per sq. k.m. of area. The density of population has increased steadily from 117 persons in 1951 to 216 persons in 1981, 274 persons in 1991, and 324 persons in 2001. Since density of population indicates the land-man ratio, it is clear that this ratio has been declining over the years.

1.5 Population as a Retarding Factor in Development

The present size and the growth rate of India's population is a drag on available economic resources. It is hindering the development process and defeating the twin objectives of removal of poverty and unemployment. The pressure of population is being felt in a variety of ways. As the Eighth Five Year Plan (1992-97) observed, "It is tempting to think that if only India had succeeded in containing her population growth rate after 1951 to around one percent per annum i.e. the rate China has achieved, how much difference this factor alone would have meant in terms of per capita income, consumption and levels of living." [8]

1.5.1 Population and Per Capita Income: A strong relationship exists between population and per capita income. National income/population=Per capita income. Economic development is generally defined in terms of increase in real per capita income. The high growth rate of population has depressed the increase in per capita income in India. During the post-Independence period, national income has increased, on the average, by 3-4 percent per annum, called by late Professor Raj Krishna as the *Hindu rate of growth*. With population growing at the rate of around 2 percent per annum, the increase in per capita income has been in the range of 1-2 percent per year.

1.5.2 Population and Food Supply: The rapid increase in India's population has called for tremendous efforts to augment food supplies. Total foodgrains production in the country was 50 million tonnes in 1951. In 1999-2000, it was 208.9 million tonnes and is expected to be 233.88 million tonnes in 2008-09. [9] In spite of this remarkable increase in foodgrains production, shortages are felt in different parts of the country and rationing system is continuing and being strengthened in backward districts of the country.

1.5.3 Population and Land-Man Ratio: The pressure of population has adversely affected the land-man ratio. Presently, the per capita availability of cultivable land is 0.17 hectare. The growing pressure of population has also led to sub-division and fragmentation of holdings. The widespread disguised unemployment in the agricultural sector is also indicative of the burden of population on land.

1.5.4 Population and Unemployment: An increase in population is invariably accompanied by an increase in labour force. The growing unemployment in India reflects the failure of the economy to absorb the net additions to the labour force. Given the present backlog of unemployment, the continuing increase in population will further aggravate the unemployment in the years to come.

1.5.5 Population and Basic Amenities: Unabated growth of population has exerted great pressure on the demand for basic amenities of life such as housing, and medical and educational facilities. Considerable resources are being diverted to meet basic needs of the teeming millions. This has adversely affected the availability of resources for developmental projects.

1.6 Population Policy

The alarming growth of India's population calls for a systematic and effective population policy to curb the undesirable trend. The post-Independence population explosion has nullified, to a large extent, the gains of developmental efforts.

The policy of the Government of India to control population has relied excessively on family planning programme. Ever since the launching of the First Five Year Plan (1951-56), family planning has occupied an important place in the development strategy of the Government. Successive plans have allocated more and more resources for the implementation of family planning schemes. In 1966, a separate Department of Family Planning was created in the Union Ministry of Health. However, the results have not been encouraging.

Eighth Five Year Plan (1992-97) sounded a distressing note on country's population growth. It warned against the disastrous consequences of population growth with regard to social and economic justice. Aptly summarising the adverse impact of population growth on the India economy, it lamented, "A sustained high growth rate has pushed the Indian population to unsupportable numbers. The 1991 Census revealed a population of 844 million. Such dizzying rate of population growth negates whatever gains the nation has been able to achieve in agriculture, industrial and services sectors. Also, this leads to an unbearable burden on health, education, and housing sectors. If this trend is not halted, it will never be possible to render social and economic justice to millions of our masses. The current rate of population growth is simply not sustainable." [10] In nutshell, the population explosion has proved a damper on the developmental efforts of the economy.

The National Population Policy (NPP) 2000 outlined the long-term objective of attaining a stable population by 2045, a level consistent with the requirements of sustainable economic growth, social development and environment protection. Apart from implementation of the National Population Policy involving all social sector programmes, the State Governments too will have to play an important role in improving the social, economic and demographic indicators especially in the high fertility regions. In the long-run, it is necessary to have an explicit demographic vision of attaining less than half percent annual growth rate of population by the end of next decade. This would involve significant upgradation of the status of women in the society and attainment of almost 100 percent literacy among adult females.

Satisfactorily, the decadal growth of population at 21.34 percent between 1991 and 2001 was the sharpest decline in the rate of growth of population witnessed since Independence, with the average exponential growth rate declining from 2.14 percent per annum during the previous decade to 1.93 percent per annum. The declining trends indicate that the country is entering a phase of rapidly declining fertility in its process of demographic transition.

Sounding a note of optimism on demographic trends in India, the Approach Paper to the Eleventh Five Year Plan (2007-12) remarked, "In the longer run, there is another important potential strength arising from our demographic trends. Our dependency rate (ratio of dependent to working age population) is falling whereas that of industrialised countries and even China is rising. The presence of a skilled young population in an environment where investment is expanding and the industrial world ageing could be a major advantage. It is however important to realise that we can only reap this demographic dividend if we invest massively on human resource development and skill formation and create an economic environment capable of absorbing our relatively young working population in productive employment." [11]

Population stabilisation is crucial for the achievement of the goal of sustainable development and an equitable distribution of resources/opportunities. Though Government initiatives exist in the form of suitable public policies on education, health and family welfare along with economic incentives and facilities for small and micro-families, these measures have had a limited impact on the fertility, net reproduction rates and the family size. Improved access to primary and secondary education extension of basic amenities, the empowerment of women, awareness gene-ration and a better standard of living would ultimately contribute towards inculcation of the required consciousness regarding the desirability of a small family size.

1.7 Measures to Control Population

The teeming millions of India pose a serious challenge to country's development efforts. The urgency to arrest the expansion of population is almost unanimously felt and a multi-pronged attack on the vexatious problem is needed.

1.7.1 Economic Measures: On the economic front, gigantic efforts are required to expand the industrial base of the economy. Particular attention has to be paid to develop small-scale and cottage industries in every corner of the country. This policy will help absorb the backlog of unemployment in urban areas and reduce pressure of population on land.

1.7.2 Social Measures: On the social plane, a frontal attack on illiteracy is required to remove superstitions and orthodoxy associated with marriage and family size. Under the Child Marriage Restraint Act, 1903 the minimum age of marriage was 18 years for men and 15 years for women. The Act was amended in 1978, raising the minimum age to 21 years for men and 18 years for women. Unfortunately, the implementation of these provisions has remained ineffective and child marriage is still prevalent in many parts of the country. It is also being felt that the minimum age of marriage for both men and women should further be raised to curb the growth of population.

1.7.3 Family Planning: Family planning programme is the linchpin of any efforts to control population growth. In

China, the one-child norm approved by the government has succeeded in lowering the birth-rate to around 20 per thousand. Similarly, in Sri Lanka, and Thailand family planning methods have been successfully used to control population growth. India can very well gain from the experience of its neighbouring countries to tackle stubbornly high birth-rate. This would require widespread use of contraceptives and improvement in the status of women. For this, a wide network of family planning centres is required, particularly in rural and tribal areas. Economic incentives/disincentives should also be used to motivate people to have small families.

1.8 Conclusion

In India, the fairly high rate of growth of population has offset to a significant extent the fruits of economic growth and used up part of the potential savings which could have been utilized to raise capital per head and the productivity of the labour force at a faster pace. Effective measures to reduce the rate of growth of population are imperative and must command priority of action. Apart from the expansion of family welfare services, sustained improvement in education and health care facilities and improved status of women in social and economic life are essential for the success of the family welfare programme and voluntary acceptance of the small family norm.

Notes

1. Government of India, Planning Commission, *Seventh Five Year Plan* (1985-90), Vol. I, para 2.20.
2. According to the theory of demographic transition, propounded by A. J. Coale and E. M. Hoover, every country passes through the following three stages of demographic transition.

   First Stage: During the first stage, the economy is rural and agriculture is the main occupation of the people. Techniques of production are primitive and per capita income is low. This type of economy is characterised by high birth rate and high death rate. High birth rate is attributable to widespread illiteracy, superstitions, absence of family planning methods and deep-rooted social and religious beliefs about family size. Likewise, death rate is also high on account of lack of medical facilities, poor sanitation and malnutrition. Thus, high birth rate is balanced by high death rate, and population remains stable or increases marginally. The first stage is marked by high growth potential of population but low actual growth.

Second Stage: It marks the beginning of the process of economic development. Living standard of the people starts improving. In this stage, death rate declines sharply owing to improved medical facilities, particularly eradication of mass-killing diseases like smallpox, cholera and plague. However, birth rate continues to remain at high levels because social and religious beliefs about marriage and family size take much longer time to change. Hence, high birth rate and falling death rate accelerate the growth of population. This stage is termed as the stage of *population explosion*. The high growth potential of the first stage is realised in the form of high actual growth of population.

Third Stage: In this stage, the economy moves from an agrarian to an industrial society. There is an increasing trend toward urbanisation and small families for achieving a higher standard of living. The economy is characterised by low birth rate and low death rate. Birth rate declines due to the spread of education and family planning methods. Otherwise also, a large family is a burden in urban industrial areas. Thus, the third stage is marked by low birth rate and low death rate, resulting in stable or marginally increasing population.

These three stages of demographic transition explain the transformation of a primitive high birth and high death rate economy into a low birth rate and low death rate economy

3. Government of India, *Economic Survey, 2001-02*, p. 252.
4. Government of India, Planning Commission, *Ninth Five Year Plan* (1997-2002), Vol. I, p. 20.
5. Government of India, *Economic Survey, 2000-2001*, p. S-1.
6. *Ibid.*, p. S-2.
7. Government of India, Planning Commission, *Eighth Five Year Plan* (1992-97), Vol. I, p. 7.
8. Government of India, Planning Commission, *Eighth Five Year Plan* (1992-97), Vol. I,, pp. 22-23.
9. Government of India, *Economic Survey, 2009-10*, p.181.

10. *Eighth Five Year Plan* (1992-97), *op cit.*, p. 7.
11. Government of India, Planning Commission, *An Approach to the Eleventh Five Year Plan*, November 2006, p. 5.

2

Work Force Participation and Occupational Structure

2.1 Work Force Participation

Total population of a country may be divided into two categories: (a) working population, and (b) non-working population. The size of working population or work force is important in relation to the level of economic activities. This is so because labour being an active factor of production, is the source of all wealth.

The size of labour force is determined by the number of people in the age group 15-60 years. Traditionally, children below the age of 15 and old persons above the age of 60 are excluded from the definition of work force. The work force participation rate in a country depends on factors such as age composition, sex ratio, attitude toward work, and availability of employment opportunities. Apparently, these factors differ from country to country.

The well-known "demographic dividend" for the country will manifest in the proportion of population in the working age group of 15-64 years increasing steadily from 62.9 per cent in 2006 to 68.4 per cent by 2026.

Labour force participation rates (LFPR) for the year 2004-05 are given in Table 2.1.

Table 2.1: Labour Force Participation Rates in India: 2004-2005

(*in percentage*)

	Rural areas	Urban areas
Males	53.1	56.1
Females	23.7	15.0

Source: Government of India, *Economic Survey, 2007-08*, Table 10.11 (excerpted), p. 249.

It is discernible that labour force participation rate in India is low as compared to developed countries of the world where it ranges between 45 to 50 percent. The low rate is reflective of the social and economic backwardness of India.

The main features of the work force participation rate in India are the following:

1. Worker-population ratio in India is low in comparison to developed countries on account of higher proportion of child population, exclusion of unpaid family workers, and low female participation.
2. Participation rate in rural areas is higher than in urban areas. Lack of educational facilities in rural areas force people to join family work in the fields/crafts at an early age.
3. Female participation rate is much smaller than male participation rate. This is reflective of the low social status of the women in Indian society.
4. Female participation rate in rural areas is higher than the female participation rate in urban areas. Women belonging to affluent families in urban areas generally do not work.

2.1.1 Women in the Work Force: According to 2001 Census, women (495.7 million) comprise 48.3 percent of the country's population. Similarly, India is home to more than 350 million children accounting for nearly 30 percent of the population. Women and children together constitute more than 60 percent of the total population of the country. The Department of Women and Child Development, set up in 1985, acts as a nodal agency for formulating policies and programmes, enacting and amending legislation and implementing various interventions for the overall development of women and children.

A majority of women workers in the country are employed in the rural areas, primarily as labourers and cultivators. In the urban areas, a majority of the women workers are employed in the unorganized sector, in household industries, petty trades and services, buildings and construction etc. The employment of women in the organized sector (both public and private) as on March 31, 2001 was 4.9 million, constituting about 17.8 percent of the total organized sector employment in the country and registering an increase of 0.5 percent over the previous year.

The distribution of women employees across industries reveals their community, social and personnel services sectors employed 55.6 percent of women workers followed by manufacturing (20.7 percent) agriculture and allied occupations (10.9 percent) and finance, insurance, real estate and business (4.7 percent).

There are about 775 institutes (224 Women Industrial Training Institutes and 551 Women Wings in General Industrial Training Institutes (ITI)/Private ITI with about 47,500 training seats for providing vocational training facilities for women at craftsman level. Statutory provisions have also been made in existing labour laws for organizing Child Care Centres for the benefit of women workers.

The Female Work Participation Rate (FWPR) was very low at 22.3 in 1991 against 51.6 for males. The provisional results of the Census 2001 have shown a moderate rise of FWPR to 25.6 percent.

2.1.2 Child Labour: The problem of child labour is a major social concern. The number of working children in the country declined from 2 percent of the total population and 6 percent of the total workforce in 1981 to 1.34 percent of the population and 3.59 percent of the total work force in 1991. The estimated number of working children in the country as per the 55th Round of the NSSO Survey (1999-2000) is 10.4 million. Children continue to be employed in the unorganized and home-based industries and domestic services. The state with the highest child labour population in the country is Andhra Pradesh. Other states having a child labour population of more than a million a million (as per 1991 Census) are Madhya Pradesh, Maharashtra and Uttar Pradesh.

The child population (0-14 years) as per the 1991 Census accounts for 319 million (37 percent, which include 154.00

million female children. Of the total child population, 18.9 million (5.9 percent) are below 1 year (infant), 38.1 million (11.9 percent), are in the age group 1-2 years (toddlers), 73 million (22.8 percent) are in the age group 3-5 years (pre-school), and another 189.6 million (59.4 percent) are in the age group 6-14 years.

According to the 1981 Census, the estimated figure of working children was 13.6 million. This figure rose to 17.02 million according to the estimates of the 43rd Round of the NSSO conducted in 1987-88. According to the 1991 Census the number of working children in the country was of the order of 11.28 million. The results of the 55th round of NSSO (1999-2000) indicate a reduction in this number.

The Human Development in South Asia Report 1998 puts the figure of working children in South Asia at 100 million in 1994. The policy of the government is to ban the employment of children below the age of 14 years in factories, mines and hazardous employment and regulate the working conditions of children in other areas of employment. There are currently about 100 National Child Labour Projects (NCLPs) covering 2.11 lakh children in 13 states where child labour use is relatively high.

Major activities undertaken under the NCLP is the establishment of special schools to provide non-formal education, vocational training, supplementary nutrition, etc. to children withdrawn from employment. Under the scheme of NCLPs, so far about 1.5 lakh children have been mainstreamed to a formal education system.

The Report on Human Development in South Asia for 1997 described the plight of children in South Asian countries as follows:

1. To be a child in South Asia is to suffer a life of constant denial. Children are often born without their mothers being attended by trained health personnel. In fact, nearly 70 percent of the mothers struggle alone, surrounded by untrained though anxious relatives, at the time of their

greatest need.

2. In their survival and development, these children face even more formidable hurdles than those they face at birth. Half of the world's malnourished children (83 million) are to be founded in just three countries: Bangladesh, Pakistan and India.
3. About 85 million children in South Asia have never seen the inside of a school. Only half of the total number of school-age children enrolled in schools. Of these, 42 percent drop out before reaching Grade 5. (In India the percentage of primary enrolment went up to 102 in 1992, but the percentage of children who drop out of schools before grade 5 was as high as 34). While many children are forced to leave school due to family circumstances and the compulsion to provide economic support to the household at a tender age, one of the main reasons for the high rates of school dropout in South Asia is that both parents and children realise the poor quality of education they receive. Dramatic improvements are required in teacher training and supervision, in learning materials and school facilities.
4. Even more worrying than the state of education is the fact that there are an estimated 134 million children in South Asia, employed as child labour, sometimes in inhuman conditions and for paltry wage.
5. Many children have to work over fifteen hours a day and are often physically abused. Rape and beatings are frequent. Once bonded, these children are traded like livestock and sometimes shipped to distant areas. 70 percent of South Asia's children are employed in agriculture, mainly victims of an entrenched system of bonded labour, where whole families are enslaved in order to pay off debts.

Pressures are now emerging, both from governments and from civil society organizations within these countries, to stop the use of child labour. Here, we would like to emphasise that a National Scheme may be designed for the payment of children's allowance on a universal basis, subject to a means test, to persons below the poverty line. This would be one way of integrating social security schemes with poverty alleviation programmes. Special measures should be taken to prevent sickness and promote the overall well being of children, specially the girl child.

The Government of South Africa is reported to have introduced a Scheme of State Support of Children of Poor Families. There are similar schemes in India for members of Scheduled Castes and Tribes who are given monetary incentives for sending their children to school. The Study Group has suggested that the scope of these schemes may be extended to cover all families below the poverty line whereby the parents maybe given a cash allowance for the maintenance of children. According to the 1991 Census, the total population of children was about 320 million. Assuming that this number has gone up to 350 million by the year 2001 and that 25 percent of them are below the poverty line, the number of children for whom such assistance would have to be given, would be about 90 million per month. Assuming again, that the rate of children's allowance to be paid would be Rs. 30 per child per month, the total cost of the scheme would be about Rs. 5400 crore per month.

A special scheme was initiated during the Annual Plan 2002-03 for 'Welfare of Children in Need of and Protection'. The objective of this scheme is to cater to child workers and potential child workers (such as street children, children of pavement dwellers, migrants, sex workers, destitute children etc.) and provide opportunities to them to facilitate their entry into main stream education through non-formal education, bridge education, and vocational training.

The Central Adoption Resource Agency (CARA) has also initiated various steps in promotion of in-country adoption. These include strengthening the Voluntary Coordinating Agencies (VCAs) by providing them grant-in-Aid.

2.2 Occupational Structure

During 1951-81, the occupational structure remained almost unaltered, except some marginal changes. The share of agriculture in working population hovered in the vicinity of 72 percent. However, it declined to 68.8 percent in 1981 and further down to 66.8 percent in 1991. Since the initiation of economic reforms in 1991, the share of agriculture sector declined to 56.64 in 1999-2000 and further down to 52.06 in 2004-05.

This clearly indicates that agriculture is still the dominant occupation of the working population. This is reflective of the continuing backwardness of the Indian economy. The excessive dependence of the work force on agriculture has resulted into widespread disguised unemployment, low productivity and poverty in the agricultural sector.

The industrial sector constitutes a relatively small source of employment for the people. In 1971, the share of secondary sector in the labour force was 11.2 percent. It marginally increased to 13.5 percent in 1981 but then declined to 12.7 percent in 1991. The share of manufacturing sector stood at 12.13 and 12.90 in 1999-2000 and 2004-05 respectively. In spite of massive investments under the Five Year Plans, the industrialisation process has remained weak in terms of employment generation. This is attributable to the excessive preference shown for the capital-intensive industries.

The share of the tertiary sector in the labour force was 16.7 percent in 1971. It increased to 17.8 percent in 1981 and further up to 20.5 percent in 1991. Over the period 1993-94 to 2004-05, the share of transport, storage and communications apart from financial, insurance, real estate, business and community, social and personal services has increased immensely. The share of trade, hotel and restaurant stood at 12.62 in 2004-05.

From the present structure and trends in the Indian economy, it is likely that significant changes in the occupational structure would occur in the foreseeable future.

3

Nature and Extent of Unemployment

Economic security is one of the main components of human security. It constitutes the crux of social security in the conventional sense. Economic security requires employment and an assured source of a basic income adequate for meeting one's basic needs.

The growth process should generate greater productive work opportunities by concentrating on sectors, sub-sectors and technologies which are labour-oriented, and in regions characterised by higher rates of unemployment and under-employment. Recognising the high incidence of under-employment and increasing casualisation of labour, there is a need to enhance employment opportunities for the poor, particularly for those who are in seasonal occupation.

3.1 Nature of Unemployment in India

As in other developing countries, unemployment is a serious problem of the Indian economy. The poverty of the masses in India is closely related to the problem of unemployment.

Unemployment is a situation when willing workers fail to get jobs at the prevailing wage rates. In other words, unemployment means involuntary idleness. From social point of view, unemployment means wastage of the precious labour resources of the country. For an individual, unemployment is a painful and demoralising experience. Employment to be gainful and sustainable has to be productive in character.

Unemployment is a multi-dimensional phenomenon in India. It is not restricted to one sector or group of population. Instead, it is a widespread disease touching almost every segment of the society.

3.1.1 Urban Unemployment: Urban unemployment may be classified into two categories: (a) industrial unemployment and (b) educated unemployment. Industrial unemployment is the result of slow growth of industrial development vis-à-vis growth of labour force. Till the mid-1960s, industrial expansion in the country was quite satisfactory and hence labour could be absorbed in the urban industrial pockets. However, the deceleration in the rate of industrial growth since mid-1960s aggravated the problem of industrial unemployment. Lately, there has been a tendency for the rural people to migrate to cities in search of employment. This has led to further competition in the job market.

Another facet of urban unemployment is the lack of job opportunities for the educated people. University degree holders and even professionally trained people are finding it difficult to get jobs. Unemployment among the educated is mainly due to over emphasis on theoretical aspects of various subjects. The education system is cut-off from ground realities of the Indian economy.

3.1.2 Rural Unemployment: Unemployment in the agricultural sector is the most serious aspect of unemployment in the Indian economy. First of all, there is open unemployment among the landless agricultural workers. With the decline of cottage industries and handicrafts, the rural population has no alternative means of livelihood. They have to fall back on the agricultural sector which is already overcrowded. There is also considerable disguised unemployment in the agricultural sector. It means more people are engaged in agricultural operations than required. In technical language, the marginal productivity of many hands in the agricultural sector is zero. Yet another dimension of rural unemployment is the problem of seasonal unemployment among Indian farmers. Agriculture by its very nature is a seasonal activity. For a significant part of the year, farmers are out of work. In the absence of supplementary sources of employment, they have to remain unemployed during slack agricultural season.

3.2 Causes of Unemployment

The causes of unemployment in India are various.

3.2.1 Labour Force Pressure: It is well-known that India is passing through the second stage of demographic transition. The death-rate has declined sharply while birth-rate is still at a high level of around 3 percent. Broadly speaking, population in the country has increased at an annual rate of 2 percent during the post-Independence period. The population explosion has created an army of labour force which is difficult to absorb given the land and other resources of the country.

3.2.2 Slow Growth of the Economy: By and large, the rate of growth of the Indian economy has remained sluggish during the last five decades. It has on the average progressed at an annual rate of 4 to 5 percent. The lack of buoyancy in the economy has failed to absorb the ever-increasing labour force.

3.2.3 Capital-intensive Technology: In the initial stages of the development planning, Indian policy makers showed bias in favour of capital-intensive technology. This was contrary to the availability of resources in the country. The scarce capital of the country was used for certain heavy industries which could not create sufficient jobs for the teeming millions.

3.2.4 Defective Education System: The education system of India is still colonial in nature. It is tailored to produce clerks in tune with the requirements of the British Government in India. There is hardly any correspondence between the needs of the economy and the class room teaching.

3.3 Three Approaches to Estimates of Unemployment

During the 1950s and 1960s, estimates of unemployment were provided by the Planning Commission. These estimates suffered from both conceptual and statistical limitations. In view of various objections, the Planning Commission discontinued giving regular estimates of unemployment. Presently, estimates of the rates of unemployment are provided by the National Sample Survey Organisation (NSSO) on the basis of its quinquennial surveys. Unemployment rate is defined as the number of persons unemployed per 1000 persons in the labour force. Three kinds of estimates for the unemployed are obtained following the three different approaches. These are explained below:

3.3.1 Usual Status (US) Basis: A person is considered unemployed on Usual Status (US) basis if he/she was not working, but was either seeking or was available for work for a relatively longer time period during the reference year.

This estimate indicates the magnitude of persons unemployed for a relatively longer period during a reference period of 365 days and approximates to an estimate of chronically unemployed. Some of the unemployed on the basis of this criterion might be working in a subsidiary capacity during the reference period. The former is called as the usually unemployed according to the principal status (P.S.) and the latter, the usually unemployed excluding the subsidiary status workers (U.S. adjusted) which admittedly is lower than the former.

3.3.2 Current Weekly Status (CWS): A person is considered unemployed by Current Weekly Status (CWS) if he/she had not worked even for one hour during the reference week, but was seeking or available for work.

This estimate based on the weekly status gives the average weekly picture during the survey year and includes both chronic unemployment and also the intermittent unemployment, of those categorized as usually unemployed, caused by seasonal fluctuations in the labour market.

3.3.3 Current Daily Status (CDS): Current Daily Status (CDS) unemployment is estimated in terms of the total persondays of unemployment, i.e. the aggregate of all the unemployment days of all persons in the labour force during the week.

This estimate based on the daily status concept gives average level of unemployment on a day during the survey year. It is the most inclusive rate of 'unemployment' capturing the unemployed days of the chronically unemployed, the unemployed days of the usually employed who become intermittently unemployed during the reference week, and the unemployed days of those classified as employed according to the priority criterion of current weekly status.

3.4 Extent of Unemployment

3.4.1 Eighth Plan Estimates and Objectives: The estimates of unemployment given in the Eighth Five Year Plan (1992-97) are presented in Table 3.1. A mixed trend in unemployment rates is discernible from the Table. Usual Principal Status (UPS) increased from 2.77 percent in 1983 to 3.77 percent in 1987-88. The weekly status unemployment increased from 4.51 percent to 4.80 percent. However, unemployment rate by daily status declined from 8.28 percent to 6.09 percent. These trends suggest that there was a shift from the state of widespread underemployment towards greater open unemployment between 1983 and 1987-88.

Table 3.1: Unemployment Rates in India: 1983 and 1987-88

(as percentage of labour force)

S. No.	Status	1983	1987-88
1.	Usual Principal Status (UPS)	2.77	3.77
2.	Current Weekly Status	4.51	4.80
3.	Current Daily Status	8.28	6.09

Source: Government of India, Planning Commission, *Eighth Five Year Plan* (1992-97), Volume I, Table 6.7, p. 134.

The Eighth Five Year Plan (1992-97) aimed at reducing unemployment to negligible level within the next ten years. To quote, "It is considered necessary and reasonable to set the goal of employment for all for achievement in a time span of the next ten years. Assessment of the present backlog of unemployment and likely additions to the labour force suggest that this goal will require generation of additional ten million employment opportunities per year on an average, or about a three percent average annual growth of employment." [1] The main elements of the strategy towards expansion of employment opportunities during the Eighth Plan included, *inter alia,* the following.

1. A faster and geographically diversified growth of agriculture.
2. Development of Infrastructure and marketing arrangements for agro-based activities.
3. Greater attention to the needs of the small manufacturing sector as a major source of industrial growth.
4. Revamping of training systems to introduce greater flexibility to labour market trends.

Unfortunately, the goal set by the Eighth Plan was not achieved.

3.4.2 Ninth Plan on Employment: Presenting an optimistic scenario of employment situation during the first decade of the new century, the Ninth Five Year Plan (1997-2002) observed, "Every effort would need to be made in attaining full employment in the post-Plan period. Since labour force growth is expected to be at its peak in the Ninth Plan period, attainment of near full employment by the year 2007 may not be an unreasonable target provided that the conditions are created for further acceleration in the growth rate and the intensity of labour absorption is not substantially reduced both sectorally and in terms of the sectoral structure of growth." [2]

Population, labour force, employment and unemployment figures during Eighth Plan, Ninth Plan and Tenth Plan are set out in Table 3.2.

3.4.3 Second National Commission on Labour: Estimates of unemployment in India (for the year 1999-2000) were made available in the Report of the Second National Commission on Labour and the same are reproduced in Table 3.3.

Table 3.2: Population, Labour Force, Employment and Unemployment

(million)

	Eight Plan (1992-97)#	Ninth Plan (1997-2002)#	Tenth Plan (2002-07)#
Population@	951.2	1,028.9	1,112.9
Labour force	374.2	423.4	478.8
Employment	367.2	416.4	474.7
Unemployment	7.0	7.0	4.1
Unemployment rate (percent)	1.87	1.66	0.86

Note: Estimates of labour force and employment are on usual status concept and pertain to 15 years and above.

@ Population at the terminal year of the Plan.

Labour force, employment and unemployment are stated as annual averages during the Plan period.

Source: Government of India, Planning Commission, *Ninth Five Year Plan* (1997-2002), Vol. I, p. 191, Table 4.9 (excerpted).

Table 3.3: Unemployment Rates in India by Various Criteria: 1999-2000

(percentage to labour force)

Unemployment rate	Males				Females			
	UPS	UPSS	CWS	CDS	UPS	UPSS	CWS	CDS
Rural areas	2.1	1.7	3.9	7.2	1.5	1.0	3.7	7.0
Urban Areas	4.8	4.5	5.6	7.3	7.1	5.7	7.3	9.4

UPS=Usual Principal Status; UPSS=Usual Status taking into account the work done in subsidiary capacity; CWS=Current Weekly Status; CDS=Current Day Status.

Source: Government of India, Ministry of Labour, *Report of the National Commission on Labour*, Vol. I (Part-I), 2002, p. 62, Table 2.13 (excerpted).

3.4.4 60th Round of NSSO Survey on Employment and Unemployment: Results of 60th Round of NSSO Survey on employment and unemployment (January-June 2004) brought out the following facts.

1. About 72 percent of households belonged to rural India

and accounted for nearly 75 percent of total population. The average household size for the rural sector at 5.0 is higher than the urban average of 4.5.

2. Male literacy was 62 percent and 80 percent in rural and urban areas respectively. In females, corresponding rates were 43 percent and 68 percent.
3. According to the usual principal and subsidiary statuses taken together (called 'all' usual status), nearly 44 (37) percent of the rural (urban) persons were in the labour force. The corresponding percentages for males (females) were 55 (32) in rural areas and 56 (16) in urban areas.
4. In the usually employed ('all' workers) category, 57 percent among males and nearly 62 percent among females were self-employed. The corresponding proportions in urban India were 44 percent for males and 45 percent for females.
5. In the rural areas, about 66 percent of usually employed males and 84 percent of usually employed females were engaged in the agricultural sector.
6. In urban India, the tertiary sector engaged 59 percent of male workers while secondary sector accounted for 35 percent of the usually employed males. For females, the corresponding proportions were lower at 53 and 31 percent.
7. In rural India, on an average, per day, a male casual labourer earned Rs. 56.53, Rs. 20.38 more than a female causal labourer who earned Rs. 36.15.
8. In urban India, wage difference was more prominent. A male casual labourer in the urban areas earned Rs. 75.51 in a day and female, Rs. 44.28 in a day.

3.4.5 Tenth Plan on Employment: One of the important objectives of the Tenth Plan was to provide gainful high quality employment to the labour force. The main approach in the Tenth Plan was to bring about a qualitative change in the structure and pattern of employment in terms of promoting growth of good quality work opportunities. The future prospects of employment situation were brought out by the Tenth Five Year Plan (2002-07) when it observes, "The first unique feature of the Plan is its explicit recognition that the Indian economy is in a phase where the growth process alone will not to be able to provide adequate work opportunities for the emerging work force, let alone reduce the back-log of unemployment. Even at an average annual growth rate of 8 percent, the economy is likely to generate 30 million work opportunities during the Tenth Plan period as compared to the estimated 35 million people who will be added to the work force. It, therefore, becomes necessary to devise suitable strategies which can accelerate the pace of work creation by modulating the growth process itself." [3]

3.4.6 Eleventh Plan Projections: The Eleventh Five Year Plan (2007-08 to 2011-12) also released projections of population, labour force, employment and unemployment and the same are presented in Table 3.4.

Table 3.4: Population, Labour Force, and Employment Projections

('000)

	Basis	2006-07	2011-12	2016-17
Population (age 0+)		11,28,313	12,07,971	12,83,242
Population (age 15-59)		6,87,120	7,60,110	8,20,570
Labour Force	UPSS	4,92,660	5,41,840	5,86,440
Labour Force	CDS	4,38,948	4,83,669	5,24,057
Employment Opportunities	CDS	4,02,238	4,60,310	51,820
Unemployed (000)	CDS	36,710	23,348	5,853
Unemployment Rate (%)	CDS	8.36	4.83	1.12

UPSS = Usual Principal and Subsidiary Status.

CDS = Current Daily Status.

Source: Government of India, Planning Commission, *Eleventh Five Year Plan* (2007-12), Vol. I, p. 75

Notes

1. Government of India, Planning Commission, *Eighth Five Year Plan* (1992-97), Vol. I, p. 10.
2. Government of India, Planning Commission, *Ninth Five Year Plan* (1997-2002), Vol. I, p. 190.
3. Government of India, Planning Commission, *Tenth Five Year Plan* (2002-07), Preface.

4

Employment-generating Policies and Programmes

The solution of the problem of unemployment lies in reversing the causes of unemployment. It means controlling the population growth, speeding up the pace of industrialisation, adoption of labour-intensive technology and making the education system job-oriented.

Generation of employment opportunities is directly linked to the process of growth in economic activities. Faster growth is, therefore, necessary to productively employ the increase in the labour force and also for improving the quality of existing employment. An employment policy, therefore, must also consider the policies required for accelerating the overall growth in the economy.

Since the initiation of reforms in early 1990s, many changes have taken place in the social life and the institutions that govern the economy. In science and technology, information system and communications, revolutionary changes have occurred in recent times. New ideas have emerged which have changed the way people all over the world look at old ideas and the old institutions.

Government's strategy and policy approach to employment generation and social development was spelt out by the President in his address to the Parliament on October 25, 1999. The elements of social policy included the following.

1. Creation of 1 crore additional employment opportunities per year.
2. A thrust to female literacy and primary education. Building of primary school buildings in all un-served habitations.
3. Provision of primary health services to all citizens and

stabilisation of population.

4. Strengthening of welfare and child health services.
5. Greater attention to welfare of the disabled and aged in cooperation with NGOs.
6. Provision of clean drinking water to all villages in the next five years.
7. Rural connectivity through all weather roads.

To deal with the unemployment problem, Government of India has launched, from time to time, various employment schemes. Huge amount of public money is being spent by the government on recurring annual basis to support wage employment programmes. A constant monitoring of these programmes is necessary to evaluate their contribution to employment generation vis-à-vis expenditure incurred on them.

The major schemes are explained below:

4.1 National Rural Employment Guarantee Act (NREGA), 2005

NREGA was notified on September 7, 2005. The Act came into force on February 2, 2006 when 200 selected districts of the country were brought under its purview (Phase I, 2006-07). NREGA was extended to additional 130 districts in Phase II during 2007-08. The remaining rural areas were notified with effect from April 1, 2008.

4.1.1 Objectives and Significance of NREGA: The objective of the NREGA is to enhance the livelihood security of the people in rural areas by guaranteeing 100 days of wage employment in a financial year to a rural household whose members volunteer to do unskilled manual work. The Act further aims at creating durable assets and strengthening the livelihood resource base of the rural poor. The choice of works suggested in the Act address causes of chronic poverty like drought, deforestation, soil erosion, etc. so that the process of employment generation is on a sustainable basis.

The significance of NREGA lies in the fact that it creates a right-based framework for wage employment programmes and makes the Government legally bound to provide employment to those who seek it. In this way the legislation goes beyond providing a social safety net, and towards guaranteeing the right to employment. By prioritizing natural resource management and emphasizing the creation of durable assets it holds the potential of becoming a growth engine for sustainable development of an agriculture-based economy.

Under NREGA, employment is dependent upon the worker exercising the choice to apply for registration, obtain a job card and then to seek employment through a written application for the time and duration chosen by her. The legal guarantee has to be fulfilled within the time limit prescribed and this mandate is underpinned by the provision of unemployment allowance. The Act is thus designed to offer an incentive structure to the States for providing employment as ninety percent of the cost for employment provided is borne by the Centre, and there is a concomitant disincentive for not providing employment, if demanded, as the States then bear the double indemnity of unemployment and the cost of unemployment allowance. Earlier wage employment programmes were allocation based. However, NREGA is not supply driven but demand driven. Resource transfer under NREGA is based on the demand for employment and this provides another critical incentive to States to leverage the Act to meet the employment needs of the poor. The delivery system has been made accountable, as it envisages an Annual Report on the outcomes of NREGA to be presented by the Central Government to the Parliament and to the State Legislature by the State Government.

4.1.2 Funding of the Programme: The Central Government bears the costs on the following items:

1. The entire cost of wages of unskilled manual workers.
2. 75 percent of the cost of material, wages of skilled and semi skilled workers.
3. Administrative expenses as may be determined by the

Central Government, which will include inter alia, the salary and the allowances of the Programme Officer and his supporting staff, work site facilities.

4. Expenses of the National Employment Guarantee Council.
5. The State Government bears the costs on the following items:
6. 25 percent of the cost of material, wages of skilled and semi skilled workers (As a ratio of 60:40 is to be maintained for wages of the unskilled manual workers and the material, skilled/semi skilled workers' wages, the State Government has to bear only 25 percent of the 40 percent component, which means a contribution of 10 percent of the expenditure).
7. Unemployment allowance payable in case the State Government cannot provide wage employment on time.
8. Administrative expenses of the State Employment Guarantee Council.

4.1.3 Expression of Demand for Employment: Since NREGA is a right-based programme, expression of demand for employment by the rural poor is the basic premise of its operation, especially if the wage seekers are illiterate and unorganized. Generating awareness about the programme among local rural communities becomes critical for enabling the rural poor to express demand. States have adopted various methods for communication and social mobilisation that include preparation of communication material on NREGA processes in simple local language, orientation of sarpanches/ward members, convening gram sabhas, using district teams for village level interactions, local vernacular newspapers, TV and radio spots, pamphlets and brochures, local cultural forums, fixing a Rozgar Day in a week and establishing a helpline. The full knowledge of the rights that NREGA confers on the rural poor is the most important pre-requisite to enable them to seek employment as per their choice of time and duration.

4.1.4 Labour Budget, Inventory of Projects and Perspective Plan: NREGA guarantees providing employment within 15 days of demand and the instrument for providing employment is unskilled manual work selected from the list of permissible works. This legal guarantee has implication for the way in which works have to be planned.

A labour budget, as stipulated under the Act, is required to be prepared to facilitate advance planning, whereby districts estimate their labour demand for the ensuing financial year by December end.

National Guidelines indicate the way in which the annual shelf of projects may be prepared to meet the estimated labour demand. Districts should keep a list of works ready to meet employment demand. Estimated benefits in terms of person days need to be assessed, so that the employment expected to be generated through the works planned may be clearly matched with the estimated employment demand. Physical improvement envisaged (land/water conservation etc.) has to be quantified so that the focus remains on creating durable and productive assets that support further self-sustaining employment. Displaying the list of approved works at the Gram Panchayat Office and the details of works taken up on the work site has been stipulated so that the workers know the work opportunities locally available.

National Guidelines lay down the broad principles of preparing a Five Year District Perspective Pan that must have the following components, viz. village mapping of natural resources and social infrastructure, identification of gaps and works that can be taken up as per NREGA permissible list, assessment of works that respond to what local people want, what will build a livelihood base to enable them to move out of NREGA to sustainable employment and assessment of labour demand.

4.1.5 Work Record, Payment of Wages and Preventing Bogus Muster Rolls: The legal guarantee of NREGA mandates that wages due to workers be paid within 15 days of work completion. This requires that a fair record be maintained for the work done. To ensure that authentic muster rolls are used, numbered muster rolls are to be issued for each sanctioned work by programme officer and maintained on the work site by the executing agency. Muster rolls must mention job card numbers of workers, days worked, quantum of work done, amount paid and must have space for recording inspections.

Muster rolls should be read out on the work site during measurement and wage payment to prevent bogus records. Entries of the muster roll should be correspondingly recorded in the job cards of the workers. Updating of muster roll data at the block level computers in a 15 days cycle needs to be ensured. Regular measurement and supervision of works should be done by qualified technical personnel on time.

4.1.6 Women Empowerment: NREGA stipulates that priority shall be given to women. In terms of implementation it mandates that a minimum of one-third of the beneficiaries shall be women who have registered and have requested for work.

4.1.7 Vigilance and Transparency: Vigilance and transparency have been strongly emphasized in NREGA. The field verification of NREGA processes is through external and internal agencies and the feedback is shared with the States for follow up. Independent concurrent studies have also been taken up. Monitoring at the State level is required and States are expected to ensure 100 percent verification at block level, 10 percent at district level and 2 percent at the state level, especially of work muster rolls, and records. Guidelines for muster roll verification have been evolved. The setting up and training local vigilance and monitoring committees is also required for bringing in lateral transparency.

A web-enabled MIS www.nrega.nic.in has been developed that seeks to place all information in public domain. It is a household level database and has internal checks for ensuring consistency and conformity to normative processes. All critical parameters get monitored in public domain.

Since the MIS places all critical data on the web and this data is software engineered, it has significant advantages in terms of transparency as it allows cross verification of records and generation of reports on any parameter of the Act.

4.1.8 Public Accountability: NREGA contains specific provisions for public accountability. This has to be accomplished through the provisions made in the Act and guidelines regarding right to information, proactive disclosure of information and a transparent social audit process. The right to information should be followed in both letter and spirit in all matters relating to NREGA. Section 17 of NREGA provides for social audit of all works in a Gram Panchayat (GP) by the Gram Sabha and the Gram Panchayat has to provide records for social audit.

4.1.9 Grievance Redressal: Enforcement of the right to employment requires setting up an effective grievance redressal system. NREGA vests the responsibility for grievance redressal with the programme officer. To ensure prompt grievance redressal, certain basic arrangements must be ensured, such as setting up a grievance redressal cell at the Programme Officer (PO)/District Programme Co-ordinator (DPC) offices, preferably with a toll free helpline. The PO and DPC must review the disposal of complaints on a monthly basis and the persons concerned must be informed.

4.1.10 Financial Management: A non-lapsable Central Employment Guarantee Fund has been set up to ensure that availability of funds match working season demands. Districts have dedicated accounts for NREGA funds and submit their proposals based on clearly delineated guidelines so that funds may be devolved efficiently at each level, and adequate funds may be available to respond to demand. The funds are released on the basis of demand for employment received in a district and are based on an appraisal of both financial and physical indicators of outcomes.

4.1.11 Other Processes of NREGA:

A. Right-based Framework:

1. Adult members of a rural household who are willing to do unskilled manual work may apply for registration to the local Gram Panchayat, in writing, or orally.
2. Gram Panchayat after due verification will issue a job card. The job card will bear the photograph of all adult members of the household and is free of cost
3. A job card holding household may submit a written application for employment to the Gram Panchayat, stating the time and duration for which work is sought.

B. Time-bound Guarantee:

1. Gram Panchayat will issue a dated receipt of the written application for employment, against which the guarantee of providing employment within 15 days operates. If employment is not provided within 15 days, daily unemployment allowance in cash has to be paid. Liability of payment of unemployment allowance is of the States.
2. Work should ordinarily be provided within 5 km radius of the village or else extra wages of 10 percent are payable
3. Wages are to be paid according to minimum wages. Disbursement of wages has to be done on weekly basis and not beyond a fortnight.

C. Work Site Facilities:

Work site facilities such as crèche, drinking water, shade have to be provided.

D. Labour-intensive Works:

A 60:40 wage and material ratio has to be maintained. Contractors and use of labour displacing machinery is prohibited.

E. Permissible Works:

1. Water Conservation
2. Drought Proofing (including plantation and afforestation)
3. Irrigation Canals
4. Minor Irrigation, horticulture and land development on the land of SC/ST/ -BPL/IAY and land reform beneficiaries

5. Renovation of traditional water bodies
6. Flood Protection
7. Land Development
8. Rural connectivity
9. Any other work that may be notified by the Central Government in consultation with the State Government.

F. Rozgar Jagaran Puruskar: The objective of the award is to acknowledge the outstanding and exemplary contribution made by a registered Civil Society Organizations (CSO) in the effective implementation of the NREGA at state, district, block and gram panchayat levels. The award includes a medal, scroll and cash (gram panchayat, Rs. 1,000; intermediate panchayat, Rs. 2,000; district panchayat, Rs. 5,000 and State level, Rs. 25,000).

4.2 Sampoorna Grameen Rozgar Yojana (SGRY)

SGRY was launched on September 25, 2001 by merging the then schemes of Jawahar Gram Samridhi Yojana (JGSY) and Employment Assurance Scheme (EAS).

4.2.1 Merger of SGRY in NREGS: SGRY programme in 330 districts was subsumed in NREGS (National Rural Employment Guarantee Scheme)—200 districts in the year 2006-07 and 130 Districts in 2007-08. SGRY programme was entirely subsumed in NREGS with effect from April 1, 2008.

4.2.2 Objectives: The objectives of the Programme were to provide additional wage employment in the rural areas, as also food security, alongside the creation of durable community, social and economic infrastructure in the rural areas. The programme was self-targeting in nature with special emphasis in providing wage employment to women, scheduled castes (SCs), scheduled tribes (STs) and parents of children withdrawn from hazardous occupations.

4.2.3 Strategy: The Scheme was exclusively implemented by the Panchayti Raj Institutions (PRIs). The programme resources were shared by all the three tiers, namely District Panchayat, Intermediate Panchayat and the Village Panchayat in the proportion of 20:30:50. Each level of Panchayat was an independent unit for formulation of Action Plan and executing the scheme.

4.2.4 Salient Features of SGRY

1. SGRY was Centrally Sponsored Scheme (CSS) on cost sharing basis between the Centre and the States in the ratio of 75:25. In case of UTs, the Centre provided entire funds. Foodgrains were provided, through Food Corporation of India (FCI), free of cost to States and UTs.
2. Payment of foodgrains was made by the Ministry of Rural Development to the FCI directly.
3. Every worker seeking employment under the SGRY was provided minimum 5 kgs of foodgrains (in kind) per manday as part of wages. However, due to shortage of foodgrains, 3 kgs of foodgrains per day was being provided from November 1, 2005.
4. Balance of wages was paid in cash so that they were assured of the notified minimum wages. Minimum 25 percent of the wages was paid in cash.
5. State Governments and UT Administrations were free to calculate the cost of foodgrains (paid as part of wages) at either BPL rates or APL rates or anywhere between the two rates.
6. Panchayati Raj Institutions (PRIs) took up works as per the felt need of the areas.

4.2.5 Special Safeguards for Weaker Sections and Women of the Community

1. 22.5 percent of the annual allocation (inclusive of foodgrains) allocated both at the level of District and Intermediate Panchayats was earmarked for Individual/group beneficiary Schemes of SC/ST families living Below the Poverty Line (BPL).
2. Minimum 50 percent of the Village Panchayat allocation (inclusive of foodgrains) was earmarked for the creation of need-based village infrastructure in SC/ST habitations/wards.

3. Efforts were made to provide 30 percent of employment opportunities for women.
4. A specified percentage, as indicated by Ministry of Rural Development, of the annual allocation (inclusive of foodgrains) allocated both at the District and Intermediate Panchayats were earmarked for individual/group beneficiary schemes for minority community families living Below the Poverty Line.
5. If a rural disabled person was willing to do manual unskilled work, efforts were made to provide him/her work under the programme according to his/her ability. Provisions of the Persons with Disabilities (Equal Opportunities, Protection of Rights and Full Participation) Act, 1995 were kept in view and implemented.

4.2.6 Ban on Contractors and Machinery: No contractors were permitted to be engaged for execution of any of the works and no middle men/intermediate agencies employed for executing works under the Scheme. Use of machinery which displaced manual labour was also not permissible with a view to create maximum possible additional employment opportunities.

4.2.7 Worksite Facilities: Facilities like drinking water, rest sheds for the workers and crèches for the children coming with working mothers were provided.

4.2.8 Annual Action Plan: Each District Panchayat/DRDA, Intermediate Panchayat and Village Panchayat was required to prepare and approve independently, before the beginning of each financial year, an Annual Action Plan equivalent in value of about 125 percent of its share of funds allocated in the preceding year. No work could be taken up unless it formed part of the Annual Action Plan. The exercise of approval of Annual Action Plan was completed by the end of February of the preceding financial year.

4.2.9 Works Taken Up: The works taken up were labour intensive, leading to the creation of additional wage-employment, durable assets and infrastructure, namely water conservation and water harvesting; drought proofing, including afforestation and tree plantation; irrigation canals, including micro and minor irrigation works; renovation of traditional water bodies, including de-silting of tanks; land development; flood-control and protection works, including drainage in waterlogged areas; rural connectivity to provide all-weather access. While taking up the works, emphasis was placed on labour-intensive works. Purely material-oriented works were not taken up.

4.2.10 Works Prohibited: Following works were prohibited under the Scheme:

1. Buildings for religious purposes and the like.
2. Monuments, memorials, statues, idols, arch gates, welcome gates and the like.
3. Bridges.
4. Buildings for higher secondary schools/senior secondary schools.
5. Buildings for colleges.
6. Black topping of roads.

SGRY was fully planned and implemented by the Panchayati Raj Institutions (PRIs) in the spirit of the 73rd Constitution Amendment Act. The quality of delivery mechanism of the programme also rested with the implementing agencies, i.e. the PRIs.

4.3 Swarnjayanti Gram Swarozgar Yojana (SGSY)

The employment created through the self employment programmes is more sustainable. Beneficiaries under these programmes get assistance for starting up their own ventures which gives him employment on a sustainable basis. The crucial point here is identification of beneficiaries and proper project formulation.

Persistent efforts made by the government to fine-tune the self-employment programmes during various plan periods yielded some new concepts that emerged at various times and got consolidated. The need to integrate the cluster approach, capacity building, skill upgradation, infrastructure including marketing development and technology penetration were felt more acutely with every passing year. Emphasis also was necessary to be laid on micro enterprise development with effective forward and backward linkages, so as to ensure best returns on the investment.

4.3.1 Objectives of SGSY: SGSY is a major on-going programme for the self-employment of rural poor. The programme was started from April 1, 1999 after restructuring the erstwhile Integrated Rural Development Programme (IRDP), Training of Rural Youth for Self Employment (TRYSEM), Development of Women and Children in Rural Areas (DWCRA), Supply of Toolkits in Rural Areas (SITRA) and Ganga Kalyan Yojana (GKY), besides Million Wells Scheme (MWS).

The basic objective of the SGSY is to bring the assisted poor families (Swarozgaris) above the Poverty Line by providing them income-generating assets through a mix of bank credit and governmental subsidy. The programme aims at establishing a large number of micro enterprises in rural areas based on the ability of the poor and potential of each area.

SGSY was launched to bring the assisted poor families above the Poverty Line by ensuring appreciable sustained level of income over a period of time. This objective was to be achieved by organising the rural poor into Self-help Groups (SHGs) through the process of social mobilization, their training and capacity building and provision of income generating assets. The SHG approach helps the poor to build their self-confidence through community action. Group processes and collective decision were to enable them in the identification and prioritization of their needs and resources. This process would ultimately lead to the strengthening and socio-economic empowerment of the rural poor as well as improve their collective bargaining power.

The SGSY is, by design, meant to create widespread income generating activities, through the empowering mechanism of self help groups, where group dynamics are expected to compensate for the basic weaknesses of the individual rural poor and present them as credit worthy and financially accountable units. The system of grading the SHGs through a rigorous process is expected to separate the more vibrant of the SHGs and eventually give them a capital subsidy assistance so that they undertake self-employment oriented livelihood opportunities.

4.3.2 Funding Pattern: SGSY is financed on 75:25 cost sharing basis between the Centre and the States.

4.3.3 Strategy: SGSY is different from earlier programmes, in terms of the strategy envisaged for its implementation. It has been conceived as a holistic programme of self-employment. It covers all aspects of self-employment of the rural poor viz. organisation of the poor in to Self-help Groups (SHGs) and their capacity building, training, selection of key activities, planning of activity clusters, infrastructure build up, technology and marketing support.

4.3.4 Social Mobilization of the Poor: A major shift of the SGSY from the erstwhile programmes is in terms of its emphasis on social mobilization of the poor. The programme focuses on organization of the poor at grassroots level through a process of social mobilization for poverty eradication. Social mobilization enables the poor to build their own organizations into Self-help Groups (SHGs), in which they participate fully and directly and take decisions on all issues that will enable them to cross the poverty line.

A SHG may consist of 10-20 persons belonging to families below the Poverty Line. A person should not be a member of more than one group. In the case of minor irrigation schemes, disabled persons, and in difficult areas i.e. hills, deserts and sparsely populated areas, the number of persons in a group may range from 5-20. However, if necessary 20 percent and in exceptional cases up to 30 percent of the members in a group may be from Above Poverty Line; (marginally above the poverty line and residing contiguously with BPL families) if agreed to by BPL members of the group. Efforts have to be made to involve women members in each SHG. 50 percent of Self-Help Groups in each block should be exclusively for women. Group activities are to be given preference and progressively, majority of the funding should be for SHGs.

4.3.5 SGSY: Main Criteria for SHG Formation

- SHG has to be a group of rural poor who volunteer to organize themselves in a group.
- Group may consist of 10-20 members (5-20 members in case of minor irrigation project, disabled persons and in difficult areas like desert hills and areas with scattered and sparse population).
- Members of group to be from BPL family, however maximum of 20 percent and in exceptional case 30 percent of the group members can be from families marginally above poverty line.
- Only one member from a family is eligible for membership of group.

4.3.6 Role of NGOs/Banks in Group Formation

- NGOs etc. are to be involved in Group Formation and even for SHG's capacity building.
- Rs. 10,000 per group to be paid to NGOs etc. for formation and development of SHG in four instalment.
- 20 percent at the beginning of group formation
- 30 percent when group qualifies for Revolving Fund
- 40 percent when group takes up economic activity
- 10 percent after start of economic activity and on adherence of group to repayment of bank loan.

4.3.7 Selection of Key Activities: SGSY emphasizes assistance to the Swarozgaris for those activities which have been identified and selected as key activities in terms of their economic viability in the area. Each Block may select about 10 key activities but focus should be on 4-5 Key Activities based on local resources, occupational skills of the people and availability of markets so that the Swarozgaris can draw sustainable incomes from their investments.

Block Level SGSY Committees are mainly responsible for selection of key activities which should be done through participative approach. Selection of Key Activity should be done in consultation with Banks, industrial/technical Organizations, local Khadi and Village Industries officials and district industry centre. The selected key activities are to be recommended by Panchayat Samiti and finally are to be approved by District Level SGSY Committee. Any new activity can be added to list of key activity by the District Level SGSY Committee but ordinarily selected key activities should not exceed 10 in a block.

4.3.8 Cluster Approach: SGSY stresses on cluster approach for taking up economic activities. The key activities are to be taken up in clusters. The cluster may not merely be geographic agglomerations but limits where backward and forward linkages can effectively be established. Separate clusters are to be taken up for each activity. More and more Swarozgaris can be added to the cluster each year. The cluster approach in the programmes is adopted to facilitate infrastructure and marketing support to the activity.

4.3.9 Project Approach: SGSY adopts a Project approach for each Key Activity. Project Reports are to be prepared in respect of each identified Key Activity. The Banks and other financial institutions have to be closely associated and involved in preparing these Project Reports, so as to avoid delay in sanctioning of loans and to ensure adequacy of financing. Project report should include all aspects like level of investment required at Swarozgaris level, economies of group lending, return from the activity, repayment schedule, technical input required by Swarozgaris, training requirement and mode of training, credit, infrastructure and marketing requirement and identification of resources to develop them, net accruable income from activity.

4.3.10 Target Group: Families below the Poverty Line (BPL) in rural areas constitute the target group of the SGSY. Within the target group, special safeguards have been provided to vulnerable sections, by way of reserving 50 percent benefits for SCs/STs, 40 percent for women and 3percent for disabled persons.

4.3.11 Financial Assistance: Assistance under the SGSY, to individual Swarozgaries or Self-help Groups, is given in the form of subsidy by the government and credit by the banks. Credit is a critical component of the SGSY, subsidy being a minor and enabling element. Accordingly, the SGSY envisages greater involvement of the banks. They are to be involved closely in the Planning and preparation of Project Reports, identification of activity clusters, infrastructure planning as well as capacity building and choice of activity of the SHGs, selection of individual Swarozgaries, pre-credit activities and post-credit activities and post-credit monitoring including loan recovery.

Subsidy under the SGSY to individuals is uniform at 30 percent of the Project Cost subject to a maximum of Rs. 7500. In respect of SCs/STs and disabled persons, the subsidy is 50 percent of the Project Cost, subject to a maximum of Rs. 10,000. For groups of Swarozgaries (SHGs), the subsidy is 50 percent of the cost of the scheme, subject to per capita subsidy of Rs. 10,000 or Rs. 1.25 lakh whichever is less. There is no monetary limit on subsidy for Irrigation Projects. Subsidy is back ended.

Credit targets under the SGSY are fixed every year by a Committee having representatives from the Ministry of Finance, NABARD, Reserve Bank of India (RBI), State Bank of India (SBI) and Ministry of Rural Development.

A close coordination between different agencies responsible for implementation of SGSY is critical for the success of the programme. In order to ensure coordination amongst Rural Development functionaries. Bankers and PRIs etc. various Committees are constituted under SGSY. At Central Level, Central Level Coordination Committee (CLCC) has been constituted to review and ensure effective implementation of the programme. It consists of representatives from State Governments and various Banks to discuss the progress of the programme. Likewise, at State Level, SGSY Committee has been constituted which meets every quarter to ensure proper follow up and effective implementation of the programme. At District Level, there is the district SGSY Committee under the Chairmanship of District Collector/Chief Executive Officer which meets every month to review the progress of SGSY and suggest corrective action wherever necessary. There are block level SGSY Committees in each block which meets once in a month.

4.3.12 Training: SGSY is a process-oriented scheme which involves organization of rural poor into Self-help Groups (SHGs), their training and capacity building to enable them to evolve into a self managed organization. Here the role of facilitators/Self-help Promoting Institutions (SHPIs), field level functionaries of banks and development functionaries is critical in successful implementation of the scheme. It has also been observed that large number of development functionaries do not have access to well-organized training programmes.

Training and capacity building of Swarozgaris is an important component of SGSY. Under SGSY, 10 percent of financial allocation is earmarked for training and skill development of Swarozgaris.

4.3.13 Implementing Agencies: The SGSY is being implemented by the District Rural Development Agencies (DRDAs), with the active involvement of Panchayati Raj Institutions (PRIs), the Banks, the Line Departments and the Non-Government Organizations (NGOs).

4.3.14 Monitoring: A comprehensive system of monitoring has been adopted under the SGSY. The programme is monitored from the Central level down to the grass-roots level. At the Central level, the Central Level SGSY Committee (CLCC) monitors and reviews the implementation of the Programme and lays down Policy Guidelines for all aspects related to credit linkages for the SGSY. The Performance Review Committee of the Department of Rural Development also reviews the implementation of the SGSY. At the State level, a State Level Coordination Committee (SLCC) monitors the Programme. At the district and block level, the programme is monitored by District level SGSY Committee and Block Level SGSY Committees.

4.3.15 Gender Budgeting under SGSY: It is envisaged that 50 percent of the Groups formed in each block should be exclusively for women who will account for at least 40 percent of the swarozgaries. Under the Scheme, women are encouraged in the practice of thrift and credit which enables them to become self-reliant. Through assistance in the form of Revolving Fund, bank credit and subsidy, the Yojana seeks to integrate women in the economy by providing increasing opportunities of self-employment. On an average, 52.45 percent of swarozgaries assisted in a year are women.

4.3.16 Persons with Disabilities: SGSY stipulates that disabled persons will account for at least 3percent of the total Swarozgaris. The groups formed should ideally be disability-specific wherever possible, however, in case sufficient number of people for formation of disability-specific groups are not available, a group may comprise persons with diverse disabilities or a group may comprise both disabled and non-disabled persons below poverty line.

4.4 Prime Minister Employment Generation Programme (PMEGP)

This is a new programme launched recently by merging the Rural Employment Generation Programme (REGP) and Prime Minister's Rozgar Yojana (PMRY). It aims at creating employment opportunities in both urban and rural areas. An allocation of Rs. 4,485 crore has been made for the four years (2008-09 to 2011-12) of the Eleventh Five Year Plan (2007-08 to 2011-12).

4.5 Sectoral Policies for Employment Generation

While improvement in the overall growth performance has

a direct bearing for faster and better quality employment generation, equally important is the sectoral structure of the growth. To the extent a larger share of growth can be derived from labour intensive sectors/sub-sectors/industries, the pace of generation of employment opportunities for any given overall rate of growth can be increased. The characteristics of the different segment of the labour force in terms of their skill base, residential status, aspirations from the job etc. also have implications for the sectoral structure of growth which can most suitably and productively employ the labour force. The requirements of employment opportunities to be created for among the rural unskilled labour force on the one hand and among the educated youth on the other are different and this needs to be kept in mind.

4.5.1 Agriculture: Approximately 60 per cent of the work force continues to be employed, though the share has declined in recent years. The growth of this sector is important not only to support the high growth target but also for the attainment of employment objectives. A large proportion of the labour force in the country is illiterate and does not possess any marketable skill. The sector will continue to play the role of single largest employer for the incremental labour force. It is therefore only appropriate that adequate attention is paid to scope of productive employment generation in agriculture sector.

While it is true that incidence of underemployment in agriculture is significant, it is basically due to lack of diversification in this sector and concentration on crop production. It is possible to productively employ rural labour force in activities such as development of wasteland, watershed development, forestry, animal husbandry, sericulture, horticulture and floriculture, herbal and medicinal plants etc.

The improvement in productivity is necessary to improve the wage of workers and earnings of the self-employed. Improvement in productivity and generation of employment, however, requires investment in areas such as irrigation, water conservation, land development, drainage etc. The slowing down of the public investment in real terms in agriculture needs to be reversed and also private investment needs to be encouraged. Such investments are specially needed in regions of the country where potential of agriculture sector has largely remained unexploited due to lack of such facilities.

4.5.2 Agro-processing Industries: Despite being the second largest producer of fruits and vegetable in the world, the food processing industry in India has not developed to its full potential. Food processing is a high value addition activity and is also very labour-intensive. The likely fruits from development of this sector in terms of employment generation, diversification of rural economy and a general improvement in the rural economy are widely known.

The exploitation of the growth potential of this sector, however, has not been possible so far due to lack of general physical infrastructure facilities like establishment of cold chains, specifically essential for the sector.

The sector as it exists today is dominated by small and traditional producers, who are not able to make even the minimum necessary investments necessary for a sustainable and profitable unit. There is a need to evolve a comprehensive package to give boost to an organised growth of food processing industry. The elements of the package must include, among other things, promotion of R&D, promotion of a formal relationship between growers of farm produce and the industry, entry of larger units in the food processing activities, credit facilities and support for marketing. The role of cooperatives in development of post-harvest preservation, silos and warehouses, cold storage facilities and air conditioned transport should also be encouraged.

4.5.3 Small-scale Industries: Promotion of SSIs has been one of the important strategies for employment generation since the early years of planned development process. Small Units have widely been acknowledged to employ more labour per unit of capital invested. However, the ability of the sector to stand up to the competition of more open economy has recently been in question. While the modern SSIs have by and large stood the test of the time, smaller and more traditional units have been facing problems of survival in the new environment. It is essential, therefore, for the traditional units, to modernise in terms of technological improvement, managerial practices and quality improvement.

International experience suggests that the cluster approach provides the most enabling environment for growth of SSI sector. Government should therefore identify areas where there exists sufficient conglomeration of small scale units for developing common facilities for technical and marketing support, credit facilities etc. Such an approach is not only economical in delivery of the services to the entrepreneurs but also takes care of many obstacles of non economic nature faced by the entrepreneurs.

4.5.4 Construction: Construction is one of the most labour-intensive sector. Also, there exists large unmet demand for housing in both rural and urban areas. Similarly in rural areas too there are such shortages. A boost to this sector is necessary to meet the housing demand, which constitute one of the basic necessities. In the process significant employment opportunities can be generated at different skill levels, though largely for unskilled labour.

A number of steps have been taken by the Government to promote construction sector. These include fiscal incentives in terms of benefit in personal income taxation and legislative steps like repeal of Urban Land Ceiling and Regulation Act.

4.5.5 Travel and Tourism: While Tourism and travel is one of the fastest growing industries in the world and employs close to 11 per cent of the global workforce, yet it has not found its appropriate place in India's development agenda. This sector has enormous potential for employment generation.

Promotion of domestic as well as international tourism can contribute to substantial expansion in productive employment. Development of tourism industry is linked to provision of necessary facilities. Some of the initiatives required to encourage the growth of the sector are:

1. Development of tourist circuits, covering all the infrastructural facilities required, as one investment project and in coordination with concerned agencies. Private sector should be motivated to invest in different types of allied activities.
2. Necessary changes in the existing bilateral air service agreements, which are too restrictive in granting additional seats to foreign airlines. This is necessary to introduce competition, which would lead to cut in air travel costs and improved facilities for potential international tourists.
3. Increasing the supply of hotel rooms of a reasonable standard, through public and private investment.

4.5.6 Employment Generation in Social Sectors: There is vast scope for improvement in the reach and quality of certain services is social sector especially in rural areas, such as (a) elementary education services, (b) vocational training services, (c) skill development services, (d) basic health services, (e) drinking water supply and (f) basic municipal services

The reach of the general population to basic health services and access to primary health care facilities is also very narrow. Though substantial infrastructure for health care has been created over the years, large gaps exist between the requirement and the availability of such services. The requirements for health care infrastructure like number of Primary Health Care Centre. Sub Centres, Community Health Centres etc. set for the year 1991 has not been achieved. In the years since 1991 requirements must have gone up. Even the infrastructure created over the years is functioning sub optimally; shortage of critical manpower being one of the reasons behind it.

Filling the infrastructural gaps in provision of health care facilities and improving the functioning of existing centres will require the trained manpower in these areas. There exists critical shortage of the specialists and paramedical staff. Social sectors like primary education and basic health care have the potential of absorbing a large number of educated manpower, if the Government is committed to universalizing their access.

The manpower planning for health sector has not received adequate attention so far. The facilities for imparting training should be created to meet the manpower requirements of health sector.

Gaps exist in many of the municipal services for the population, which need to be expanded and strengthened. The crucial point here is to channelise investment in these areas and to determine the roles of public and private sector in provision of these services.

Part II: Human Development and Social Security

5

Poverty and Poverty Alleviation Programmes

The final objective of all economic efforts is human development. The emphasis on the achievement of higher economic growth along with social justice is manifest in the renewed focus on development initiatives in the social sectors. Human development encompasses quality of life, the level of well being and access to basic social services.

5.1 Human Development Indicators

Human Development Report (HDR), 2002 of United Nations Development Programme (UNDP) highlighted that rapid growth in the two largest countries—China since the 1970s and India since the late 1980s—has enabled them to catch up to some extent with rich countries. In the 1990s, only 24 countries, including China and India, achieved a 3.7 percent annual growth in per capita GDP.

The Human Development Index (HDI) measures the overall achievements in a country in three basic dimensions of human development, viz. GDP per capita (PPP US$), life expectancy at birth and education and knowledge. As per the UNDP Human Development Report, 2009, India has been ranked 134th out of 182 nations and in terms of the UNDP's Human Development Index (HDI) it is classified in the group Medium Human Development with an HDI of 0.612 for the year 2007.

In India, the first ever National Human Development Report (NHDR) brought out by the Planning Commission has estimated the value of Human Development Index (HDI) for the States and the Union Territories in the country for the years 1981, 1991 and 2001. The HDI is a composite of variables capturing attainments in three dimensions of human development, namely economic, education and health.

The HDI for the country as a whole improved from 0.302 in 1981 to 0.472 in 2001. Kerala remains at the top of the NHDR table with an HDI of 0.638 in 2001 while Orissa is almost at the bottom of the list, with an index of 0.267 in 1981, 0.345 in 1991 and 0.404 in 2001. The HDI for Bihar has been the lowest with the HDI for 2001, registering an improvement over the earlier years.

Amongst the North-eastern States, Mizoram had the highest HDI and Arunachal Pradesh the lowest, in 1991. States which have done well in terms of HDI in 2001 are Punjab (0.537), Tamil Nadu (0.531) and Maharashtra (0.532). The national index for the rural areas between 1981 and 1991 has gone up from 0.263 to 0.340 and for urban areas from 0.442 to 0.511. The rural-urban gap was the minimum in case of Kerala and maximum for Madhya Pradesh in the early 1990s.

A comparison of indicators of human development followed by UNDP and NHDR is presented in Table 5.1.

Table 5.1: Indicators of Human Development

UNDP Indicators	NHDR Indicator
Life expectancy at birth	Life expectancy at 1 and Infant mortality rate
Adult literacy rate combined with enrolment ratio	Literacy rate 7+ and intensity of formal education
Real GDP per capita (PPP US$)	Per capita real consumption expenditure adjusted for inequality. Worker-Population ratio in the case of Gender-Equality Index.

Source: Government of India, Planning Commission, *National Human Development Report,* 2001.

5.2 Millennium Development Goals: Deadline 2015

The Millennium Development Goals (MDGs) comprise quantifiable, monitorable targets to assess progress achieved against standards set by the international community.

Goals for development and poverty eradication set at the UN General Assembly in 2000:

Eradicate extreme poverty and hunger.

- Halve the proportion of people living on less than US$ 1 a day.
- Halve the proportion of people suffering from hunger.

Achieve universal primary education.

- Ensure that children everywhere—boys and girls alike—complete a full course of primary education.

Promote gender equality and empower women.

- Eliminate gender disparities in primary and secondary education, preferably by 2005, and in all levels of education by 2015.

Reduce child mortality.

- Reduce infant and under-five mortality rates by two-thirds.

Improve maternal health.

- Reduce maternal mortality ratios by three-quarters.

Combat HIV/AIDS, malaria and other diseases.

- Halt and begin to reverse the spread of HIV/AIDS
- Halt and begin to reverse the incidence of malaria and other major diseases.

Ensure environmental sustainability.

- Integrate the principles of sustainable development into country policies and programmes and reverse the loss of environmental resources.
- Halve the proportion of people without sustainable safe drinking water.
- Achieve, by 2020, a significant improvement in the lives of at least 100 million slum dwellers.

Develop a global partnership for development

5.3 Social Security in India's Constitution

The Fundamental Rights that our Constitution guarantees to every citizen include the right to life, and as the Supreme Court has pointed out, the right to livelihood is inherent in the right to life. The ultimate object of social security is to ensure that everyone has the means of livelihood. It follows, therefore, that the right to social security is also inherent in the right to life. According to the Supreme Court of India, India is constitutionally a socialist state. The principal aim of socialism is to eliminate inequality of income and status and to provide a decent standard of living to the working people.

5.3.1 Directive Principles of State Policy: These principles which form part of our Constitution (Part IV) direct that:

1. The State under Article 38, shall strive to promote the welfare of the people by securing and protecting, as effectively as it may, a social order in which justice, social, economic and political, shall inform all the institutions of the national life. The State shall, in particular, strive to minimum inequalities in income, and endeavour to eliminate inequalities in status, facilities and opportunities not only amongst individuals, but also amongst groups of people residing in different areas or engaged in different vocations.
2. The State shall in particular direct its policy towards securing:

- that the citizens, men and women equally, have the right to an adequate means to livelihood.
- that the health and strength of workers, men and women and the tender age of children are not abused and that citizens are not forced by economic necessity to enter avocations unsuited to their age and strength;
- that children are given opportunities and facilities to develop in a healthy manner and in conditions of freedom and dignity and that childhood and youth are protected against exploitation and against moral and material abandonment.

3. That State shall make within the limits of its economic capacity and development effective provision for securing the right to work, to education and to public assistance in case of unemployment, old age, sickness and disablement

and in other cases of under-served want under Article 41.

4. Under Article 43, the State shall endeavour to secure by suitable legislation or economic organization or in any other way to all workers, agricultural, industrial or otherwise, work, a living wage, conditions of work ensuring a decent standard of life and full enjoyment of leisure and social and cultural opportunities.

In the light of these Principles, no one can argue that the Indian Constitution does not visualise a regime of social security for the citizens in general, and the workforce in particular. In fact, as long as these Principles and Fundamental Rights remain in the Constitution, the Indian State, and the policies of any government that may be in power, will be judged by their commitment to these Principles and Rights. Changes in policy cannot abrogate the responsibility of the State in this area.

Moreover, it does not seem likely that any proposal to amend the Constitution to abridge or dilute these Rights and Principles will get the requisite popular or parliamentary mandate. As long as these are part of the Constitution, we cannot overlook them or depart from them. No political party or responsible thinker has suggested the deletion or dilution of these commitments in the Constitution. Nor can we hold the view that since governments have not been adhering to many of the Directive Principles, we have the right to select and respect the sanctity of some, and question the sanctity of others.

It has been rightly pointed out that the Directive Principles are not justiceable, and therefore they do not have the same force as the Fundamental Rights. It has also been pointed out that the difference in the status that has been accorded in the Constitution to Fundamental Rights and Directive Principles was not the result of difference in degrees of faith or commitment, but of the belief that the financial implications of making the Directive Principles justiceable could not be laid on the state all of a sudden, that the responsibility for implementation had to be matched with the accrual or acquisition of the requisite financial resources, and that there was, therefore, an inevitable need to provide for gradualness.

Fundamental Rights and Directive Principles leave no doubt about the concern and commitment of the Constitution to the right of citizens to enjoy social security that the security that is envisaged is not only against aggression and violation of sovereignty by other countries, but also security against deprivation. The concept of social security and the commitment to social security are thus implicit in the Constitution. The judgements of the Supreme Court that clearly declare that the right to life includes the right to livelihood should remove any doubt about the commitment to social security. The right to livelihood includes the right to work, and the right to education that equips us with the skills that we need for employment as well as the ability to fulfil one's civic and social responsibilities.

5.4 The Problem of Poverty

The root cause of social insecurity in India is poverty and that is largely due to lack of adequate or productive employment opportunities. It is described as 'chronic or structural social insecurity, arising from insufficient degree of overall economic development.' It is associated with other insecurities 'emanating from conventional contingencies such as the loss of employment, disability, old age, death, etc., which are called the 'second-order' type of insecurities or conventional social insecurity. We have to address both.

The provision of adequate and stable incomes will enable the poor to satisfy their basic needs and thereby, their other social security needs as well. Till then, the State has to assume the basic responsibility of providing social security, especially in respect of those contingencies, which would be difficult for individuals to cover without assistance from the State. The State also has the responsibility to provide the means of livelihood to those who cannot work and earn their living due to childhood, old age or other infirmities.

Poverty is a widespread social evil in underdeveloped countries of the world, particularly in Asia and Africa. There is no standard definition of poverty for all the countries of the world. Being a relative concept, the meaning of poverty differs from country to country. The concept, incidence and causes of poverty in India are examined below. Government measures to deal with this national problem are also described.

5.4.1 Meaning of Poverty Line: In India, poverty is defined in terms of a minimum (subsistence) level of living rather than a reasonable level of living. Thus, minimum physical quantities of cereals, pulses, clothing etc. are determined for a subsistence level. These physical quantities are multiplied by their prices and converted into monetary terms, determining the per capita consumption/income for subsistence level. Persons whose income/consumption is below this determined figure are considered to be below the poverty line.

Hence, poverty line is based on the definition of a norm which takes nutritional requirements into account and all persons below the norm are classified as poor. The present basis of the estimation of poverty line is based on the desired requirements of calories of 2400 per person per day in the rural areas and 2100 per person per day in the urban areas. The monetary expenditure per capita needed for meeting these calorie requirements is revised upward periodically taking into consideration the rise in the prices of consumption goods.

Based on the foregoing procedure, the poverty line for a household worked out to Rs. 6,400 per annum for the rural sector and Rs. 7,300 per annum for the urban sector in 1984-85 at 1984-85 prices. In other words, poverty line for a household worked out to Rs. 533.5 per month for the rural areas and Rs. 611 per month for the urban areas. Or, Rs. 17.70 per day for rural households and Rs. 20.36 per day for urban households. Assuming that an average household consists of five members, the figures turned out to be Rs. 3.55 per capita per day for rural areas and Rs. 4.07 per capita per day for urban areas. According to this definition, nearly 37 percent of the people in the country were living below the poverty line in 1984-85. [1]

The Government increased the annual household income/expenditure for computing poverty line to Rs. 11,060 at 1991-92 prices during the Eighth Five Year Plan (1992-97). [2] Earlier, the income for the purpose was Rs. 6,400 at 1984-85 prices. In this connection, the Eighth Plan observed, "Views vary on the concept of poverty line and the method of estimating poverty. However, irrespective of the concept and measurement, there is evidence that poverty is on decline since the middle of the seventies. In 1987-88, as per the official methodology, around 30 percent of the population was poor. Assuming that by 1991 poverty proportion declined to 27 percent, even then about 230 million people were poor and not capable of providing bare essentials of existence....The target is to eliminate poverty by the turn of the century." [3]

5.5 Incidence of Poverty

Widespread poverty in India has attracted the attention of a number of economists and organisations. Leading studies on poverty have been conducted by Dandekar and Rath, B.S. Minhas, P.K. Bardhan, World Bank and the Planning Commission of India.

5.5.1 Estimates of Dandekar and Rath: In their book *Poverty in India* (1971), Dandekar and Rath made a path-breaking study of the poverty phenomenon in India. Using the NSS data on consumption, they concluded that in 1960-61, about 40 percent of the rural population and about 50 percent of the urban population lived below the poverty line.

5.5.2 Estimates of Planning Commission: The Planning Commission has been estimating the incidence of poverty at the national and state level using the methodology contained in the report of the Expert Group on Estimation of Proportion and Number of Poor (Lakdawala Committee) and applying it to consumption expenditure data from the large sample surveys on consumer expenditure conducted by the National Sample Survey Organization (NSSO) at an interval of approximately five years.

The Ninth Five Year Plan (1997-2002) gave estimates of incidence of poverty for the year 1993-94. These were based on the National Sample Survey (NSS) consumer expenditure data of 50th Round (July 1993 to June 1994). Table 5.2 presents poverty ratios and the number of poor at the all-India level for different years. With reference to Table 5.2, the Ninth Plan remarked, "The incidence of poverty expressed as percentage of people below the poverty line is observed to have declined from 56.4 percent in 1973-74 to 37.3 in 1993-94 in rural areas and from 49.0 percent in 1973-74 to 32.4 percent in 1993-94 in urban areas. For the country as a whole, the percentage of people below the poverty line declined from 54.9 percent in 1973-74 to 36 percent in 1993-94. However, the number of poor in the country remained more or less stable at around 320 million due to the rise in population. This fact should not over-shadow the 300 million persons who joined the non-poor group during the twenty year period between 1973-74 and 1993-94, but underlines the need for containment of the growth rate of population." [4]

Table 5.2: Percentage and the Number of Poor in India

Year	Poverty ratio			Number of poor (million)		
	Rural	Urban	Combined	Rural	Urban	Combined
1973-74	56.4	49.0	54.9	261.3	60.0	321.3
1977-78	53.1	45.2	51.3	264.3	64.6	328.9
1983	45.7	40.8	44.5	252.0	70.9	322.9
1987-88	39.1	38.2	38.9	231.9	75.2	307.1
1993-94	37.3	32.4	36.0	244.0	76.3	320.3

Note: The estimates are based on the methodology recommended by

the Expert Group on Estimation of Proportion and Number of Poor as adopted by the Planning Commission.
Source: Government of India, Planning Commission, *Ninth Five Year Plan, 1997-2002*, Vol. I, p. 27, Table 1-9.

Estimates of poverty incidence in India were made available in *Economic Survey,* 2002-03. These are reproduced in Table 5.3. To quote, "The success of the anti-poverty strategy is reflected in the decline in the combined poverty ratio from 54.9 percent in 1973-74 to 36 .0 percent in 1993-94. The poverty ratio declined by nearly 10 percentage points in the 5 year period between 1993-94 to reach 26.1 percent in 1999-2000. While the proportion of poor in the rural areas declined from 56.4 percent in 1973-74 to 27.1 percent in 1999-2000, the decline in urban areas has been from 49 percent to 23.6 percent during this period. The poverty reduction target set by the Planning Commission for the Tenth Five Year Plan aims at achieving a poverty ratio of 19.3 percent for the country as a whole by 2007, 21.1 percent for the rural and 15.1 percent for the urban areas." [5]

Table 5.3 Estimates of Incidence of Poverty in India

Year	Poverty ratio (percent)		
	Rural	Urban	Combined
1973-74	56.4	49.0	54.9
1993-94	37.3	32.4	36.0
1999-00	27.1	23.6	26.1
2007 (projection)	21.1	15.1	19.3

Source: Government of India, *Economic Survey,* 2002-03, p. 213, Table 10.6 (excerpted).

Apart from an indicative target of an 8 percent average GDP growth rate, specific monitorable targets for key indicators were finalised for the Tenth Five Year Plan (2002-07) and beyond. One of these pertained to the reduction in poverty ratio by five percentage points by 2007 and by 15 percentage points by 2012. The poverty reduction target set by the Planning Commission for the Tenth Plan aimed at achieving a poverty ratio of 19.3 percent for the country as a whole by 2007, 21.1 percent for the rural, and 15.1 percent for the urban areas.

Poverty projections of the Tenth Plan for different States for the year 2006-07 are presented in Table 5.4.

A. Percentage Share of Poor in the Population: Over the years, the headcount ratio of the poor has steadily declined. In this connection, Eleventh Five Year Plan (2007-12) observed, "India has successfully reduced the share of the poor in the population by 27.3 percentage points from 54.8 in 1973 to 27.5 in 2004. Between 1973 and 1983, the headcount ratio of the poor had declined from 54.8 percent to 44 percent, and it fell further to 36 percent in 1993-94 and to 27 percent by 2004-05 (Table 5.5). Thus, sixty years after Independence, over a quarter of our population still remains poor. There is growing consensus that the poverty line (Rs. 356 monthly per capita consumption expenditure for rural areas and Rs. 458 for urban areas in 2004-05) in India is much too low, and continues to be based on a consumption basket. If the poverty line was higher, the share of the population below the poverty line would be accordingly higher." [6]

B. Absolute Number of the Poor: Though the percentage of poor in the population has fallen appreciably over the last three-four decades, the absolute number of poor has registered only a marginal fall. This is clear from Table 5.6. In this context the Eleventh Five Year Plan (2007-12) remarked, "India is a nation of over 300 million poor people, a number that has barely declined over the last three decades of development. It is therefore essential that the Eleventh Five Year Plan addresses the task of reducing the numbers of the poor frontally. All growth benefits the poor, but the appropriate definition of pro-poor growth should be that it benefits them disproportionately. It is clear that rapid growth will be essential to reduce the number of the poor and

Table 5.4: Poverty Projections for Different States: 2006-07

State/UT	Rural		Urban		Combined	
	percent of poor	No. of poor (lakh)	percent of poor	No. of poor (lakh)	percent of poor	No. of poor (lakh)
AP	4.58	26.97	18.99	41.75	8.49	68.72
Arunachal	37.89	3.54	4.48	0.14	29.33	3.68
Assam	37.89	95.36	4.48	1.78	33.33	97.14
Bihar	44.81	482.16	32.69	54.74	43.18	536.91
Goa	2.00	0.13	2.00	0.16	2.00	0.29
Gujarat	2.00	6.88	2.00	4.38	2.00	11.25
Haryana	2.00	3.30	2.00	1.51	2.00	4.81
HP	2.00	1.18	2.00	0.14	2.00	1.32
J&K	N.A	N.A	N.A	N.A	N.A	N.A
Karnataka	7.77	28.66	8.00	16.34	7.85	45.00
Kerala	1.63	4.03	9.34	8.01	3.61	12.04
MP	28.73	192.07	31.77	74.46	29.52	266.54
Maharashtra	16.95	101.61	15.20	72.68	16.18	174.30
Manipur	37.89	8.10	4.48	0.27	30.52	8.37
Meghalaya	37.89	7.99	4.48	0.24	31.14	8.23
Mizoram	37.89	1.88	4.48	0.23	20.76	2.12
Nagaland	37.89	8.01	4.48	0.21	31.86	8.22
Orissa	41.72	139.12	37.46	23.57	41.04	162.69
Punjab	2.00	3.40	2.00	1.95	2.00	5.35
Rajasthan	11.09	54.41	15.42	23.44	12.11	77.86
Sikkim	37.89	2.08	4.48	0.03	33.78	2.12
Tamil Nadu	3.68	12.46	9.64	31.61	6.61	44.07
Tripura	37.89	10.70	4.48	0.28	31.88	10.98
UP	24.25	373.16	26.17	111.25	24.67	484.41
WB	21.98	137.53	8.98	22.21	18.30	159.73
A&N Island	3.68	0.10	9.64	0.14	5.82	0.24
Chandigarh	2.00	0.02	2.00	0.19	2.00	0.21
Dadra & NH	2.00	0.04	2.00	0.02	2.00	0.06
Daman & Diu	2.00	0.03	2.00	0.01	2.00	0.04
Delhi	2.00	0.19	2.00	3.18	2.00	3.38
Lakshadweep	1.63	0.01	9.34	0.02	4.59	0.03
Pondicherry	3.68	0.13	9.64	0.70	7.72	0.83
All India	21.07	1705.26	15.06	495.67	19.34	2200.94

Source: Government of India, Planning Commission, *Tenth Five Year Plan* (2002-07), Volume I, p.45.

sustainable poverty reduction, but for growth to benefit the poor disproportionately, it will have to be accompanied by more rapid employment expansion than hitherto, greater investment in health, education, water/sanitation and child nutrition than so far, and directly targeted poverty-reduction programmes." [7]

Table 5.5: Percentage of Population below Poverty Line in India (1973-2004)

Year	Rural	Urban	Combined
1973	56.4	49.0	54.9
1983	45.7	40.8	44.5
1993	37.3	32.3	36.0
2004	28.3	25.7	27.5

Source: Government of India, Planning Commission, *Eleventh Five Year Plan* (2007-12), Vol., III, p. 79.

Table 5.6: Number of Persons below Poverty Line in India (1973-2004)

(in Lakh)

Year	Rural	Urban	Combined
1973	2612.90	600.46	3213.36
1983	2519.57	709.40	3228.97
1993	2440.31	763.37	3203.68
2004	2209.24	807.96	3017.20

Source: Government of India, Planning Commission, *Eleventh Five Year Plan* (2007-12), Vol., III, p. 80.

It is discernible from Table 5.6 that the number of poor in rural areas in the country has declined from 2612 lakh in 1973 to 2209 lakh in 2004. However, in urban areas the number of poor has gone on increasing from 600 lakh in 1973 to 709 lakh in 1983, to 763 lakh in 1993 and to 807 lakh in 2004. Giving explanation for these trends, the Eleventh Five Year Plan (2007-12) observed, "The fact that the numbers of the poor have slightly declined in rural areas, and increased in urban areas over the last three decades suggests that to escape rural poverty, the poor migrate to urban areas. In fact, the total number of *migrant workers* in India in 1999-2000 was 10.27 crore, a staggering number. The number of seasonal or cyclical migrants in India may be 2 crore or so. But migration, both rural-rural (from relatively poor to relatively richer states and districts) and rural-urban, has the effect of disenfranchising the poor, leaving them without a safety net. Nevertheless, rural-urban migration will, and should continue; the policy imperative is that migrants are provided the basic social services that all citizens are entitled to according to the Constitution of India." [8]

From the statistical and other information available on the subject, the following facts emerge regarding the geo-social aspects of poverty in India.

1. The incidence of poverty is more in rural areas than in urban areas.
2. Incidence of poverty is the greatest among small farmers and landless workers in rural areas.
3. Poverty in urban areas is largely the overflow of rural poor into the urban areas.
4. Urban poverty is concentrated in the casual labour households.
5. Wide inter-state disparities are visible in the poverty ratios. Uttar Pradesh, Bihar, Madhya Pradesh, Orissa and Rajasthan account for most of the poor in India
6. Among the social groups, scheduled castes, scheduled tribes and backward castes account for more percentage of the poor than their share in the population

Thus, poverty in India is a chronic and multi-dimensional Phenomenon. There is geography of poverty, with poverty being concentrated in the rural areas of certain states. There is sociology of poverty, with certain social groups suffering the most. There are identifiable occupational features of the poor: they are concentrated in agricultural labour and artisanal households in rural areas, and among casual labourers in urban areas. Casual labourers in urban areas are essentially distress migrants from rural areas in States where agricultural land-man ratio is very adverse, and where agricultural incomes have not been growing

There has been controversy around the measurement of poverty, as presented in the official statistics of the Planning Commission. There are many unresolved issues regarding measurement of poverty in India and upon the question of poverty line itself, which necessitate a revisit of this entire question. Keeping this in view, two committees were constituted to look into these issues.

5.5.3 Important Recommendations of the Expert Group to Review the Methodology for Estimation of Poverty, November 2009 (Tendulkar Committee):

- Poverty estimates to continue to be based on private household consumer expenditure of Indian households collected by the National Sample Survey Organization (NSSO).
- Need to move away from anchoring the poverty lines to a calorie *intake* norm.
- Since for canvassing household expenditure on a recall basis, the NSSO has decided to shift to an MRP-based estimates for all its consumption surveys in future, there is need to adopt the MRP-based estimates of consumption expenditure as the basis for future poverty lines as against the previous practice of using URP estimates. This change captures the household consumption expenditure of poor households on low- frequency items of purchase more satisfactorily.
- The all-India rural headcount ratio and all-India combined headcount ratio using the recommended procedure is 41.8 per cent and 37.2 per cent in comparison with official estimates of 28.3 per cent and 27.5 per cent respectively. Poverty at all-India level in 1993-94 was 50.1 per cent in rural areas, 31.8 per cent in urban areas and 45.3 per cent in the country as a whole as compared to the 1993-94

official estimates of 37.2 per cent rural, 32.6 per cent urban and 36.0 per cent combined. Thus, even though the suggested new methodology gives a higher estimate of rural and combined rural-urban headcount ratio at the all-India level for 2004-05, the extent of poverty reduction in comparable percentage point decline between 1993-94 and 2004-05 is not very different from that inferred using the old methodology.

5.6 Causes of Poverty

Widespread poverty in India is attributable to a host of factors, viz. population explosion, lack of industrialisation, failure of land reforms and failure of fiscal policy to narrow the gap between the rich and the poor.

Industrial development of the country has neither been on desirable lines nor at expected rate. Undue emphasis on capital-intensive industries has failed to generate sufficient jobs for the labour force.

Land reforms programme was started with great fanfare soon after Independence. However, it has failed to achieve the desired results. The incidence of poverty in rural areas is mainly due to the failure of land reforms.

Similarly, taxation and expenditure policies of the government have not been used effectively to bridge the gap between the rich and the poor.

5.7 Poverty Alleviation and Employment Generation Programmes

Poverty eradication may either be left to the automatic mechanism of growth process and/or to programmes aimed at direct assault on poverty.

The initial thinking of the Government relied on the automatic benefits of growth coupled with a progressive taxation policy. However, this strategy did not work on desired lines. As the Eighth Five Year Plan (1992-97) observed, "The equity objective was sought to be pursued through redistribution of assets. But, land reforms could not be implemented effectively. The problem of poverty could not be tackled through growth, which itself was slow over a long period of time. Hence, direct intervention through poverty alleviation programmes became necessary." [9] Lately, the Government has increasingly resorted to direct attack on poverty through rural development and rural employment schemes. Integrated Rural Development Programme (IRDP) was launched in 1978-79 as a programme of total rural development.

Some major anti-poverty programmes of the Government of India are the following:

5.7.1 Jawahar Rozgar Yojna: The National Rural Employment Programme (NREP) was started as a part of the Sixth Five Year Plan to help those who depended largely on wage employment in the agricultural sector. Similarly, Rural Landless Employment Guarantee Programme (RLEGP) was launched on August 15, 1983 with a view to expanding the employment opportunities for the rural landless. In February 1989, Government announced a new scheme called Jawahar Lal Nehru Rozgar Yojna for employment creation in 120 backward districts of the country. On April 1, 1989, the three employment schemes, viz. NREP, RLEGP and Jawahar Lal Nehru Rozgar Yojna were merged into a single rural employment programme named Jawahar Rozgar Yojna.

5.7.2 Pradhan Mantri Gramodaya Yojana (PMGY): PMGY was launched in 2000-2001 in all States and Union Territories (UTs) in order to achieve the objective of sustainable human development at the village level. The PMGY envisages allocation of Additional Central Assistance (ACA) to the States and UTs for selected basic minimum services in order to focus on certain priority areas. PMGY initially had five components viz., primary health, primary education, rural shelter, rural drinking water and nutrition. Rural electrification was added as an additional component from 2001-02. For 2002-03 as well as 2003-04, the allocation of ACA for PMGY was Rs. 2,800 crore. Both financial and physical monitoring of the programme is being carried out by the Planning Commission.

5.7.3 Swarnajayanti Gram Swarozgar Yojana (SGSY): After a review and restructuring of the erstwhile Integrated Rural Development Programme and allied schemes, SGSY was launched in April, 1999. It is the only self- employment programme currently being implemented for rural poor. The objective of the SGSY is to lift the assisted Swarozgaris above the poverty line by providing them income-generating assets through bank credit and Government subsidy. The Scheme is being implemented on a 75:25 cost sharing between the Centre and the States.

Up to December 2009, 36.78 lakh self-help groups (SHGs) had been formed and 132.81 lakh swarozgaris have been assisted with a total investment of Rs. 30,896.08 crore.

5.7.4 Sampoorna Grameen Rozgar Yojana (SGRY): The SGRY was launched in September 2001, by merging the ongoing Schemes of Jawahar Gram Samridhi Yojana (JGSY) and Employment Assurance Scheme (EAS). The objective of the programme is to provide additional wage employment in the rural areas as also food security, along with the creation of durable community, social and economic infrastructure in rural areas. The SGRY is open to all rural poor who are in need of wage employment and desire to do manual and unskilled work in an around the village/habitat. The Scheme is implemented through Panchayati Raj Institutions. The scheme envisages generation of 100 crore man-days of employment in a year. The cost of each component of the programme is shared by the Centre and States in the ratio of 75:25.

The SGRY scheme has a cash and a foodgrains component, and the Centre bears 75 per cent and 100 per cent of the cost of the two with the balance borne by the States/UTs. During the year 2003-04 an amount of Rs. 4,121 crore as cash component and 49.97 lakh tones of food grain were released to the States/UTs and 76.45 crore persondays were generated as reported by the States/UTs. Under the Special Component of the SGRY, 65.84 lakh tonnes of foodgrains were released to 12 calamity affected States during 2003-04.

In 2004-05, 82.23 crore persondays were generated with the Centre releasing Rs. 4,496 crore as cash component and about 50 lakh tonnes of foodgrains to the States/UTs. Besides, under the special component of the SGRY, with the States/UTs meeting the cash components, Centre released 26 lakh tonnes of foodgrains to the 13 calamity affected States. In 2007-08, up to December 2007, the number of persondays of employment generated under SGRY was 11.60 crore, while the Centre's contributions in terms of the cash and foodgrains components up to December 31, 2007 were Rs. 1142.27 crore and 9.55 lakh tonnes, respectively. The SGRY has been entirely subsumed in NREGS with effect from April 1, 2008.

5.7.5 Rural Housing Schemes: Rural housing schemes such as Indira Awaas Yojana (IAY) aim at providing dwelling units, free of cost, to the poor families of the Scheduled Castes (SCs), Scheduled Tribes (STs), freed bonded labourers and also the non SC/St persons Below Poverty Line (BPL) in the rural areas. The Scheme is funded on a cost-sharing basis of 75:25 between the Centre and States. Till the end of 2003-04, the ceiling on construction assistance under IAY was Rs. 20,000 in plain areas and Rs. 22,000 in hilly areas, which has been increased to Rs. 25,000 per unit for plain areas and Rs. 27,500 for hilly areas from April 1, 2004. Twenty percent of the allocation is allowed for upgradation of unserviceable Kutcha houses for which ceiling of Rs. 12,500 per unit applies since April 2004. Credit-cum-Subsidy Scheme for rural housing targeting rural families having annual income up to Rs. 32,000 was launched on April 4, 1999. In addition, the innovative scheme of Rural Housing and Habitat Development and Rural Building Centres (RBCs) was introduced to encourage innovative, cost effective and environment friendly solutions in building/housing sectors in rural areas. A National

Mission for Rural Housing and Habitat has also been set up to address the critical issues of 'housing gap' and induction of science and technology inputs into the housing/construction sector in rural areas. Since inception (up to June 1, 2004) 113.96 lakh houses have been constructed/upgraded by incurring an expenditure of Rs. 19,869 crore. During 2003-04, against the target of 14.84 lakh, 12.54 lakh (provisional) houses have been constructed/upgraded.

During 2008-09, Rs. 8795.79 crore was released till March 31, 2009 and 21.05 lakh houses have been constructed during 2008-09.

5.7.6 Pradhan Mantri Gram Sadak Yojana (PMGSY): The PMGSY, was launched in December, 2000, to provide road connectivity to 1.6 lakh unconnected habitations with population of 500 persons or more (250 in case of hilly, desert and tribal areas) in the rural areas by the end of the Tenth Plan period. It is being executed in all the States and six UTs. Although the initial estimates indicated a requirement of Rs. 60,000 crore for the program, the present indications are that about Rs. 1,30,000 crore will be needed for achieving the intended connectivity.

As per the Budget announcements of 2003-04, the diesel cess which is the source for funding the programme, was increased from Re 1 per litre to Rs. 1.50 per litre, in order to provide additional funds for the programme. Since the inception of the programme, project proposals for Rs. 14,417 crore have been cleared and 88.685 Kms. of rural roads have been taken up under this program. 20,740 road works had been completed till March 2004, and an expenditure of over Rs. 6,547 crore has been incurred by the States/UTs. Up to March 2009, a total length of 2,14,281.45 km. of roadways has been completed with a cumulative expenditure of Rs. 46,807.21 crore. The National Rural Roads Development Agency (NRRDA), registered under the Societies Registration Act, provides Operations and Management supports for the programme.

The Asian Development Bank (ADB) has agreed to support the development of rural roads in Madhya Pradesh and Chhattisgarh, which have been identified as recipient States for the first tranche. The ADB Board has approved a loan of US$ 400 million (in a project size of US$ 571 million). The States of Assam, Orissa and West Bengal have been identified for the second tranche of ADB assistance, of the order of US$ 500 million.

5.7.7 Drought Prone Areas Programme (DPAP), Desert Development Programme (DDP) and Integrated Wastelands Development Programme (IWDP): These are being implemented for the development of wastelands/degraded lands. DPAP was launched in 1973-74 to tackle the special problems faced by those areas constantly affected by drought conditions. DDP was launched in 1977-78 to mitigate the adverse effects of desertification. IWDP has been under implementation since 1989-90. These programs were implemented on a sectoral basis till 1994-95. Since April 1995, these programs are being implemented on watershed basis. For the project DPAP, total number of the projects sanctioned was 2,535, with funds released by the Centre at Rs. 295 crore. Under DDP, 1,562 projects have been sanctioned with funds of amount of Rs. 215 crore; and under IWDP, 190 projects with funding of Rs. 306 crore, were sanctioned.

The cost norms for all the three schemes have been revised to Rs. 6,000 per hectare. Under DPAP and DDP, the cost is shared between the Centre and the States in the ratio of 75:25, while in the case of IWDP, Rs. 5,500 is borne by the Central Government and Rs. 500 is shared by the States.

5.7.8 Antyodaya Anna Yojana (AAY): AAY was launched in December 2000. Under the scheme 1 crore of the poorest among the BPL families covered under the targeted public distribution system are identified. Twenty five kilograms (kg) of good grains were made available to each eligible family at a highly subsidized rate of Rs. 2 per kg for wheat and Rs. 3 per kg for rice. This quantity has been enhanced from 25 to 35 kgs with effect from April, 2002. The scheme has been further expanded in June 2003 by adding another 50 lakh PL families. Under the scheme, during 2002-03, against an allocation of 41.27 lakh tones of foodgrains, 35.39 lakh tones have been lifted by State Governments, and during 2003-04, 38.24 lakh tones of food-grain have been lifted against an allocation of 45.56 lakh tones.

5.7.9 Swarna Jayanti Shahari Rozgar Yojana (SJSRY): The Urban Self-Employment Programme and the Urban Wage Employment Program are two special schemes of the SJSRY initiated in December 1997, which replaced various programs operated earlier for urban poverty alleviation. The government recently revamped the Scheme with effect from April 1, 2009. Between the Centre and the States, SJSRY is funded on 75:25 basis. In 2009-10, out of an allocation of Rs. 515 crore, Rs. 363.12 crore had been utilized until December 31, 2009.

5.8 Conclusion

The socio-economically disadvantaged are yet to benefit from economic reforms. The challenge to overcome the scourge of poverty remains a daunting task. The support of the poor for reforms and their involvement in the development process can be achieved only if they start benefiting from the policies. It is necessary to ensure that the poor and the deprived have an even greater stake in economic reforms than at present for mobilising their enthusiastic participation in the development process. Economic reforms must be guided by compassion and distributive justice. Improvement of living conditions of the poorest and the weakest sections of society should be high priority areas in the first decade of the new millennium.

The entire gamut of the existing poverty alleviation and employment generation programmes need to be restructured to meet the newly emerging demand for employment. An anti-poverty strategy that is fiscally sustainable should be devised which directly targets those who are unable to benefit from the opportunities offered by growth. Safety nets should focus on those who either cannot participate in the growth process (for reasons of extreme deprivation or vulnerability combined with poverty) or face continuing exposure to risks.

The Union Finance Minister while presenting the 2005-06 budget to the Parliament made the following observations regarding assault on poverty and unemployment in his budget speech: "India is not a poor country, yet a significant proportion of our people are poor. Poverty is not only income poverty. Other indicators of poverty are illiteracy, disease, infant mortality, malnutrition, absence of skills and unemployment. The whole purpose of democratic government is to eliminate poverty and give to every citizen the opportunity to be educated, to learn a skill and to be gainfully employed. The Government holds that it is its sacred duty to empower the poor and eliminate the scourge of poverty." [10]

Notes

1. Statement of the Minister of State for Planning in the Rajya Sabha, November 28, 1985.
2. Statement of the Minister of State for Planning in the Rajya Sabha, March 9, 1992.
3. Government of India, Planning Commission, *Eighth Five Year Plan* (1992-97), Vol. I, p. 31.
4. Government of India, Planning Commission, *Ninth Five Year Plan* (1997-2002), Vol. I, p. 27.
5. Government of India, *Economic Survey,* 2002-03, p. 213.
6. Government of India, Planning Commission, *Eleventh Five Year Plan* (2007-12), Vol., III, p. 79.
7. Ibid., p. 79.
8. Ibid., p. 80.
9. *Eighth Five Year Plan* (1992-97), op cit., p. 7.
10. Government of India, Budget Papers, 2005-06, *Speech of the Finance Minister*, p. 3.

6

Health, Family Welfare and Nutrition

6.1 Introduction

Health security is one of the major components of human development. Good health is not only an end product of development but also a necessary condition for economic development. Improved health contributes to economic growth by reducing production losses due to illness of workers. There is a significant relation between income growth and health.

Health care is also an important component of social security. Indeed medical care is widely regarded as the primary branch of social security since health is of concern to all age groups and all categories of employees. All comprehensive social security programmes, therefore, make provision for medical care. [1]

Entry 6 in the State List (List II) in the Seventh Schedule of the Constitution of India reads: "Public health and sanitation, hospitals and dispensaries." Thus public health is a State subject in India. However, population control and family planning are areas of common interest for the Central and State Governments as they find place in the Concurrent List (List III) [entry 20A] in the Seventh Schedule of the Constitution

According to the Directive Principles of State Policy laid down in the Constitution, raising the level of nutrition, and the standard of living and the improvement of public health are among the primary duties of the State. Improvement in the health status of the population has been one of the major thrust areas for the social development programmes of the country.

Public spending on health in India at 1 percent of GDP is amongst the lowest in the world whereas its proportion of private spending on health is one of the highest. Households in India spend about 5-6 percent of their consumption expenditure on health. The cost of services in the private sector makes it unaffordable for the poor and the underprivileged.

6.2 World Health Assembly, 1977

World Health Assembly held in 1977 adopted a resolution which said that the main social target in the coming decades should be the attainment by every citizen of the world of a level of health that will permit him to lead a socially and economically productive life. The Assembly had set the year 2000 as the target date for achieving the objective. Subsequently, the Conference on Primary Health Care held at Alma Ata declared that primary health care is the key to attaining this target as part of development, and in the spirit of social justice. Since then, many countries have adopted primary health care as the strategy for social security. India has also adopted primary health care as the main instrument for achieving the goal of *health for all*. A vast network of institutions at primary, secondary and tertiary levels has been established for this purpose. The provision of primary health care services constitutes one of the seven Basic Minimum Services included in the national agenda.

6.3 Health Indices of India and Selected Asian Countries

The comparative picture with regard to health indicators such as life expectancy, Total Fertility Rate (TFR), Maternal Mortality Ratio (MMR) and Infant Mortality Rate (IMR) reveals that India is lagging behind other Asian countries such as Indonesia, Sri Lanka and China (Table 6.1).

6.4 Trends in Health Care in India

Improvement in the health status of the population is a major thrust area under the social development programmes being undertaken in the country. This is sought to the achieved through improvement in the access to and utilization of health services in the country with special focus on under-served and under-privileged segments of the population. India has built up a vast health infrastructure and manpower at primary, secondary and tertiary care in government, voluntary and private sectors. Technological advances and improvement in access to health care technologies have resulted in a substantial improvement in health indices of the population and a steep decline in mortality (Table 6.2).

Table 6.1: Health Indicators among Selected Asian Countries

Country	Life expectancy (years)		TFR	MMR	IMR
	Male	Female			
Japan	78.9	86.1	1.35	10	3
Sri Lanka	72.2	77.5	1.89	92	15
China	70.6	74.2	1.72	56	32
Indonesia	66.2	69.9	2.25	230	36
India	63.9	66.9	2.90	301	58
Pakistan	64.0	64.3	3.87	500	73

TFR = Total Fertility Rate; MMR = Maternal Mortality Ratio per 1,00,000 live births; IMR = Infant Mortality Rate per 1,000 live births.

Source: Government of India, Planning Commission, *Eleventh Five Year Plan* (2007-12), Vol., II, p. 58, Table 3.1.1 (excerpted).

Table 6.2: Time Trends (1951-2000) in Health Care in India

	1951	1981	2000
SC/PHC/CHC	725	57,363	1,63,181
Dispensaries and Hospitals (all)	9,209	23,555	43,322
Beds (Private and Public)	1,11,198	5,69,495	8,70,161
Nursing Personnel	18,054	1,43,887	7,37,000
Doctors (Modern system)	61,800	2,68,700	5,03,900
Malaria (cases in million)	75	2.7	2.2
Leprosy (cases/10,000 population)	38.1	57.3	3.74
Small Pox (No., of cases)	44,887	Eradicated	
Guinea worm (No. of cases)	39,792	Eradicated	
Polio (No. of cases)	29,709	265	---

Source: National Health Policy 2002.

However, the extent of access to and utilization of health care has varied substantially between States, districts and different segments of society.

India has entered an era of *dual disease burden*. While communicable diseases have become more difficult to combat due to insecticide resistance among vectors, resistance to antibiotics in many bacteria and emergence of new diseases such as HIV increasing longevity and the changes in life style have resulted in the increasing prevalence of non-communicable diseases.

6.5 Health Indices in Rural and Urban India

Public health care system in rural areas in many States and regions is in shambles. Extreme inequalities and disparities persist both in terms of access to health care as well as health outcomes (Table 6.3). This large disparity across India places the burden on the poor, especially women, scheduled castes and tribes. Inequity is also reflected in the availability of public resources between the advanced and less developed States.

Table 6.3: Rural-Urban Health Indicators in India

	CBR	CDR	IMR	Anaemia among Children (6-35 months) (percent)	Anaemia among Pregnant Women (percent)
Urban	19.1	6.0	40	72.7	54.6
Rural	25.6	8.1	64	81.2	59.0
Total	23.8	7.6	58	79.2	57.9

CBR = Crude Birth Rate per 1,000; CDR = Crude Death Rate per 1,000; IMR = Infant Mortality Rate per 1,000 live births.

Source: Government of India, Planning Commission, *Eleventh Five Year Plan* (2007-12), Vol., II, p. 61, Table 3.1.3.

Urban growth has led to increase in number of urban poor. Though the coverage of health and family welfare services in urban areas is much better than the rural, lack of water and sanitation and the high population density in slums leads to rapid spread of infections. These settlements have high incidence of vector borne diseases, asthma, TB, malaria, coronary heart diseases, diabetes etc. Poor housing conditions, exposure to heat and cold, air and water pollution and occupational hazards add to the environmental risks for the poor. They are further made vulnerable, as they have no back up savings, food stocks or social support systems to tide over the crisis of illness. Despite the presence of so many private and government hospitals in urban areas, large chunk of homeless and those living in slums or temporary settlements are left out of the proper health care system. Thus, even though there is a concentration of health care facilities in urban areas, the urban poor lack access; initiatives in the country to date have been limited and fragmented.

6.6 Primary Health Care

Primary health care infrastructure is intended to provide integrated promotive, curative and rehabilitative services to the population close to their residence. It is estimated that over 80 percent of the health care needs of the population can be met by the primary health care infrastructure; only the rest may require referral to the secondary or tertiary health care institutions.

Nearly 30 percent of India's population lives in urban areas. Due to the massive inflow of population to the towns and cities, the health status of urban slum dwellers is, at times, worse than that of the rural population. There has been a dearth of well-planned and organized effort to provide primary health care services to the urban population within 2-3 kms of their residence and to link primary, secondary and tertiary care institutions in geographically defined areas. While an elaborate network of health services based on population norms has been established in the rural areas through group centres, primary health centres and community health centres, the services provided in these centres have, however, not been satisfactory.

Primary health care system faces persistent gaps in manpower and infrastructure. Sub-optimal functioning of the available infrastructure and poor referral services are the other problems.

In spite of these deficiencies, primary health care is regarded as the most appropriate strategy for attaining the goal of health for all, within a reasonable time frame. Basic health security has to be provided by the primary health care infrastructure. It may be supplemented by one or more of the various other options such as health insurance.

The reproductive and child health services reach community and household levels through the primary health care infrastructure. Inadequacies in the existing health infrastructure have led to gaps in coverage and outreach services in rural areas. The Pradhan Mantri Gramodaya Yojana (PMGY) for Primary Health Sector is an initiative to strengthen and revitalize the primary health infrastructure.

6.7 Incidence of Major Diseases in India

A brief description of the incidence of major diseases in the country and the efforts made to control them is given below.

6.7.1 Malaria: This is a major public health problem. The National Anti-malaria Programme (NAMP) is being implemented all over the country on a 50:50 sharing basis, barring North Eastern States, where 100 percent Central Funding is being provided for disease control. Full funding is also provided to 100 tribal districts covering 1,045 Primary Health Centres (PHCs) in 8 States where a 5 year Enhanced Malaria Control Project with assistance from World Bank is in operation. The goal is to bring about a 50 percent reduction in mortality due to malaria by 2010 according to National Health Policy (NHP), 2002.

6.7.2 Kala Azar: This disease is endemic in West Bengal, Jharkhand and Bihar, with high mortality. However, there has not been a significant decline in number of reported cases and deaths due to inadequate insecticide spraying operations and poor outreach of diagnostic services. There is a shift in focus from control of Kala Azar to its elimination. NHP, 2002 envisages its elimination by 2010.

6.7.3 Tuberculosis (TB): Phase-I of the Revised National TB Control Programme (1997-2002) was implemented with an outlay of Rs. 749 crore with World Bank funding. This was the largest public health programme against TB in the World. Phase-II (2003-04) of this programme was approved with World Bank assistance. NHP, 2002 envisages a 50 percent reduction in mortality due to TB by 2010.

6.7.4 Leprosy: The prevalence rate for the country as a whole declined from 24 per 10,000 population in 1992 to 3.36 per 10,000 population in September 2002. The second phase of the World Bank assisted National Leprosy Eradication Programme was approved for 2000-03 with a provision of Rs. 250 crore, with the objective of elimination of leprosy for the country as a whole. The Tenth Plan goal was to eliminate leprosy as a public health problem by bringing the prevalence rate to less than 1 per 10,000 population.

6.7.5 Blindness: Out of the total estimated 45 million blind persons in the world, 7 million are in India. Due to the large population base and increased life expectancy, the number of cataract cases is expected to increase in the coming years. India is committed to reduce the burden of avoidable blindness by the year 2020 by adopting strategies advocated in "Vision 2020". The Right to Sight Initiative was launched in October 2001. The prevalence of blindness has come down from 1.49 percent in 1980 to 1.1 percent in 2002 based on a survey done in 15 districts of the country. Cataract and refractive errors presently constitute over 82 percent of the blindness in the country, as against 91 percent earlier. Prominent emerging causes of blindness are diabetic retinopathy and glaucoma.

The World Bank assisted Cataract Blindness Control Project was successfully completed in June 2002. As against its target of 11 million cataract operations, 15.3 million operations were conducted. Construction of eye operation theatres/eye wards in districts, supply of ophthalmic equipment, Intra Ocular Lens (IOL), implantation in district hospitals, training of surgeons in IOL surgery and assistance to NGOs for setting up eye care services, were some activities undertaken in the Project.

6.7.6 HIV/AIDS: AIDS is not only a serious health problem but also a major development issue on account of its potential impact on productivity and economic growth within the country. A nation-wide HIV sentinel surveillance conducted by National AIDS Control Organization in all States/UTs has indicated that HIV infection is prevalent in all States/UTs. Six States have emerged as high prevalence States where HIV prevalence rate is recorded to be 1 percent and above, viz. Karnataka, Tamil Nadu, Andhra Pradesh, Maharashtra, Manipur and Nagaland. The National AIDS Control Programme (NACP) Phase-II (1999-2004) was implemented with an estimated outlay of Rs. 1,425 crore with funding by World Bank and USAID.

The focus of this programme is to reduce HIV transmission among the poor and marginalised high-risk groups by adopting following measures:

1. Condom promotion.
2. Reduction in blood-borne transmission.
3. Voluntary testing and counselling.
4. Developing capacity for community-based low-cost care for people living with HIV/AIDS.
5. Strengthening implementation capacity at the National, State and Panchayat levels.
6. Forging inter-sectoral linkages between public, private and voluntary sectors.

The goal of NHP, 2002 is to achieve a zero level of growth for HIV/AIDS by the year 2007.

6.8 Major Public Health Programmes in India

6.8.1 Universal Immunization Programme: First

launched in the urban areas in 1985, the coverage of the programme was progressively extended to cover the entire country by 1990. Between 1988 and 2006, there was a decline of 83 percent in diphtheria, 83 percent in pertussis, 59 percent in measles, 94 percent in neo-natal tetanus and 97 percent in poliomyelitis. Hepatitis-B vaccination programme which was started in 2002 in 33 districts and 15 cities as a pilot project was expanded to all districts of good performing States. Vaccination against Japanese encephalitis was started in 2006.

6.8.2 Pulse Polio Immunization Programme: An outbreak of polio was witnessed in 2006 with the spread of polio virus. During 2007 a total of 471 cases were reported. To respond to this, supplementary immunization activities were intensified in the high risk areas. The initiatives included use of Monovalent Oral Polio Vaccine in the high risk districts and States to enhance immunity against P1 and P3 virus, vaccinating the children in transit and covering children of migratory population from Uttar Pradesh and Bihar.

6.8.3 National Vector Borne Disease Control Programme (NVBDCP): NVBDCP is being implemented for prevention and control of vector borne diseases like malaria, filariasis, kala-azar, Japanese encephalitis, dengue and chikungunya. Most of these diseases are epidemic prone and have seasonal fluctuations. To achieve NHP, 2002 goal of Elimination of Lymphatic Filariasis by 2015, the Government. of India initiated Annual Mass Drug Administration (MDA) with single dose of Diethylcarbamazine citrate tablets to all individuals living at risk of filariasis excluding pregnant women, children below 2 years of age and seriously ill persons.

Kala-azar is endemic in 4 States of the country, namely Bihar, West Bengal, Jharkhand and Uttar Pradesh. However, about 80 percent of the total cases are reported from Bihar. NHP, 2002 envisages kala-azar elimination by 2010. Under the elimination programme the Central Government provides 100 percent operational cost to the State Governments, besides anti-kala-azar medicines, drugs and insecticides.

Acute Encephalitis Syndrome (AES)/Japanese encephalitis (JE) has been reported frequently from 12 States/UTs. Dengue is prevalent in different parts of the country but the outbreak of the disease is reported mainly in urban areas. However, in the recent past, dengue is reported from rural areas as well. During 2006, chikungunya fever re-emerged in the country in epidemic proportions after a quiescence of about three decades. The Government has taken various steps to tackle the vector borne diseases (VBDs) including dengue and chikungunya which, include implementation of strategic action plan for prevention and control of chikungunya by the State Governments.

6.8.4 Revised National Tuberculosis Control Programme (RNTCP): RNTCP using Directly Observed Treatment Short-course (DOTS) is being implemented with the objective of curing at least 85 percent of the new sputum positive patients initiated on treatment, and detecting at least 70 percent of such cases. Since its inception, RNTCP has initiated more than 8.4 million TB patients on treatment, thereby saving over 1.4 million additional lives. Deaths have been reduced from over 5 lakh per year at the beginning of programme to less than 3.7 lakh per year currently. Good quality assured anti-TB drugs are provided in the patient-wise drug boxes, free of cost. Padiatric Patient Wise Drug Boxes were introduced in the programme from January 2007. The treatment success of new infectious TB cases under RNTCP has consistently exceeded the global benchmark of 85 percent.

6.8.5 National AIDS Control Programme: Nearly 20,408 AIDS cases were reported in 2007, out of which, 87.4 percent of the infections were transmitted through the sexual route and pre-natal transmission accounted for 4.7 percent of infections. About 1.8 percent and 1.7 percent of infections were acquired through injecting drug use and contaminated blood and blood products respectively.

Government of India has launched National AIDS Control

Programme Phase III, with the goal to halt and reverse the epidemic in the country over the next 5 years by integrating programmes for prevention, care, support and treatment.

6.9 Shortcomings of the Public Health System

The public health system in India has various drawbacks. The Eleventh Five Year Plan (2007-12) pointed out the following drawbacks:

- "Centralised planning instead of decentralised planning using locally relevant strategies.
- Institutions based on population norms rather than habitations.
- Fragmented disease specific approach rather than comprehensive health care.
- Inflexible financing and limited scope for innovations.
- Semi-used or dysfunctional health infrastructure.
- Inadequate provision of human resources.
- No prescribed standards of quality.
- Inability of system to mobilize action in areas of safe water, sanitation, hygiene and nutrition (key determinants of health in the context of our country) – lack of convergence.
- Inability to mobilize AYUSH and RMPs and other locally available human resources." [2]

[AYUSH = Ayurveda, Yoga & Naturopathy, Unani, Siddha and Homeopathy; RMPs = Registered Medical Practitioners]

6.10 National Health Policy, 2002

The Department of Health has formulated the National Health Policy (NHP), 2002 which was approved by the Cabinet in 2002. The National Health Policy, 2002 aims at achieving an acceptable standard of good health amongst the general population of the country and has set the goals for the next two decades (Table 6.4).

Areas of attention in the Tenth Plan included the reorganization and restructuring of existing health care infrastructure at primary, secondary and tertiary levels so that they have the capacity to render health care services to the population residing in well defined geographical areas and have appropriate referral linkages with each other. Appropriate delegation of powers to Panchayati Raj institutions to ensure local accountability of public health care providers, horizontal integration of all aspects of the current vertical disease control programme, including supp-lies monitoring, IEC, training and administrative arrangements, development of appropriate two-way referral system utilizing information technology, exploring alternative systems of health care financing, and defining the role of various stakeholders—government, private and voluntary sectors—are the other focus areas.

Table 6.4: National Health Policy 2002: Goals to be Achieved

Goal	Year
Eradicate Polio and Yaws	2005
Eliminate Leprosy	2005
Eliminate Kala Azar	2010
Eliminate Lymphatic Filariasis	2015
Achieve zero level growth of HIV/AIDS	2007
Reduce mortality on account of TB, malaria and other vector and water-borne diseases by 50 percent	2010
Reduce prevalence of blindness to 0.5 percent	2010
Reduce IMR to 30/1000 and MMR to 100/100,000 live births	2010
Increase utilization of public health facilities from the current level of <20 percent to > 75 percent	2010
Establish an integrated system of surveillance of National health accounts and health statistics	2005

Source: National Health Policy, 2002.

6.11 Growth of Private Sector in Health Care

Growth of private health sector in India has been considerable in both provision and financing. There is diversity in the composition of the private sector, which ranges from voluntary, not-for profit, for–profit, corporate, trusts, stand-alone specialist services, diagnostic services to pharmacy shops and a range of highly qualified to unqualified providers, each addressing different market segments.

Private sector is flourishing primarily because of the failure of the public sector. The growth of private hospitals and diagnostic centres was also encouraged by the Central and State governments by offering tax exemptions and land at concessional rates, in return for provision of free treatment for the poor as a certain proportion of outpatients and inpatients. Apart from subsidies, private corporate hospitals receive huge amounts of public funds in the form of reimbursements from the public sector undertakings, the Central and the State governments for treating their employees.

The cost of health care in the private sector is much higher than the public sector. Many small providers have poor knowledge base and tend to follow irrational, ineffective and sometimes even harmful practices for treating minor ailments. Bulk of the qualified medical practitioners and nurses are subject to self-regulation by their respective State Medical Councils under central legislation. In practice, however, regulation of these professionals is weak and close to non-existent.

6.12 Health Insurance

India with her huge geographical area, very large population and inequity of resources, ensuring good health for all, particularly the poor, is a complex issue. Health system is a mix of the public and private sectors, with the NGOs and civil society still playing a very small, though important, role.

Coverage of health insurance in India is pathetically limited. Traditionally health care insurance in the country has been limited to the Employees State Insurance Schemes (ESIS) for industrial workers, the Central Government Health Scheme (ECHS) for employees and pensioners of the Central Government and the Ex Servicemen Contributory Health Scheme (ECSH) for the former Armed Forces Personnel.

After general insurance was opened up to the private sector and further to FDI, there has been a considerable expansion of health insurance, covering mainly the urban upper-middle class. However, health care insurance schemes have experienced problems such as high premium, delay in settling claims and non-transparent procedures in deciding reimbursements. The system of Third Party Administrators (TPAs) has facilitated cash payments and expanded access to providers and as a result delivery of health care services to the upper middle class has improved. Other segments of the population, the Below Poverty Line (BPL) categories in particular, have remained deprived of the benefits of health insurance in the country.

Side by side with the development of health insurance on a commercial basis the country has seen the emergence of Community Based Health Insurance (CBHI). CBHI is a not-for-profit insurance scheme managed by the members themselves on the basis of collective pooling of health risks. CBHI schemes are being operated by organizations such as ACCORD, BAIF, Karuna Trust, SEWA, DHAN Foundation and VHS.

India has a huge working population of about 400 million. Almost 93 percent of this work force is in the unorganized sector. There are numerous occupational groups in economic activities, passed on from generation to generation, scattered all over the country with differing employer-employee relationship. Those in the organized sector of the economy, whether in the public or private sector, have access to some form of health service coverage. The unorganized sector workers have no access. The National Commission for Enterprises in the Unorganized Sector (NCEUS) had recommended a specific health scheme in incidences of illness and hospitalization for workers and their families.

6.13 National Urban Health Mission (NUHM)

The National Urban Health Mission (NUHM) will meet

health needs of the urban poor, particularly the slum dwellers by making available to them essential primary health care services. This will be done by investing in high calibre health professionals, appropriate technology through public-private partnership and Health Insurance for Urban poor.

Recognizing the seriousness of the problem, Urban Health will be taken up as a thrust area for the Eleventh Five Year Plan. NUHM will be launched with focus on slums and other urban poor. At the State level, besides the State Health Mission and State Health Society and Directorate, there would be a State Urban Health Programme Committee. At the district level, similarly there would be a District Urban Health Committee and at the city level, a Health & Sanitation Planning Committee. At the ward slum level, there will be a Slum Cluster Health and Water and Sanitation Committee. For promoting public health and cleanliness in urban slums, the Eleventh Five Year Plan will also encompass experiences of civil society organizations working in urban slum clusters. It will seek to build a bridge of NGO-GO partnership and develop community level monitoring of resources and their rightful use.

NUHM would ensure the following:

- Resources for addressing the health problems in urban areas, especially among urban poor.
- Need based city specific urban health care system to meet the diverse health needs of the urban poor and other vulnerable sections.
- Partnership with community for a more proactive involvement in planning, implementation and monitoring of health activities.
- Institutional mechanism and management systems to meet the health related challenges of a rapidly growing urban population.
- Framework for partnerships with NGOs, Charitable hospitals and other stakeholders.
- Two-tier system of risk pooling: (a) women's Mahila

Arogya Samiti to fulfil urgent hard cash needs for treatments; (b) a Health Insurance Scheme for enabling urban poor to meet medical treatment needs.

NUHM would cover all cities with a population of more than 100,000. It would cover slum dwellers; other marginalized urban dwellers like rickshaw pullers, street vendors, railway and bus station coolies, homeless people, street children, construction site workers, who may be in slums or on sites.

The existing Urban Health Posts (UHPs) and Urban Family Welfare Centres (UFWCs) would continue under NUHM. They will be marked on a map and classified as the Urban Health Centres, on the basis of their current population coverage. All the existing human resources will then be suitably reorganized and rationalized. These centres will also be considered for upgradation.

Inter-sectoral coordination mechanism and convergence will be planned between the Jawahar Lal Nehru National Urban Renewal Mission and the National Urban Health Mission.

6.14 National Rural Health Mission (NRHM)

NRHM was launched on April 12, 2005, to provide accessible, affordable and accountable quality health services to the poorest households in the remotest rural regions. The thrust of the Mission was on establishing a fully functional, community owned, decentralized health delivery system with inter-sectoral convergence at all levels, to ensure simultaneous action on a wide range of determinants of health like water, sanitation, education, nutrition, social and gender equality. Under the NRHM, the focus was on a functional health system at all levels, from the village to the district.

The Mission aims to provide universal access to equitable, affordable and quality health care which is accountable and at the same time responsive to the needs of the people. The Mission is expected to achieve the goals set under the National

Health Policy and the Millennium Development Goals.

To achieve these goals, NRHM facilitates increased access and utilization of quality health services by all, forge a partnership between the Central, State and the local governments, set up a platform for involving the PRIs and the community in the management of primary health programmes and infrastructure and provides an opportunity for promoting equity and social justice. The NRHM establishes a mechanism to provide flexibility to the States and the community to promote local initiatives and develop a framework for promoting inter-sectoral convergence for promotive and preventive health care. The Mission has also defined core and supplementary strategies.

6.14.1 Strategies of NRHM:

A. Core Strategies: These are the following:

- Train and enhance capacity of Panchayati Raj Institutions (PRIs) to supervise and manage public health services.
- Promote access to improved health care at household level through the female health activist (ASHA).
- Health Plan for each village through Village Health Committee of the Panchayat.
- Strengthen sub-centre through an untied fund to enable local planning and action and more Multi Purpose Workers (MPWs).
- Strengthen existing PHCs and CHCs and provision of 30-50 bedded CHC per Lakh population for improved curative care to a normative standard (Indian Public Health Service Standards defining personnel, equipment and management standards).
- Prepare and implement an inter-sectoral District Health Plan prepared by the District Health Mission, including drinking water, sanitation, hygiene and nutrition.
- Integrate vertical health and family welfare programmes at National, State and District levels.
- Technical Support to National, State and District Health Missions for Public Health Management.

- Strengthen capacities for data collection, assessment and review for evidence-based planning, monitoring and supervision.
- Formulate transparent policies for deployment and career development of Human Resources for health.
- Develop capacities for preventive health care at all levels for promoting healthy life styles, reduction in consumption of tobacco and alcohol, etc.
- Promote non-profit sector particularly in underserved areas.

B. Supplementary Strategies: These include:

- Regulation of Private Sector including the informal rural practitioners to ensure availability of quality service to citizens at reasonable cost.
- Promotion of Public Private Partnerships (PPP) for achieving public health goals.
- Reorienting medical education to support health issues including regulation of Medical Care and Medical Ethics.
- Effective and viable risk-pooling and social health insurance to provide health security to the poor by ensuring accessible, affordable, accountable and good quality health care.

6.14.2 Five Planks of the National Rural Health Mission:

- The Mission is expected to address the gaps in the provision of effective health care to rural population with special focus on 18 States, which have weak public health indicators and/or weak infrastructure.
- The Mission is a shift away from the vertical health and family welfare programmes to a new architecture of all inclusive health development in which societies under different programmes will be merged and resources pooled at the district level.
- The Mission aims at effective integration of health concerns with determinants of health like safe drinking water, sanitation and nutrition through integrated District

Plans for Health. There is a provision for flexible funds so that the States can utilise them in the areas they feel are important.

- The Mission provides for appointment of Accredited Social Health Activist (ASHA) in each village and strengthening public health infrastructure, including outreach through mobile clinics. It emphasizes involvement of the non-profit sector, especially in the under served areas. It also aims at flexibility at the local level by providing for untied funds.
- The Mission, in its supplementary strategies, aims at fostering public-private partnerships; improving equity and reducing out of pocket expenses; introducing effective risk-pooling mechanisms and social health insurance; and taking advantage of local health traditions.

In the Eleventh Five Year Plan, the emphasis under NRHM will not be on numerical achievements only but also on Indian Public Health Service Standards and enforcement of guidelines for improving the functioning of infrastructure being strengthened and created. It has been felt that the Mission Directors, both at the Centre and the States, should be officials with public health background, supported by the Civil Service cadres.

NRHM has successfully provided a platform for community health action at all levels. Besides merger of Departments of Health and Family Welfare in all States, NRHM has successfully moved towards a single State and District level Health Society for effective integration and convergence. Through a concerted effort at decentralized planning through preparation of District Health Action Plans, NRHM has managed to bring about intra-health sector and inter-sectoral convergence for effectiveness and efficiency. In all the States, specific health needs of people have been articulated for local action. With the establishment of public institutions like the Village Health and Sanitation Committees (VH&SCs), Hospital Development Committees and PRI-led

Committees, it is the civil society to which the health system is being made increasingly accountable. Through untied and flexible financing, NRHM is trying to drive reforms that empower local communities to make their own decisions. It is thus a serious effort at putting people's health in people's hands.

6.15 Sarva Swasthya Abhiyan (SSA)

The Tenth Five-Year Plan (2002-2007) indicated the dismal picture of the health services infrastructure and emphasized the need to invest more on building good primary-level care and referral services. The plan emphasized on restructuring and developing the health infrastructure, especially at the primary level.

The plan highlighted the importance of the role of decentralization but did not state how this would be achieved. Programme-driven health care was in focus. Verticality and technical solutions were given more importance than the comprehensive primary health care. The multi-sectoral approach that is much needed for a vibrant health system had not been well thought out.

Eleventh Five Year Plan envisages inclusive growth by introducing National Urban Health Mission (NUHM) which along with National Rural Health Mission (NRHM) will form Sarva Swasthya Abhiyan (SSA).

NRHM was launched for meeting health needs of all age groups and reduce disease burden across rural India. NUHM will be launched to meet the unmet needs of the urban population. NUHM based on health insurance and public-private partnership will provide integrated health service delivery to the urban poor. Initially, the focus will be on urban slums. NUHM will be aligned with NRHM and existing urban schemes. Besides, Sarva Swasthya Abhiyan aims for inclusive growth by finding solutions for strengthening health services and focusing on neglected areas and groups.

6.16 Janani Suraksha Yojana (JSY)

To change the behaviour of the community towards institutional delivery, the Government of India, under NRHM in 2005, modified the National Maternity Benefit Scheme (NMBS), from that of a nutrition-improving initiative to the JSY. The scheme has the dual objectives of reducing maternal and infant mortality by promoting institutional deliveries. Though the JSY is implemented in all States and UTs, its focus is on States having low institutional delivery rate. The scheme is 100 percent centrally sponsored and integrates cash assistance with maternal care. It is funded through the flexi-pool mechanism.

While the JSY scheme is meant to promote institutional delivery, it has to take two critical factors into account, one being that India does not have the institutional capacity to receive the 26 million women giving birth each year, and the other being that around half of all maternal deaths occur outside of delivery, during pregnancy, abortions and postpartum complications. If institutions are preoccupied with handling the huge numbers of normal childbirths, there will be inevitable neglect of life-threatening complications faced by women. They will be compelled to vacate beds in the shortest time. Consequently, complications during pregnancy and after childbirth will not be given attention. Second, JSY money sometimes does not reach hospitals on time, and as a result, poor women and their families do not receive the promised money.

6.17 Health Education

In India, medical education is highly regulated and there is an access barrier for setting up new medical and dental colleges. Eligibility for setting up medical or dental colleges is limited to the following organizations:

1. A State Government/ Union territory.
2. A University.
3. An autonomous body promoted by Central and State

Government.

4. A Society registered under the Societies Registration Act, 1860 or corresponding Acts in States.
5. A public religious or charitable trust registered under the Trust Act, 1882 or the Wakf Act, 1954.

Thus, for example, the corporate sector is not eligible and only not-for-profit organizations can apply. The private sector medical and dental colleges that have been established in large numbers have all done so by setting up not-for-profit societies.

Besides the problem of the numbers of health care personnel there is an acute problem of quality as well. Some of the private colleges are producing graduates far below the standards required but the Government colleges have also deteriorated, in part because of shortage of staff, the vacancies remaining unfilled because of unattractive remuneration. In Government medical colleges another reason for deterioration of the quality of medical graduates is that they do not get the opportunity to observe the treatment of patients because of the fall in the number of patients coming to Government hospitals for treatment.

6.18 Medical Value Travel in India

Recent decades have seen a tremendous growth in private sector investment in health care. Hospitals established by the private corporate players are of world class. They have not only the latest medical technological facilities but also the services of Indian doctors and nurses with a high degree of proficiency. Corporate hospitals are completely equipped, up market and proficient and can measure up, or even outshine, any hospital in the west. India is able to offer highly cost competitive medical treatment with the most up-to-date technological advances.

The quality of service coupled with comparatively low charges for common surgeries has made India an attractive destination for medical value travel. The Indian Government has moved to provide visa facilities for the medical tourists.

The main clientele comes from the SAARC countries but an increasing number of NRIs settled in the US and the UK have also been availing of the health care services in India. There is a good prospect of patients coming from the Middle East in future. The main impediment for medical tourists coming from the UK and US for major surgeries is the fact that the insurance companies are generally not willing to cover treatment in India. However, the cost savings involved in getting treatment done in India is bound to break barriers imposed by insurance companies. Already some hospitals are entering into alliance with international insurance companies for making it possible to send patients to India for treatment.

The competitiveness of India in medical value travel is enhanced by the attractiveness of the alternative systems of medicine, Ayurveda in particular, for the foreign tourists. A large number of tourists, both domestic and foreign, undergo treatment under Ayurveda not only for improving their fitness and well-being but also for curing many types of chronic diseases. For the regulation of Ayurveda clinics and for ensuring that they employ techniques in accordance with traditional methods, the Ministry of Health has issued guidelines to be used by the States. Accordingly Kerala, the most popular destination for tourists for treatment under Ayurveda has promulgated an Ordinance regulating Ayurveda Health Centres. The Ordinance requires registration of such centres and prescribes the facilities and medical staff that they must have in order to run them. The unique position that Kerala enjoys with respect to Ayurveda is due to the fact that the treatment in the State has proved effective in dealing with certain diseases, which are incurable by other systems. The State is also well endowed with herbs and medicinal plants, which are used for treatment.

Medical tourism is an international dimension of the growth of the health care industry. Thailand has been able to attract more than 1 million medical tourists due to world class infrastructure facilities in Thailand. India should be able to replicate the Thailand example by focusing on development of good quality medical as well as tourism infrastructure. India certainly has the potential and the capacity to attract more than 1 million tourists per annum.

There are two clear advantages for India in the field of medical tourism. The first and the foremost is the cost advantage. The second unique advantage of India is that it offers holistic medicinal services. With yoga, meditation, ayurveda, allopathy and natural herbal treatments, India offers a unique basket of services to foreign patient-tourists that is difficult to match by other countries. Kerala has been the pioneering State in this area as evidenced by the fact that Kerala and Ayurveda have virtually become synonymous with each other. The preference for health tourism in Kerala is so strong that Kerala Ayurveda Centre (KAC) has been established at multiple locations in various major cities. Karnataka has also taken some very pioneering steps in promoting medical tourism. Government of Karnataka has planned to set up Bangalore International Health City Corporation in order to cater to international patients for a wide variety of health care products and treatments. The recent operations of children from Pakistan in Bangalore have not only helped boost the medical economy in the state, but also helped in fostering goodwill, peace and harmony between India and Pakistan.

In Maharashtra, there is a wide array of speciality and super-speciality hospitals that can help promote medical tourism. Some of the major hospitals already in the business of medical tourism are Lilavati Hospital, Jaslok Hospital, Breach Candy, Hinduja Hospital, Wockhardt Hospital and Apollo NUSI Wellness Retreat. The Asian Heart Institute at Mumbai's Bandra-Kurla Complex offers state-of-the-art facilities for all types of heart ailments. Hotels like Hyatt, JW Marriott, Renaissance and Resort offer extensive spa facilities for both domestic and international tourists.

The Indian Health care Federation has prepared a roadmap

for making India a world class destination for medical tourism. Accreditation of Indian hospitals is paramount for medical tourism. This will help in ensuring quality standards across a spectrum of specialty and super-specialty hospitals. In order to encourage medical tourism, air connectivity needs to be strengthened for all the major cities in the country especially Delhi, Chennai, Bangalore, Pune, Hyderabad and Kolkata. Health-support infrastructure also needs to be created at the airports and other travel junctions. It is also essential to establish Indian health care brand synonymous with safety, trust and excellence. One-stop centres need to be established in key international markets to facilitate inflow of foreign patients, and immigration process needs to be streamlined for medical visitors.

A related area which can be exploited is provision of back-end health care related services. Health care majors in the developed world, especially the US, are already outsourcing back-end health care services to Indian BPO firms. The major health care BPO operations in the country are Hinduja TMT (claims adjudication), Apollo Health Street (claims adjudication, billing and coding), Comat Technologies (transcription), Datamatics (transcription and forms processing) and Lapiz (medical billing).

6.19 Indian Medical Professionals in Foreign Countries

One of the main reasons for the international competitiveness of private health care institutions in India is the quality of Indian medical professionals. While the quality is highly variable across the country, the best professionals in India match the quality of professionals in the developed countries. For several decades Indian medical professionals have been serving not only in the Middle East but also in several English speaking developed countries including the USA and the UK. India has also emerged as a supplier of other categories of health care professionals to a number of countries, particularly radiologists, laboratory technicians, dental hygienists, physiotherapists and medical rehabilitation workers.

6.20 Issues in Health Care Sector

6.20.1 Regulation: The competitiveness of health care services in the country suffers from under-regulation on the whole but over-regulation on the medical education front. Medical professionals are regulated through Central legislation, viz. Indian Medical Councils Act, Dentist Act and Nursing Council Act. These laws provide for the setting up of regulatory councils at the National and State levels. The National Councils prescribe norms and standards of education, while the State Councils deal primarily with registration and enforcement of these standards. The Ministry of Health and Family Welfare has developed Indian Public Health Standards (IPHS) for certain Governmental clinical establishments, viz. Community Health Centres (CHC), Primary Health Centres (PHC) and Sub-Centres, which are implemented through administrative means.

Standards are also being evolved for the larger hospitals, up to 500 beds. A few States and Union Territories have enacted laws (The Bombay Nursing Homes Act, 1949; Delhi Nursing Homes Act, 1953; and Tamil Nadu Private Clinical Establishments Act, 1997) for registration and regulation of nursing and clinical establishments, but they were not comprehensive in that they did not cover laboratories and diagnostic centres, and there were deficiencies in laying down minimum standards. More importantly their implementation has remained ineffective. There has been resistance from some stakeholders against the introduction of law for the regulation of health care service providers because of the fear of Inspector Raj. Opposition to regulation of health service providers has also been fuelled by the exemption provided in some of the State laws for the public health institutions. On the other hand, there is scepticism among policy makers whether publicly funded health care institutions will be able to adhere to the standards. The multiplicity in the types of clinical establishments has also daunted policy makers from undertaking the task of formulating minimum standards, which are a prerequisite for effective regulation. At the Central level, some specific aspects of health care services have been regulated through legislation, such as management of medical waste, setting up of blood banks, and pre-natal diagnostic tests, but there is absence of an overall statutory framework for the licensing of health care establishments such as hospitals, nursing homes and clinics, and laying down the minimum standards that must be met.

6.20.2 Licensing: There are rules for the registration of medical practitioners and separate regulations for professional conduct, etiquette and ethics. The latter contain certain recommendatory rules, such as use of generic names of drugs, but also mandatory rules, such as for the maintenance of medical records of indoor patients for minimum period of three years and maintenance of a register of certificates issued. There is however a serious regulatory gap in the country in that there are no mandatory standards prescribed and enforced for hospitals, nursing homes, clinics, as well as establishments undertaking diagnosis or treatment of disease. The standards for hospitals, for instance, should cover all aspects ranging from building and fire safety to availability of potable water and from basic laboratory services to employment of health professionals. According to international best practices license is granted initially on the basis of some form of external evaluation of compliance with the prescribed minimum standards.

6.20.3 Accreditation: The commencement in 2006 of an accreditation programme for secondary and tertiary hospitals by the National Accreditation Board for Hospitals and Healthcare Providers (NABH), a constituent board of the Quality Council of India, represents a strong attempt to improve the quality of health care establishments in the country. Accreditation is a voluntary process, involving evaluation of an organization's compliance with pre-established performance standards. The organization is granted accreditation if it is assessed to meet an acceptable level compliance, or it may be given a conditional accreditation.

NABH has 120 qualified assessors on its panel, comprising senior clinicians, hospital administrators and nursing supervisors, who are assigned the task of carrying out the evaluation.

An accreditation system such as what has been established in India is the best way of improving the quality of performance of clinical establishments. The challenge in the country is for more and more clinical establishments to take advantage of the accreditation system in order to improve the quality of healthcare service in the country. As for clinical establishment run by the Central and State Governments, the first step should be that they adhere to the minimum standards prescribed under the proposed legislation, but as a subsequent step they should also come forward and take advantage of the accreditation system.

6.21 Family Planning and Welfare

As per the Census of India, 2001, the population of India as on March 1, 2001 was 1027 million, with males at 531 million and females at 496 million. Viewed globally, India constitutes 16.87 percent of the world population. India is following the demographic transition pattern of all developing countries from initial levels of *high birth rate–high death rate* to the intermediate transition stage of *high birth rate–low death rate* which manifests in high rates of population growth, before graduating to *low birth rate–low death rate* stage. The improvement in the quality of health care over the years is reflected in some of the basic demographic parameters (Table 6.5).

The current high population growth rate is due to (a) the large size of the population in the reproductive age-group, (b) higher fertility due to unmet need for contraception and (c) high wanted fertility due to prevailing high IMR.

Table 6.5: Trends in India's Demographic Indicators

Indicator	1951	1981	1991	Current
Crude birth rate (per 1,000 population)	40.8	33.9	29.5	22.8 (2008)
Crude death rate (per 1,000 population)	25.1	12.5	9.8	7.4 (2008)
Total fertility rate (per woman)	6.0	4.5	3.6	2.7 (2007)
Maternal mortality rate (per 1,00,000 live births)	NA	NA	437	254 (2004-06)
Infant mortality rate (per 1,000 live births)	146	110	80	53 (2008)
Child (0-4 years) mortality rate per 1,000 children	57.3	41.2	26.5	16.0 (2007)
Life expectancy at birth (Male)	37.2	55.4*	59.0#	63.5^
(Female)	36.2	55.7*	59.7#	64.2^

*(1981-85); #(1989-93); ^(2002-06)

Source: Government of India, *Economic Survey, 2009-10*, Table 11.9 (excerpted), p. 284.

The goal of population stabilization can be achieved only when child survival, maternal health and contraception issues are addressed simultaneously and effectively. Actual success in containing the growth of population would, however, depend upon: (a) publicly-related support from community leaders, (b) resources available for the family welfare programmes, (c) efficiency and accountability in the States health system for ensuring effective delivery of services to citizens and (d) women's education and status in the family. All these inputs have so far not been uniformly available to the required extent for the family welfare programmes, thereby not allowing the optimal benefits to be reaped from the same.

6.21.1 Family Welfare in the Tenth Five Year Plan (2002-07): The Tenth Plan envisaged the following measures to enable families to achieve their reproductive goals:

- Method-specific contraceptive targets to meet all the

unmet needs for contraception to reduce unwanted pregnancies.

- Health care for women and children by integrating numerous vertical programmes for family planning and child health.
- Implementation of Reproductive and Child Health care (RCH) programme to reduce infant mortality and reduce high desired fertility.
- Predominantly women-centred programmes to meet the health care needs of the family with emphasis on involvement of men in planned parenthood.

6.21.2 Family Welfare in the National Population Policy (NPP), 2000: NPP adopted in February 2000 affirmed the commitment of the Government towards stabilizing the population of the country by providing for its citizens voluntary and informed decisions about their family size. The policy envisaged certain National Socio-Demographic goals to be achieved by 2010 for paving the way for a stable population in the country by 2045, at a level consistent with the requirements of sustainable economic growth and social development. It also provided a policy for advancing goals and prioritizing strategies during the next decade, to meet the reproductive and child health needs of the people of India, and to achieve net replacement levels of fertility (Total Fertility Rate =2:1) by 2010.

It was decided to relocate the National Population Stabilization Fund (NPSF) from the National Commission on Population to the Department of Family Welfare. The NPSF was created with core funding of Rs. 100 crore from Government of India and will invite funds from the voluntary and corporate sectors.

An Empowered Action Group (EAG) was constituted in the Ministry of Health and Family Welfare with Union Minister for Health and Family Welfare as Chairman on March 20, 2001. The EAG aims at assisting States with weak socio-demographic indicators to attain the goals listed in the

National Population Policy, 2000. In the first instance, the States of Bihar, Uttar Pradesh, Madhya Pradesh, Rajasthan, Orissa, Jharkhand, Uttaranchal and Chhattisgarh were chosen for focussed attention.

Population Census 2001 showed a decline in the sex ratio in the age group 0-6 years in several States. For the country as a whole the child sex ratio is 927 girls per 1000 boys which is much less than 945 recorded in the 1991 Census. The Government is keen to strengthen the implementation mechanism of Pre-Natal Diagnostic Techniques (Regulation and Prevention of Misuse) Act, 1994.

The Reproductive and Child Health Programme (RCH) was launched on October 10, 1997 which combines fertility regulation, safe motherhood, child survival and Reproductive Tract Infections (RTI)/Sexually Transmitted Infections (STI). This programme is primarily implemented through the primary health care infrastructure.

Vitamin A deficiency, which can lead to blindness, has been prevalent in the country, especially among the pre-school children. Under the programme for prevention and control of vitamin A deficiency among children, five doses of vitamin A are administered to all children under 3 years of age.

Iron deficiency (anaemia) is widely prevalent not only in women of child-bearing age but also in young children. The National Family Health Survey-II (1998-99) revealed that 74.3 percent children under the age of 3 years were anaemic. There is a marginal difference in the prevalence in the rural and urban areas. While 75.3 percent of rural children were found to be anaemic, the prevalence in urban children was 70.8 percent. Iron folic acid tablets containing 20 mg of elemental iron and 0.1 mg of folic acid are provided at the sub-centre level.

It is estimated that prior to the Pulse Polio Immunization Programme around 2.5 lakh children used to get afflicted by polio each year. In order to establish a better surveillance system, National Polio Surveillance Project (NPSP) was launched in October 1997 under which a network of 8,000 reporting units have been established which is being supervised by over 220 Surveillance Medical Officers. The NPSP has been able to sustain an international standard surveillance system for polio since then. The number of reported polio cases declined considerably from 28,257 reported in 1987 to 268 in 2001. However, during 2002, 1,211 polio cases were reported out of which 990 cases were from Uttar Pradesh, and 81 from Bihar.

The agenda for population stabilization is multi-sectoral which necessitates decentralization and convergence across sectors. In cooperation with State Governments, the Department of Family Welfare is bringing about a convergence between the NGOs, the Self-help Groups, Zila Saksharta Samitis and Panchayati Raj Institutions, to improve integrated service delivery at community and household levels.

6.22 Nutrition Support

Although the country has been able to eliminate nutritional deficiency syndrome like pellagra, beriberi, scurvy etc. yet chronic energy deficiency among adults, under-nutrition among children and micronutrient deficiencies are still prevalent across all section of the population. The country has adopted a multi-sectoral and multi-pronged strategy to combat these problems and to improve the nutritional status of the population.

One half of the children under the age of 5 years in India are moderately or severely malnourished, 30 percent of newborn children are significantly under weight and nearly 60 percent of women are anaemic. Under the Integrated Child Development Scheme (ICDS), the Department of Women and Child Development implements the food supplementation programme for improving nutritional status of mothers and children. Ministry of Health and Family Welfare implements programmes for tackling major micronutrient deficiencies such as vitamin A and iodine deficiency etc.

To address the needs of under-nourished infants and

children below 3 years, 15 percent of the total Additional Central Assistance (ACA) is earmarked for the nutrition component under the Pradhan Mantri Gramodaya Yojana (PMGY). ACA under the nutrition component of PMGY is an additionality for providing nutrition to children in 0-3 years. States are required to ensure that all below poverty line (BPL) children in 0-3 years are registered for PMGY and provided requisite nutrition.

The programme of Nutritional Support to Primary Education, popularly known as Mid-day Meal Scheme, was launched in 1995 as a fully-funded Centrally Sponsored Scheme. Under this scheme, all children in primary schools in government and government-aided schools are covered. Ideally, a hot meal is provided to the children at school for 10 months in a year. The foodgrains are delivered directly at the district level by the Food Corporation of India, under instructions from the Department of Education in the Government of India.

6.22.1 National Nutrition Mission (NNM): The Prime Minister, in his Independence Day speech on August 15, 2001 announced the setting up of NNM. Under this Mission, subsidized foodgrains are made available to adolescent girls and expectant and nursing mothers, belonging to below-poverty-line families. NNM is headed by the Prime Minister and its Executive Committee is under the Human Resource Development Minister.

6.23 Towards e-Health

Eleventh Five Year Plan (2007-12) has ambitious programmes to use information technology for health services and usher India into the age of e-health. To quote, "Appropriate use of IT for an enhanced role in health care and governance will be aimed at during the Eleventh Five Year Plan. It is feasible to set up a National Grid to be shared by health care providers, trainers, beneficiaries and civil society. The country already has the advantage of a strong fibre backbone and indigenous satellite communication technology with trained human resources in this regard. A number of pilot projects on e-Health over the past years by private concerns, corporate, NGOs, medical colleges and research institutions have been set up. The successful outcome of many of these initiatives needs to be evaluated and scaled up.

Health Management Information System (HMIS) would be an important new initiative utilizing developments in the field of information technology. A computerized web enabled data capturing and analytical system will be established to provide valid and reliable data and reports for use at all levels. This would not only facilitate proper monitoring and evaluation of different programmes under implementation but will also help in various aspects of service delivery. The HMIS will also integrate the various vertical systems having their own reporting machinery into an integrated umbrella of holistic monitoring and evaluation to cater to the needs of Sarva Swasthya Abhiyan. The data will flow directly from the periphery. The Integrated Disease Surveillance Project (IDSP) will eventually be a by-product of the HMIS. As the system stabilizes and the penetration of computerization at the Block level increases, the system will be modular enough to expand the scope to the remotest areas. Wastage of drugs due to date expiry also needs to be curtailed by demand driven management and redistribution of medicines nearing date of expiry. Health Management Information System (HMIS) when fully developed and implemented will track demand and supply and continuously monitor the drug situation.

Telemedicine could help to bring specialized health care to the remotest corners of the country. Telemedicine is likely to provide the advantages of tele-diagnosis, especially in the areas of cardiology, pathology, dermatology and radiology besides continuing medical education. It will be of immense use for diagnostic and consultative purposes for patients getting treatment from the secondary level health care facilities. The efficacy of telemedicine has already been shown through the network established by the Indian Space Research Organization (ISRO), which has connected 42 super-specialty hospitals with 8 mobile telemedicine vans and 200 rural and remote hospitals across the country through its geostationary satellites. So far about 3 Lakh people have benefited from this programme. Facility of telemedicine will be provided in district hospitals and Government Medical Colleges.

The e-Health initiatives to be taken up during the Eleventh Five Year Plan are:

- Training, Education & Capacity Building for e-Health.
- Monitoring by e enabled Health MIS (HMIS) to ensure timely flow of data and collation to be used at various levels.
- GIS Resource Mapping of various health facilities (Allopathic & AYUSH), Laboratories, Training Centres, Health Manpower and other inputs to optimize utilisation.
- Providing service delivery and other e-enabled activities like, disease surveillance, tele-consultations, health helpline, district hospital referral net and e enabled mobile medical units. [3]

6.24 Time-bound Goals of the Eleventh Five Year Plan

- Reducing Maternal Mortality Ratio (MMR) to 1 per 1000 live births.
- Reducing Infant Mortality Rate (IMR) to 28 per 1000 live births.
- Reducing Total Fertility Rate to 2.1.
- Providing clean drinking water for all by 2009 and ensuring no slip-backs.
- Reducing malnutrition among children of age group 0-3 to half its present level.
- Reducing anaemia among women and girls by 50 percent.
- Raising the sex ratio for age group 0-6 to 935 by 2011-12 and 950 by 2016-17.

6.25 Conclusion

Since Independence in 1947, India has built up a vast health infrastructure and health personnel at primary, secondary and tertiary care in public, voluntary and private sectors. Health of a nation is an essential component of development, vital to nation's economic growth and internal stability. Assuring a minimal level of health care to the population is a critical constituent of the development process.

Considerable achievements have been made over the last six decades to improve health standards; such as in life expectancy, child mortality, infant mortality and maternal mortality. Small pox and guinea worm have been eradicated and there is hope that poliomyelitis will be contained in the near future. Nevertheless, problems abound. Malnutrition affects a large proportion of children. An unacceptably high proportion of the population continues to suffer and die from new diseases which are emerging apart from continuing and new threats posed by the existing ones. Pregnancy and childbirth related complications also contribute to the suffering and mortality.

The strong link between poverty and ill health needs to be recognized. The onset of a long and expensive illness can drive the economically well-off into poverty. Ill health creates immense stress even among those who are financially secure. High health care costs can lead a family into poverty. The importance of public provisioning of quality health care to enable access to affordable and reliable heath services cannot be underestimated. This is specially so, in the context of preventing the non-poor from entering into poverty and reducing the suffering of those who are already below poverty line.

Public institutions played a dominant role in the Indian Healthcare sector in the past, in the urban as well as in the rural areas. However, the public healthcare has been on a serious decline during the last two or three decades because of non-availability of medical and paramedical staff, diagnostic services and medicines. Equally distressing is the fact that essential therapeutic drugs are not supplied in most public health institutions with the exception of some States. Consequently there has been a pronounced decline in the percentage of cases of hospitalized treatment in Government hospitals and a corresponding increase in the percentage treated in private hospitals. Despite higher costs in the private sector, this shift shows the people's growing lack of trust in the public system. Critical shortage of health personnel, inadequate incentives, poor working conditions, lack of transparency in posting of doctors in rural areas, absenteeism, long wait, inconvenient clinic hours, poor outreach, time of service, insensitivity to local needs, inadequate planning, management, and monitoring of service/facilities appear to be the main reasons for low utilization'.

India has to deal with rising costs of health care and growing expectations of the people. The challenge of quality health services in remote rural regions has to be urgently met. Given the magnitude of the problem, there is the need to transform public health care into an accountable, accessible and affordable system of quality services.

Special attention needs to be given to the health of vulnerable groups like adolescent girls, women, children, older persons [4], disabled and primitive tribal groups. The contribution of the private sector in providing primary, secondary and tertiary services should be enhanced through various measures including partnership with the Government. Good governance, transparency and accountability in the delivery of health services should be ensured through involvement of Panchayati Raj Institutions (PRIs), Community and Civil Society Groups.

Rising income levels and the emergence of health insurance has facilitated the growth of high quality health care sector in India although the capacity to pay for health services remains limited to middle and high income brackets. With the opening of the insurance market in 2000 to private players, health and medical insurance has shown significant growth. Though at present, only 2.5 million people are covered under voluntary medical insurance. Cashless claim facilities offered by many players have led to a significant rise in health insurers.

The public health care system is not able to meet the growing demands for health care facilities. The gap between demand and supply has to be bridged by the private players, and this has facilitated the growth of the corporate health care industry in India. Emergence of strong corporate players in health care is not a substitute for expansion of public sector health facilities especially for the bulk of our population but it has led to professionalization of the industry, better hospital management and higher investments in infrastructure facilities.

Notes

1. International Labour Organization (ILO) Convention No. 130 and Recommendation No. 69 contain guidelines for the provision of medical care under social security.
2. Government of India, Planning Commission, *Eleventh Five Year Plan* (2007-12), Vol., II, p. 67.
3. Ibid., pp. 85-87.
4. In order that the elderly people keep healthy, it is necessary that they should remain gainfully active. Their services should therefore, be utilised in various activities of the community, such as manning childcare centres cultural clubs, vocational training centres etc. for which they may be paid appropriate remuneration, or allowances or honorarium.

7

Education, Training and Skill Formation

Literacy levels in a country are a measure of its degree of commitment to social justice. A literate environment is essential for ensuring universal elementary education, reducing child mortality, curbing population growth, ensuring gender equality and acquiring essential livelihood skills.

Education is a critical input for investment in human capital. As the Eleventh Five Year Plan (2007-12) observed, "The role of education in facilitating social and economic progress is well recognized. It opens up opportunities leading to both individual and group entitlements. Education in its broadest sense of development of youth is the most crucial input for empowering people with skills and knowledge and giving them access to productive employment in future. Improvements in education are not only expected to enhance efficiency but also augment the overall quality of life." [1]

7.1 Trends in Literacy Rates and Recent Initiatives

Over the decades, literacy rates have shown a substantial improvement. The total literacy rate which was only 18.33 percent in 1951, rose to 52.21 percent in 1991 and further increased to 65.4 percent in 2001. According to the Census of India, 2001, the literacy rate has gone up to 75.85 percent for males and 54.16 percent for females. Female literacy rate has shown much higher growth, increasing by 14.87 percentage points as against 11.72 for males thus reducing the male-female differential in literacy rates from 24.84 in 1991 to 21.7 in 2001 (Table 7.1).

Literacy rates in India have risen sharply from 18.3 percent in 1951 to 65.4 percent in 2001. Nevertheless, India continues to lag behind several other developing countries in the region such as China (86 percent) and Sri Lanka (92 percent).

Table 7.1: Literacy Rates in India (1951-2001)

(percent)

Census Year	Persons	Males	Females	Male-Female gap in literacy rate
1951	18.33	27.16	8.66	18.30
1961	28.30	40.40	15.35	25.05
1971	34.45	45.96	21.97	23.98
1981	43.57	56.38	29.76	26.62
1991	52.21	64.13	39.29	24.84
2001	65.38	75.85	54.16	21.70

Source: Census of India.

Plan expenditure on education has increased rapidly since the First Five Year Plan. A high priority was accorded to this sector in the Tenth Five Year Plan (2002-07), with an allocation of Rs. 43,825 crore as against Rs. 24,908 crore made available in the Ninth Five Year Plan (1997-02), representing an increase of 76 percent. During the Tenth Plan Rs. 28,750 crore were allocated for elementary education.

To enlist the support of all concerned and to mobilize extra budgetary resources for the education sector, *Bharat Shiksha Kosh*, a registered society has been set up for receiving contributions, donations or endowments from individuals, Central and State governments, NRIs and PIOs for various educational purposes.

The Constitutional (93rd Amendment) Bill, passed by both Houses of Parliament, received the President's Assent on December 12, 2002. This was a significant measure for achieving the goal of Education for All (EFA) by making free and compulsory elementary education a fundamental right for all children in the age group of 6-14 years. In order to fulfil this constitutional obligation, Sarva Shiksha Abhiyan was launched in partnership with the States. The programme is an effort towards recognition of the need for improving the performance of the school system through a community owned approach and ensuring quality elementary education in a mission mode to all children in the age group of 6-14 years by 2010. It also seeks to bridge gender and social gaps. This programme will subsume all existing programmes (except *Mahila Samakhya* and Mid-day Meal Schemes) including externally-aided programmes in due course with its overall framework with district as the unit of programmes implementation.

7.2 Elementary Education

Within the education sector, elementary education has been given the highest priority in terms of sub-sectoral allocations and a number of schemes launched by the Central Government to meet the needs of the educationally disadvantaged. These have included the following.

1. Operation Blackboard.
2. District Primary Education Programme.
3. Education Guarantee Scheme.
4. Alternative and Innovative Education.
5. *Mahila Samakhya.*
6. National Programmes of Nutritional Support to Primary Education.
7. *Lok Jumbish.*
8. *Shiksh Karmi* Project.
9. *Janashala* Programme.
10. *Pradhan Mantri Gramodaya Yojana.*

Elementary education, i.e. classes I-VIII consisting of primary (I-V) and upper primary (VI-VIII) is the foundation of the structure of the education system.

7.2.1 Elementary Education in the Tenth Five Year (2002-07) Plan: Elementary education received a major push in the Tenth Plan through the Sarva Shiksha Abhiyan (SSA). The Tenth Plan laid emphasis on Universalisation of Elementary Education (UEE) guided by the following 5 parameters:

1. Universal Access.
2. Universal Enrolment.
3. Universal Retention.
4. Universal Achievement.
5. Equity.

The major schemes of elementary education sector during the Tenth Plan included SSA, District Primary Education Programme (DPEP), National Programme of Nutritional Support to Primary Education (NP-NSPE) commonly known as Mid-Day Meal Scheme (MDM), Teacher Education Scheme and Kasturba Gandhi Balika Vidyalaya Scheme (KGBVS).

7.2.2 Elementary Education in the Eleventh Five Year (2007-12) Plan: Eleventh Plan set the following targets for elementary education during its duration:

- "Universal enrolment of 6-14 age group children including the hard to reach segment.
- Substantial improvement in quality and standards with the ultimate objective to achieve standards of KVs under the CBSE pattern.
- All gender, social and regional gaps in enrolments to be eliminated by 2011-12.
- One year pre-schools education for children entering primary school.
- Dropout at primary level to be eliminated and the dropout rate at the elementary level to be reduced from over 50 percent to 20 percent by 2011-12.
- Universalized MDMS at elementary level by 2008-09.
- Universal coverage of ICT at upper primary schools by 2011-12.
- Significant improvement in learning conditions with emphasis on learning basic skills, verbal and quantitative.
- All EGS centres to be converted into regular primary schools.
- All States/UTs to adopt NCERT Quality Monitoring Tools.
- Strengthened BRCs/CRCs: one CRC for every 10 schools

and 5 resource teachers per block." [2]

7.2.3 Select Programmes for Elementary Education.

A. Sarva Shiksha Abhiyan (SSA): Launched in November 2000, SSA is a comprehensive programme and the main vehicle for providing elementary education to all children. The goals of SSA are the following.

1. All children in School, Education Guarantee Centre, Alternate School, Back-to-School camp by 2005.
2. Bridge all gender and social category gaps at the primary stage by 2007 and at elementary education level by 2010.
3. Universal retention by 2010.
4. Focus on elementary education of satisfactory quality with emphasis on education for life.

SSA, implemented in partnership with the States, addresses the needs of 209 million children in the age group of 6-14 years. It covers 9.72 lakh existing primary and upper primary schools and 36.95 lakh teachers.

SSA is the culmination of all previous endeavours and experiences in implementing various education programmes. SSA has been the single largest holistic programme addressing all aspects of elementary education covering over one million elementary schools SSA has brought primary education to the doorstep of millions of children and enrolled them, including first generation learners, through successive fast track initiatives in hitherto unserved and underserved habitations.

According to Eleventh Plan, "SSA interventions have brought down the number of out of school children from 32 million in 2001-02 to 7.1 million in 2005-06. Forty eight districts in 10 States accounted for over 50,000 out of school children, each. The number of such districts declined to 29 in 2005-06." [3]

B. Kasturba Gandhi Balika Vidyalaya Scheme (KGBVS): KGBVS was launched in July 2004 to set up 750 residential schools at elementary level for girls belonging predominantly to the SC, ST, OBC and minorities in Educationally Backward Blocks (EBBs). All 750 KGBVs have now been sanctioned by the Government of India, with 117 KGBVs (15.6 percent) allocated to blocks with substantial minority population. A minimum of 75 percent of the enrolment in KGBVs is reserved for girls from the target groups and the remaining 25 percent is open for girls belonging to the BPL category. The Tenth Plan allocation for the scheme was Rs.427 crore.

C. District Primary Education Programme (DPEP): Started in 1994, DPEP, an externally aided project, aimed at the holistic development of primary education covering Classes I to V. It had specific objectives of reducing the dropout rate to less than 10 percent, reducing disparities among gender and social groups in the enrolment to less than 5 percent and improving the level of learning achievement compared to the baseline surveys. However, these ambitious targets could not be achieved. Still, DPEP has brought a sea change in the implementation of school education programme with its decentralized approach and focus on community participation. At its peak, DPEP covered 273 districts in 17 States. Now it continues in only 17 districts of Orissa and Rajasthan where it would be completed in 2008.

D. National Programme of Nutritional Support to Primary Education: Launched on August 15, 1995 with the objective to boost the Universalisation of Primary Education by impacting upon enrolment, attendance, retention and nutritional needs of children studying in class I–V. Under this programme more than 10 crore children are being targeted for coverage. At present, Gujarat, Kerala, Tamil Nadu, Madhya Pradesh, Chattisgarh, Orissa, Karnataka and Delhi are providing cooked meals. The remaining States and UTs are distributing foodgrains (wheat/rice).

E. Pradhan Mantri Gramodaya Yojana: This programme was launched during 2000-01 and envisages Additional Central Assistance for basic minimum services in certain priority areas. The scheme has six components covering elementary education, primary health, rural shelter, rural drinking water, nutrition and rural electrification. A minimum of 10 percent of ACA for all components except nutrition (for which it is 15 percent) has been fixed. The allocation for the remaining 35 percent of ACA would be decided by the States and UTs among the components of the Scheme, as per their priorities. Funds for elementary education sector under PMGY are utilized to further the goal of Universalisation of Elementary Education.

F. National Programme for Education of Girls at Elementary Level (NPEGEL): It is an important component of SSA. NPEGEL provides additional support by way of girl-child friendly schools, stationery, uniforms, etc. for girls' education in educationally backward blocks (EBB), and in other areas for elementary education of under privileged and disadvantaged sections. EBBs are blocks with female literacy below, and gender gap above, the national average. Apart from EBBs, NPEGEL is also implemented in blocks of districts which are not covered under EBBs but have at least 5 percent SC/ST population and where SC/ST female literacy is below 10 percent, and also in select urban slums. In the Tenth Five Year Plan, an amount of Rs.1064.80 crore was earmarked for this programme.

Launched in July, 2003 as a focused intervention aimed at enhancing girls' education, NPEGEL provides for development of a "model school" in every cluster with more intense community mobilisation and supervision of girls' enrolment in schools. Gender-sensitisation of teachers, development of gender-sensitive learning materials and provision of need-based incentives like stationery, workbooks and uniforms are some of the objectives under NPEGEL. It is being implemented in about 3,164 educationally backward blocks in 25 States.

Under NPEGEL, around 31,450 model schools have been developed and 1.97 lakh teachers gender-sensitised. Over 51,345 Early Childhood Care and Education (ECCE) centres are being supported in areas not covered by Integrated Child

Development Services (ICDS) scheme to help free girls from sibling care responsibilities and attend schools. Free uniforms have been given as a direct educational incentive to about 2 crore girls in educationally backward blocks. 1.84 crore girls have been benefited under NPEGEL till October 31, 2006.

G. Education Guarantee Scheme and Alternative and Innovative Education (EGS&AIE): Another important component of SSA is the EGS&AIE. It is specially designed to provide access to elementary education to children in school-less habitations and out-of-school children. It supports flexible strategies for out-of-school children through bridge courses, residential camps, drop-in centres, summer camps, remedial coaching, etc., and helped to provide elementary education to 85.67 lakh children in 2004-05.

H. Mahila Samakhya (MS): MS, an externally aided project for women's empowerment, was started with Dutch assistance in 1989. Since 2005-06 it is being funded by GOI. The programme endeavours to create an environment for women to learn at their own pace, set their own priorities and seek knowledge and information to make informed choices. It has strengthened women's abilities to effectively participate in village level education programmes. The programme is implemented in 9 states covering 83 districts. The States of M.P. and Chhattisgarh have registered MS societies through which the programme is initiated. It provides for vocational and skill development as well as educational development of adolescent girls and women in rural areas.

I. Prarambhik Shiksha Kosh (PSK): Department of Elementary Education and Literacy issued orders on November 14, 2005 constituting Prarambhik Shiksha Kosh (PSK) to receive the proceeds of the education cess imposed through Finance (No.2) Act, 2004. PSK is a separate, dedicated, non-lapsable fund to be maintained by the Ministry of Human Resource Development.

J. Mid-Day Meal Scheme (MDMS): Mid-Day Meal Scheme (MDMS) was launched in 1995 to enhance enrolment, retention and participation of children in primary schools, simultaneously improving their nutritional status. It is the world's largest school feeding programme involving preparation of a hot meal everyday. It provides free foodgrains, cooking cost, transport subsidy and other facilities.

The MDM scheme was revised and universalised in September 2004 and central assistance was provided @ Re. 1 per child/per school day for converting foodgrains into hot cooked meals for children in classes IV in Government, Local Body and Government-aided schools, and Education Guarantee Scheme (EGS) and Alternate and Innovative Education (AIE) centres. The maximum permissible transport subsidy was revised for Special Category States from Rs. 50 to Rs. 100 per quintal and for other States to Rs. 75 per quintal.

The scheme was further revised in June 2006 to enhance the minimum cooking cost to Rs. 2.00 per child/per school day to provide 450 calories and 12 grams of protein. The revised scheme also provided assistance for construction of kitchen-cum-stores @ Rs. 60,000 per unit in a phased manner in primary schools and procurement of kitchen devices (utensils etc) @ Rs. 5000 per school. 94,500 schools were also sanctioned kitchen sheds and 2.6 lakh schools were sanctioned kitchen equipment. The number of children covered under the programme has risen from 3.34 crore in 3.22 lakh schools in 1995 to 12 crore in 9.5 lakh primary schools/EGS centres in 2006-07.

K. Problem Areas: In education, the elementary sector is besieged by numerous systemic problems such as inadequate school infrastructure, presence of single-teacher schools, high teacher absenteeism (especially in rural areas), large-scale teacher vacancies, inadequate equipment, etc. This brings into focus the role of decentralization and people's participation in the provision of basic services. It is essential that control over schools and teachers should be transferred to local bodies, having a direct interest in teacher performance. This has also been highlighted as an area of emphasis in the Tenth Plan.

The National Policy on Education (NPE), 1986, as modified in 1992, emphasised three aspects in relation to elementary education.

1. Universal access and enrolment.
2. Universal retention of children up to 14 years of age.
3. A substantial improvement in the quality of education to enable all children to achieve essential levels of learning.

NPE emphasised that education must play a positive and interventionist role in correcting social and regional imbalance, empowering women, and in securing a rightful place for the disadvantaged and the minorities. Government is firmly committed to providing education for all, the priority areas being free and compulsory elementary education, covering children with special needs, eradication of illiteracy, education for women's equality, and special focus on the education of SCs/STs and Minorities. Allocation for elementary education in the Tenth Five Year Plan period (2002-07) at Rs. 28,750 crore was 75 percent higher than the allocation in the Ninth Plan. Resources for elementary education have been augmented through imposition of the education cess at the rate of 2 percent on direct and indirect Central taxes imposed through Finance (No.2) Act, 2004.

In the Budget 2010-11 presented on 26.02.2010, Plan allocation for school education has been increased by 16 per cent from 26,800 crore in 2009-2010 to Rs. 31,036 crore in 2010-11.

7.3 Secondary and Vocational Education

The year 2008-09 was a momentous year for secondary education when a new Centrally Sponsored Scheme to universalise education at secondary stage was launched.

7.3.1 Secondary Education: This education sector prepares students in the age group of 14-18 years for entry into higher education as well as for the world of work. The success of Sarva Shiksha Abhiyan (SSA) in achieving large scale enrolment of children in regular and alternate schools has thrown open the challenge of expanding access to secondary education. Rapid changes in technology and the demand for skills also make it necessary that young people acquire more than eight years of elementary education to acquire the necessary skills to compete successfully in the labour market. Moreover, Secondary education serves as a bridge between elementary and higher education.

Women belonging to SCs and STs and those living in rural areas are the most disadvantaged. A Constitution Amendment Bill was passed by Parliament in December, 2005, which enables the State to make special provisions, by law, for admission of students belonging to SCs, STs and socially and educationally backward classes to educational institutions, including aided and unaided private educational institutions, except minority institutions referred to in Article 30(1) of the Constitution.

A. Centrally Managed Schools: The Central Government is managing and fully funding four types of schools, viz.

- Kendriya Vidyalayas (KVs).
- Navodaya Vidyalayas (NVs).
- Central Tibetan Schools (CTSs)
- National Institute of Open School (NIOS)

There are 972 KVs with an enrolment of 9.54 lakh and staff strength of about 46,000. KVs cater to the educational needs of the wards of transferable Central Government and public sector employees.

There are 548 NVs with a total enrolment of 1.91 lakh students, selected through entrance tests. These are pace setting residential co-educational schools providing quality education to talented children predominantly from rural areas.

There are 79 CTSs with a total enrolment of 9755 children,

NIOS provides opportunities for continuing education to those who missed completing school education. 14 lakh students are enrolled at the secondary and senior secondary stages through 11 Regional Centres, 1,943 accredicated institutions for academic courses and 1,002 accredited vocational institutions for programme delivery through open learning and distance learning. NIOS Centres have also been set up in UAE, Kuwait, Nepal and China.

Central Government also supports autonomous organisations like National Council of Educational Research and Training (NCERT) and Central Board of Secondary Education (CBSE).

The thrust of secondary education during the Tenth Plan period was on improving access and reducing disparities by emphasising the Common School System in which it is mandatory for schools in a particular area to take students from low income families in the neighbourhood. The Tenth Plan also focused on revision of curricula with emphasis on vocationalisation and employment-oriented courses, expansion and diversification of the open learning system, reorganization of teacher training and greater use of information and communication technologies. These objectives have been achieved only partly.

A notable feature of secondary education is the mushrooming of private unaided schools in recent years. It indicates that parents are willing to pay for education that is perceived to be of good quality. The factors underlying this perception include better English teaching; better monitoring and supervision of students' performance, better attention, attendance and accountability of teachers.

B. Targets for the Eleventh Plan: Following are the goals of the Eleventh Plan as regards secondary education:

- To raise the minimum level of education to class X level and accordingly universalise access to secondary education.
- To ensure good quality secondary education with focus on Science, Mathematics and English.
- To reduce gender, social and regional gaps in enrolments, dropouts and schools retention.

The norm will be to provide a secondary school within 5 km and a higher secondary school within 7-8 km of every habitation. The Gross Enrolment Ratio (GER) in secondary education is targeted to increase from 52 percent in 2004-05 to 75 percent by 2011-12 and the combined secondary and senior secondary GER from 40 percent to 65 percent in the same period.

7.3.2 Vocational Education [4]: The Centrally Sponsored Scheme of Vocationalisation of Secondary Education at +2 level is being implemented since 1988. The revised scheme is in operation since 1992-93. The scheme provides financial assistances to States for setting up administrative structures, carrying out area-vocational surveys, preparing curriculum guides training manuals, organizing teacher training programmes, strengthening technical support system for research and development etc. It also provides financial assistance to NGOs and voluntary organisations for implementation of specific innovative projects for conducting short term courses. Under the scheme, an enrolment capacity of over 10 lakh students in 9583 schools with about 21000 sections have been created so far.

As reported in the Eleventh Plan, the National Skill Development Mission is on the anvil. It is envisaged to evolve a comprehensive scheme for creating a diverse and wide range of skills for our youth that would enable the country to reap the scientific and demographic dividend. The emphases will be on demand driven vocational education programmes in partnership with employers. The current programmes will be restructured with emphasis on hands-on training/exposure, vertical mobility and flexibility.

Furthermore, a National Vocational Qualification (NVQ) system, in which public and private systems of vocational education collaboratively meet the needs of industry and individuals, will be developed. Under this, modular competency based vocational courses will be offered along with a mechanism of testing skills. Bridge courses to facilitate people without any formal education to get enrolled in the regular system of courses will also be developed through NVQ system.

7.4 Higher and Technical Education

Higher education is of vital importance for the country in consolidating its comparative advantage in skill and knowledge intensive services and in building a knowledge based society.

7.4.1 Higher Education: At the time of independence, the number of universities was no more than 20, of colleges around 500 and the total enrolment was less than 1 lakh. The investment made in higher education in the 1950s and 1960s has given us a strong knowledge base in many fields and contributed significantly to economic development, social progress and political democracy in independent India.

By the end of the Tenth Plan, the Indian higher education system has grown into one of the largest in the world with 378 universities, 18,064 colleges, a faculty strength of 4.92 lakh and an estimated enrolment of 140 lakh students. The higher education institutions include 23 Central Universities, 216 State Universities, 110 Deemed Universities, 11 Private Universities and 33 Institutions of National Importance established through Central legislation and another 5 institutions established through state legislations.

Despite the expansion that has occurred, it is evident that the system is under stress to provide a sufficient volume of skilled human power, which is equipped with the required knowledge and technical skills to cater to the demands of the economy. The accelerated growth of our economy has already created shortages of high quality technical manpower. It underscores the need to expand opportunities for youth on a massive scale and in diverse fields of basic science, engineering and technology, healthcare, architecture, management etc. This is possible only if there is rapid expansion, along with long over-due reforms, in the higher, technical and professional education sectors.

The focus of the Tenth Plan was on primary education

with an expenditure of over Rs. 50,000 crore, whereas the expenditure on university and higher education was below Rs. 8000 crore.

Though the recent emergence of the private sector in higher education has helped expand capacity, it is characterized by some imbalances. Private institutions have improved access in a few selected areas like engineering, management, medicine and IT etc. where students are willing to pay substantial fees. However, the distribution across country is uneven, with some states receiving most of the growth in private institutions.

A. University Grants Commission (UGC): The UGC, a statutory body, established in 1956, operates over 100 schemes—providing a wide range of development grants to institutions, travel grants for researchers, area studies, cultural exchanges, adult education, and women studies.

B. National Accreditation Assessment Council (NAAC): It was set up in 1994 to make quality an essential element through a combination of internal and external quality assessment and accreditation. During the Tenth Plan, NAAC was strengthened with the opening of four regional centres so as to speed up the accreditation process..

C. Academic Staff Colleges (ASCs): At present there are 55 ASCs which conduct orientation programmes of 4-weeks for newly appointed teachers and refresher courses of 3-weeks for in-service teachers. The refresher courses provide opportunities for serving teachers to learn from each other and serve as a forum for keeping abreast with the latest advances in various subjects.

D. All India Council for Technical Education (AICTE): It was given statutory status in 1987 for coordinated development of Technical Education, promotion of qualitative improvement and maintenance of norms and standards. AICTE has delegated the powers of approval of Diploma level technical institutes to the State Governments.

E. Eleventh Plan Targets and Strategies: Following are

the key elements of the higher education agenda of the Eleventh Plan:

"**A. Admission, Curriculum and Assessment**

- Common calibration and admission based on CET and/other relevant criteria for at least professional and PG courses in Central Universities in the first phase.
- Universalising the semester system.
- Continuous internal evaluation and assessment to eventually replace Annual Examinations.
- Introducing Credit System - to provide students with the possibility of spatial and temporal flexibility/mobility.
- Curriculum revision at least once every three years or earlier to keep syllabi in tune with job market dynamics and research advances.

B. Accreditation and Ratings

- Introduction of mandatory accreditation system for all educational institution.
- Creation of multiple rating agencies with a body to rate these rating agencies.
- Departmental Ratings in addition to institutional rating.

C. Teachers Competence and Motivation

- Restructuring of NET/SET with greater emphasis on recruitment of adequate and good quality teachers.
- Revamping Academic Staff Colleges (ASCs) and upgrading teachers capabilities through short and long-term courses.
- Expansion of Research programmes/projects and incentivizing search faculty through funded projects/research.

D. Miscellaneous

- UGC in consultation with stakeholders to arrive at optimum size of Universities and the number of college affiliations.
- Setting up of a new Inter-university Centre on higher education to undertake specialized research for policy formulation." [5]

7.4.2 Technical Education: Technical and professional education in the country has played a significant role in economic and technical development by producing quality manpower. Strong linkages have developed between technical institutions and the industry. For strengthening technical education and improving the quality of polytechnic pass outs, various steps have been taken through Technical Education Development Programmes.

There is a widespread network of technical education institutions in India. The major among them are the following::

- 7 Indian Institutes of Technology (IITs) and 6 Indian Institutes of Management (IIMs), which are Institutions of National Importance;
- 1,617 engineering and technology colleges, 1,292 polytechnics;
- 525 institutions for Diploma in pharmacy;
- 91 Schools for Hotel Management and 4 Institutions for Architecture;
- For post-graduate courses, these are 1,147 educational institutions for MBA/PGDM and 953 for MCA;
- Deemed-to-be-Universities, namely

1. Indian Institute of Science (IISc), Bangalore.
2. Indian School of Mines (ISM), Dhanbad.
3. School of Planning & Architecture (SPA), New Delhi.
4. Indian Institute of Information Technology and Management (IIITM), Gwalior.
5. Indian Institute of Information Technology (IIIT), Allahabad.
6. Indian Institute of Information Technology, Design and Manufacturing Jabalpur Kanchipuram.

- 20 National Institutes of Technology (NITs) which are Institutions of national importance.

The Tenth Plan period saw, a big increase in the number of technical and management institutions, mainly due to private initiatives. During the Tenth Plan, the number of AICTE approved Degree Engineering/Technology institutions increased from 1,057 to 1,522 and the annual intake from 2.96 lakh to 5.83 lakh. During the Tenth Plan, University of Roorkee was upgraded to an IIT and the number of IITs increased to 7.

The Eleventh Plan has envisaged setting up of 8 new IITs, 7 new IIMs and 10 new NITs.

An Ordinance has been promulgated for establishing 15 Central Universities.

Six new Indian Institutes of Technology (IIT) have started functioning in Bihar, Andhra Pradesh, Rajasthan, Orissa, Punjab and Gujarat during 2008-09. Two more IITs in Madhya Pradesh and Himachal Pradesh are expected to commence their academic sessions in 2009-10.

With the commencement of academic sessions in the Indian Institutes of Science Education and Research (IISERs) at Bhopal and Thiruvananthapuram, all 5 IISERs announced by the Government are now functional.

Two new schools of Planning and Architecture at Vijayawada and Bhopal have already started functioning.

Teaching is expected to commence in four of the six new Indian Institutes of Management, proposed for the Eleventh Plan period, from the academic year 2009-10. These are in Haryana, Rajasthan, Jharkhand and Tamil Nadu.

As an integral part of the coordinated action plan for skill development, the Government created the National Skill Development Corporation in July 2008 with an initial corpus of Rs.1,000 crore to stimulate and coordinate private sector participation in skill development.

7.5 Adult Education

Literacy is the most essential prerequisite for individual empowerment. A new thrust was given to adult literacy in the National Policy on Education (NPE), 1986 and the Plan of Action 1992, which advocated a three-pronged strategy of adult education, elementary education and non-formal education to eradicate illiteracy. The National Literacy

Mission (NLM) was launched on May 5, 1988 as a Technology Mission to impart functional literacy to non-literates in the country in the age group of 15-35 years in a time-bound manner. This age-group has been the focus of attention because they are in the productive and reproductive period of life. NLM was set up with an initial target to make 80 million persons literate by 1995, which was later enhanced to 100 million by 1997 and the revised target is to achieve a threshold level of 75 percent literacy by 2007.

The Total Literacy Campaign (TLC) has been the principal strategy of NLM for eradication of illiteracy in the target group. These campaigns are area-specific, time-bound, volunteer-based, cost effective and outcome-oriented. They are implemented by Zila Saksharata Samities and district level literacy societies.

Keeping pace with its endeavours, campaigns and programmes, the NLM has strengthened and revitalized the States Literacy Missions which have been imparted greater autonomy. They now have the authority to plan, implement and monitor literacy programmes and sanction continuing education programmes at the State level. The NLM has also come to recognize the great potential that NGOs have in furthering its programmes and schemes. Given the major role, NGOs are now allowed to receive funds from *Zila Sakshara Samities* and actually run continuing education centres. The *Jan Shikshan Sansthans* have expanded their outreach and are also catering to the rural segment by offering vocational training courses.

At present, 137 districts are implementing TLCs, 165 districts Post-Literacy Programmes and 295 districts Continuing Education Programmes. In addition, 157 Jan Shikshan Sansthan have been set up to provide vocational training to the neo-literates and backward sections of the society, and 25 State Resource Centres established for providing academic and technical resource support for the literacy programmes.

NLM has accorded priority for the promotion of female literacy. According to 2001 Census, 47 districts in the country have female literacy rate below 30 percent. Most of these districts are concentrated in Bihar, Jharkhand, Uttar Pradesh and Orissa. Special innovative projects have been taken up to raise the level of female literacy in these areas. Special efforts have been made to target female Panchayati Raj functionaries and make them literate.

7.5.1 Jan Shikshan Sansthan (JSS): The objective of JSS Scheme is educational, vocational and occupational development of socio-economically backward and educationally disadvantaged groups of urban/rural population, particularly neo-literates, semi-literates, SCs, STs, women and girls, slum dwellers, migrant workers etc. By linking literacy with vocational training, JSSs seek to improve the quality of life of the beneficiaries. JSSs offer around 284 different types of vocational courses—from candle and agarbatti making, to computer training and hospital/health care. The total number of JSS is 198.

7.5.2 Weaknesses of Adult Education Programmes: The constraints in the implementation of adult education programmes include inadequate participation of the State Governments, low motivation and training of voluntary teachers/preraks, lack of convergence of programmes, and weak management and supervision structure for implementation of NLM. Besides, the funding for various components of NLM schemes is inadequate and the level of community participation is also low.

7.5.3 Eleventh Plan Targets and Special Focus Areas

Targets:

- Achieve 80 percent literacy rate.
- Reduce gender gap in Literacy to 10 percent.
- Reduce regional, social and gender disparities.,
- Extend coverage of NLM programmes to 35+ age group.

Special Focus Areas:

- SCs, STs, Minorities and rural women to have a special

focus.

- Focus also on low literacy states, tribal areas, other disadvantaged groups and adolescents.

7.6 Conclusion

It is widely acknowledged that the education system in India is woefully inadequate for the social and economic development of the country in general and for enhancing the competitiveness of the services sector in particular. The goal of bringing all children in the age group 6-14 to schools is still unrealised although the number of out-of-school children has been brought down from 32 million in 2001-02 to 7.1 million in July 2006. Although a great deal of progress has been made under the Sarva Shiksha Abhiyan the quality of education at the primary level still lags behind.

Recent decades have seen the emergence of private sector institutions particularly in technical education financed by large capitation fees charged by them. This development has been inequitable, as it has led to the deprivation of a large number of students who have not been able to pay the substantial sums involved in the capitation fees. While encouraging private sector initiative to expand higher education, it has become necessary for the Government to ensure that private sector institutions take measures to provide scholarships and free-ships to an adequate number of meritorious students who do not have the means to pay the fees.

One of the main reasons for falling standards of higher education is the teacher shortage in the institutions of higher learning, particularly the technical education institutions. The salaries commanded by graduates in the market are so high that they do not have the motivation to move on for post-graduation or doctoral level with the ultimate objective of becoming teachers. In order to make the teaching profession attractive and motivate bright young professionals to take post-graduate courses, it is necessary to look at the salary structure and career opportunities of teachers in colleges. Research project funds must be shared as incentive payment to the faculty and the faculty should be given maximum freedom to undertake consultancies.

The decline in standards in higher education is also due to the failure to revise the curricula to keep pace with the developments in the various fields of knowledge as well in the society. The curricula must be revised every three years and the revisions must be subjected to outside peer review. The process of revision should be streamlined and decentralised with more autonomy given to teachers.

One of the major reforms needed in the education system is a change in the method of assessment of students, which relies exclusively on examinations. The current system is inadequate because it tests memory rather than understanding and does not encourage the development of analytical and creative abilities. Assessment of students must be based on the work done throughout the year rather than being judged solely on the performance during the annual examination. Evaluation of courses and teachers by students should also be used as an input in the process of assessment of students. Semester system must be introduced in the institutions of higher education. Also important is the need to introduce a system of credits whereby a student who discontinues studies or who changes institutions may be granted recognition for the courses completed earlier, thus granting them spatial and temporal flexibility in pursuing studies.

The main instrument used by the UGC to obtain improvement in the standards of teaching in institutions of higher education is to require them to adhere to minimum standards in infrastructure and physical facilities and human resources as a condition for financial assistance. However, what is needed is to induce them to be for ever striving to undertake self-improvement on a voluntary basis to obtain better standards. With this end in view in 1994 the UGC established the National Assessment and Accreditation

Council (NAAC) to undertake accreditation of institutions desirous of undertaking such improvement. It is necessary to promote the process of accreditation by making available additional discretionary funds to the funding agencies to be utilised for the purpose.

The educational institutions are regulated by the UGC and a number of Councils such as the All India Council for Technical Education (AICTE), the Medical Council of India (MCI) etc. The Councils have their own rules and regulations and there is a large overlap of their functions with that of the UGC. It has become imperative to restructure the apex level bodies in order to streamline their functioning. There is also an acute need for reform in the structures of governance of universities.

Notes

1. Government of India, Planning Commission, *Eleventh Five Year Plan* (2007-12), Vol., II, p. 1.
2. Ibid., p. 9.
3. Ibid., p. 2.
4. Kothari Commission on Educational Reforms, 1966 had visualized that 25 percent of the students at the secondary stage would go for the vocational stream. However, according to the recent NSSO data, only 5 percent of the population of 19-24 age group in India have acquired some sort of skills through vocational education.
5. *Eleventh Five Year Plan*, op. cit., pp. 24-25.

8

Empowerment of Socially Disadvantaged Groups

8.1 Introduction

India's development efforts since Independence in 1947 have not benefited different social groups equitably. Certain social groups such as the Scheduled Castes (SCs), Scheduled Tribes (STs), Other Backward Classes (OBCs) and Minorities (particularly Muslims) have historically been disadvantaged and vulnerable. Then there are certain other groups which may be discriminated against and which suffer from handicaps. These include persons with disabilities, older persons, street children, beggars, victims of substance abuse.

The concept of inclusive growth demands that all social groups have equal access to the services provided by the State and equal opportunity for upward economic and social mobility. It is also necessary to ensure that there is no discrimination against any section of our society. The Constitution of India contains various provisions for the development of such marginalized groups. Their individual and collective growth, however, cannot be ensured without improving their surroundings and providing clean drinking water, toilets and educational opportunities.

The Ministry of Social Justice and Empowerment undertakes programmes aimed at ensuring social justice to and empowerment of the disadvantaged and marginalised sections of society such as Scheduled Castes (SCs), Scheduled Tribes (STs), Other Backward Classes (OBCs), minorities, persons with disabilities, victims of alcoholism and drug abuse, children in need of care and protection and welfare of the aged. The Ministry is also charged with the Constitutional obligation of ensuring effective implementation of laws passed for the protection of the interests of these groups. The areas covered by the Ministry are also the areas where a major role is played by the State Governments.

8.2 Scheduled Castes (SCs)

The Scheduled Castes constitute 16.23 percent of the Indian population. In the past, they have been socially ostracized, economically exploited and denied human dignity and a sense of self-worth. The socio-economic development and protection of SCs from discrimination and exploitation has been a high priority area from the very start of Independent India.

People belonging to SC communities are spread all over the country; 80 percent of them live in rural areas. They constitute more than one-fifth of the population of Uttar Pradesh, Punjab, Himachal Pradesh and West Bengal. The State of Punjab has the highest proportion of SCs to the State population. More than half the Scheduled Caste population is concentrated in the five States of Uttar Pradesh (35.1 million), West Bengal (18.4 million), Tamil Nadu (11.8 million), Andhra Pradesh (12.3 million) and Bihar (13.0 million).

8.2.1 Constitutional Safeguards for Scheduled Castes: The Constitution of India contains various provisions to protect SCs against discrimination and to ensure their socio-economic development (Table 8.1).

In addition to the above, the Parliament has enacted the Untouchability (Offences) Act, 1955, renamed as Protection of Civil Rights Act, in 1976. To check and deter the atrocities against Scheduled Castes, the Scheduled Castes and the Scheduled Tribes (Prevention of Atrocities) Act, 1989 has also been enacted.

8.2.2 Measures for Economic Advancement of SCs: The National Scheduled Castes Finance & Development Corporation (NSFDC), established in 1989 provides financial and other support to beneficiaries for taking up various income generating activities. An amount of Rs. 388.80 crore was made available to the Corporation up to 31st March, 2007 as equity share contribution against the authorized share capital of Rs. 1000 crore. The number of SC beneficiaries that were assisted during the Tenth Five Year Plan (2002-07) was 2,57,901.

Table 8.1: Constitutional Safeguards for Scheduled Castes in India

Article of the Constitution	Brief description
46	Protection from social injustice and all forms of exploitation
14	Equality before law
15 (1)	State not to discriminate against any citizen on the ground of caste
15 (2)	No citizen shall, on ground only of caste or race, be subjected to any disability and restriction
15 (4) & 15 (5)	State to make provisions for reservation in educational institutions
16 (4), 16 (4A), 16 (4B) & 335	Appointments for posts in favour of SCs
17	Untouchability is abolished and its practice in any form is forbidden
330	Reservation of seats for SCs in the Lok Sabha
332	Reservation of seats for SCs in State Assemblies
243D & 340T	Reservation of seats for SCs in Local Self-Governments

The National Safai Karamcharis Financc and Development Corporation (NSKFDC) was established in 1997, to provide financial support to the Safai Karamcharis (Scavengers) to take up various income-generating activities. During the Tenth Five Year Plan, the Corporation introduced the Micro credit Finance Scheme (MCF) and the Mahila Samridhi Yojana

(MSY), benefiting 1,02,187 persons. During 2006-07, it disbursed loans to 16,545 beneficiaries (up to December, 2006) for various income generating activities in 23 States and 2 UTs.

The scheme of Grant-in-aid to Scheduled Castes Development Corporation (SCDCs) was introduced in 1978-79 as a Centrally Sponsored Scheme for participating in the equity share of the State Corporations in the Centre: State ratio of 49:51. The SCDCs finance employment oriented schemes that cover: (a) Agriculture and allied activities including minor irrigation; (b) Small Scale Industry; (c) Transport and (d) Trade and Service Sector. They also finance projects by dovetailing the loan component from NSFDC/Banks with margin money out of their own funds and subsidy out of the Special Central Assistance (SCA).

There are about 6.53 lakh scavengers in the country. Under the National Scheme for Liberation and Rehabilitation of Scavengers, monetary resources are released for assisting scavengers for training and rehabilitation. Sanitary marts have been set-up with the objective of organizing scavengers into groups/cooperatives to take up economically viable activities. These marts cater to the sanitary needs of the common man and work for the conversion of dry latrines to sanitary latrines. Sanitary marts are being operated in Tamil Nadu and Andhra Pradesh.

8.2.3 Measures for Educational Advancement of SCs: With respect to the educational development of SCs, the Central Government has introduced major scholarship programmes. The other important schemes for educational development of SCs are (a) providing coaching facilities to students for preparing them for various competitive examinations being conducted by UPSC, State Public Service Commissions, and Banks etc. (b) Hostel facilities to both boys and girls for pursuing education from middle level onwards.

Rajiv Gandhi National Fellowship for SC students was introduced in 2005-06 to provide fellowship to 1333 SC students for pursuing higher studies leading to M.Phil. and Ph.D. degrees. The response under this scheme has been very encouraging in the last two years and this will necessitate increasing the number of fellowships. Those who cannot continue their education after schooling, or who wish to diversify should be provided with vocational training/skill training programmes in the ITIs, polytechnics, etc. These institutes should have adequate seats on population basis and should be located closer to the SC dominated communities. The stress should be not merely on subject learning but also on personality development and entrepreneur skills.

8.2.4 Scheduled Caste Sub-Plan (SCSP) and Tribal Sub-Plan (TSP): In view of the persistent and widespread socio-economic backwardness of SCs and STs, a distinct need was felt for innovative policy intervention to enable these groups to share the benefits of growth in a more equitable manner. The Government prepared a separate Development Plan called Tribal Sub-Plan for the STs in 1976. It was followed by the Special Component Plan (SCP) for the Scheduled Castes in 1978 [renamed as Scheduled Castes Sub-Plan (SCSP)].

The SCSP and TSP aim at facilitating convergence and pooling of resources from all the other development sectors in proportion to the population of SCs and STs respectively for their overall development.

Tenth Five Year Plan (2002-07) adopted the following multi-pronged approach for the socio-economic development of the SCs:

- Social empowerment through educational development.
- Economic empowerment through income and employment enhancing avenues.
- Protection through effective implementation of protective legislations.
- Eradication of occupations such as manual scavenging.
- Holistic development through earmarking of funds proportionate to the population [SCSP and TSP].

8.3 Scheduled Tribes (STs)

The population of Scheduled Tribes (STs) in India stood at 84.33 million as per the 2001 Census. ST's constitute 8.2 percent of the total population of the country with 91.7 percent of them living in rural areas and 8.3 percent in urban areas. The sex-ratio of ST population in 2001 was 978 which was much higher than the national average of 933. The proportion of the ST population to the total population had also increased from 6.9 percent in 1971 to 8.2 percent in 2001.

The proportion of STs to the total population in States/Union Territories was the highest in the North-eastern region of Mizoram (94.5 percent) and Lakshadweep (94.5 percent) followed by Nagaland (89.1 percent), Meghalaya (85.9 percent). Within major states, Chhattisgarh (31.8 percent) had the highest percentage followed by Jharkhand (26.3 percent) and Orissa (22.1 percent).

Of the total ST population in the country, Madhya Pradesh accounted for the highest proportion of ST population (14.5 percent) followed by Maharashtra (10.2 percent), Orissa (9.7 percent), Gujarat (8.9 percent), Rajasthan (8.4 percent), Jharkhand (8.4 percent) and Chhattisgarh (7.8 percent). In fact, 68 percent of the country's Scheduled Tribes population lives in these seven States only.

8.3.1 Constitutional Safeguards for Schedules Tribes (STs): The Constitution of India has made several provisions to safeguard the interests of the Scheduled Tribes in Articles 15(4), 16(4), 46, 243M, 243 ZC, 244, first and second provisos to 275(1), Articles 334, 335, 338A, 339(1), and the Fifth and the Sixth Schedules.

Besides these, several laws have been enacted by the Central Government like the Protection of Civil Rights Act 1955, the Scheduled Castes and Scheduled Tribes (Prevention of Atrocities) Act 1989, the Provisions of the Panchayats (Extension to Scheduled Areas) Act 1996, the Scheduled Tribes and Other Traditional Forest Dwellers (Recognition of Forest Rights) Act 2006], as well as by the State Governments [relating to prevention of alienation and restoration of tribal land, money-lending, reservations etc.]. The Centre has been given the authority of giving directions to the State Governments [cf. Article 339(2), Para 3 of the Fifth Schedule] in the interest of tribal people.

There are various schemes and programmes directed at the socio-economic development of the tribal population.

8.3.2 Measures for Economic Advancement of STs: The National Scheduled Tribes Development and Finance Corporation (NSTFDC) was set up in 2001 with an authorized share capital of Rs. 500 crore. The Corporation supports various income and employment generating activities though loans, marketing support, training etc. Special focus is accorded to ST women beneficiaries under programmes such as the Adivasi Mahila Shashaktikaran Yojana which facilitates income-generating activities through women's Self-help Groups.

The State ST Development Corporations (STDCs) which function as channelising agencies in identifying eligible beneficiaries and extending financial and other assistance to them are also supported by the NSTFDC. The Tribal Cooperative Marketing Development Federation of India Ltd. (TRIFED) provides marketing assistance and remunerative prices to STs for collection of minor forest produce and surplus agricultural produce to protect them from exploitative private traders and middlemen.

Though majority of the tribals are settled cultivators, their farming activity is generally uneconomic and non-viable due to lack of access to necessary agricultural inputs specially assured irrigation. Therefore, a special provision of funds under grant-in-aid under Article 275 (1) of the Constitution has been made for financing minor irrigation works.

In 1975, guidelines to States/UTs were issued by the Centre for taking steps for discontinuation of commercial vending of liquor in tribal areas in pursuance of Excise Policy, 1974. Although the States/UTs have accepted the guidelines, commercial vending of intoxicants continues in tribal areas and stringent measures are needed for its prevention.

8.3.3 Measures for Educational Advancement of STs: The Department of Elementary Education and Literacy and the Department of Higher Education in States have provided special incentives to the ST students in the form of text books, uniform, abolition of tuition fee etc. Special focus is also accorded to ST students under the District Primary Education Programme, Kasturba Gandhi Balika Vidyalaya, Mid-day Meal Programme, Navodaya Vidyalaya, National Talent Search Scheme etc.

However, the problem of adequacy of the school building both in number and in facilities still remains. The lack of education in mother language or dialect in primary classes, ignorance of non-tribal teachers about tribal language and ethos, delay in distribution of scholarships, text books, uniforms etc. continue to be sources of worry.

8.3.4 Restoration of Traditional Rights: The Government took a major initiative in enacting Scheduled Tribes and Other Traditional Forest Dwellers (Recognition of Forest Rights) Act, 2006 which was notified on January 2, 2007. Rules have also been framed for implementation of the provisions of the Act. Major rights that are granted under the Act, among others, are (a) the right to cultivate forest land to the extent under occupation, (subject to a ceiling of 4 hectares), (b) the right to own, collect, use and dispose of minor forest produce and (c) the rights inside forests which are traditional and customary e.g. grazing etc.

8.3.5 Rehabilitation and Resettlement: The Government has recently approved the National Rehabilitation and Resettlement Policy [NRRP] 2007, with the following objectives:

- Minimize displacement and promote non-displacing or least-displacement alternatives.
- Ensure adequate and expeditious rehabilitation with participation of the PAPs through an independent

authority.

- Create obligations on the State to protect the rights of weaker sections, particularly SCs and STs.
- Provide a better standard of living with sustainable income.
- Integrate rehabilitation concerns into development planning and implementation.

8.3.6 Primitive Tribal Groups: There are 75 identified Primitive Tribal Groups (PTGs) spread in 17 States/UTs living in utmost destitute conditions. Some of them in dire straits also face the threat of extinction. In order to provide focused attention to the survival, protection and development of these PTGs, a special scheme was launched in 1998-99 to provide tribe-specific services and support including housing, land, agricultural inputs, cattle rearing, health, nutritional services, and income-generating programmes.

In spite of protective measures and developmental efforts mentioned above, tribal population of the country continues to suffer from following disadvantages:

- Increasing tribal alienation on account of slipping economic resources like land, forest, common property resources (CPR).
- Displacement and dispossession of life support systems.
- General apathy of official machinery.
- Escalating atrocities, at times related to assertion of rights;
- Growing clout of market forces.
- Inadequate advancement through planned development efforts.

Since most of the tribal habitations are located in isolated villages and hamlets in undulating plateau lands coinciding with forest areas; they have limited access to critical infrastructure facilities such as roads, communication, health, education, electricity, drinking water, etc. This widens the gap between the quality of their life and the people in the country.

The Tenth Five Year Plan (2002-07) adopted the following strategy to solve the persisting problems of the tribal population.

1. Protecting the tribals from land alienation and the related problems of indebtedness and exploitation.
2. Expediting the final pronouncement of the National Policy for Rehabilitation of the Displaced Persons with a special focus on the displaced tribals.
3. Promoting tribal participation in forest-cantered activities and thereby stimulating the tribal economy without alienating tribals from the forest.
4. Protecting the precarious Primitive Tribal Groups (PTGs) with expansion of ongoing schemes and effective involvement of voluntary organizations.
5. Ensuring tribal participation in the development efforts by democratising the decision-making process by strengthening the grassroots democratic institutions.

The current situation calls for a major shift towards entrusting, enabling and empowering the tribal people to look after their own welfare and address issues of development through their own initiative. The constitutional-cum-legal framework has been enormously strengthened by the enactment of the Provisions of the Panchayats (Extension to the Scheduled Areas) Act 1996 [PESA], a charter of autonomous tribal governance, embodying rights in favour of tribal communities coupled with respect for their ethos.

Scheduled Tribes are mainly landless poor, forest dwellers and shifting cultivators, small farmers and pastoral and nomadic herders. The livelihood strategy would thus have to take into account the land structure, level of skills, socio-economic conditions, low level of human development index (HDI) along with physical infrastructure and natural resource base in the tribal areas.

8.4 Other Backward Classes (OBCs)

Considerable confusion exists regarding the percentage of OBCs population in India's total population. The Second Backward Classes Commission headed by Shri B.P. Mandal

(1980), basing its calculation on census 1931, estimated that Other Backward Classes (OBCs) constituted 52 percent of the population. Recently, NSSO 61st Round (July 2004 to June 2005) report on 'Employment and Unemployment Situation among Social Groups in India' gave an estimate of OBC to constitute 41 percent of the population.

8.4.1 Constitutional Safeguards: Though the Constitution does not make specific provisions for OBCs, it empowers the State to make provisions for reservation in appointments or posts in favour of any backward class of citizens which, in the opinion of the State, is not adequately represented in the Services under the State [Article (16(4)]. It also empowers the State to appoint a Commission to investigate into the conditions of socially and educationally backward classes (Article 340). In pursuance of the Supreme Court judgment Indira Sawhney and Others vs. Union of India (1992), the National Commission for Backward Classes was set up on August 14, 1993 under the National Commission for Backward Classes Act, 1993. Thus, Other Backward Classes got recognition as a separate group of people for the purpose of 27 percent reservation in services in Government of India and Public Sector Undertakings. The States/UTs were left free to decide the quantum of reservation based on the OBC population in their State/UTs. All State Governments/ UT Administrations were also directed by the Supreme Court of India in the same case to set up a permanent body in their State/UT and to draw their own list and decide the quantum of reservation as per the State/UTs demography.

8.4.2 Measures for Socio-economic Advancement of OBCs: In economic and occupational terms, the backward classes comprise of peasants, landless labourers, artisanal communities like handloom weavers, carpenters, metal workers, stone cutters and fishermen and those who provide various traditional services. The plight of these categories of the backward classes has worsened in recent years due to extensive mechanization and market competition. There is a need to ensure upgradation of skills of such categories so that they can compete better in the market.

Specific programmes for development of OBCs were initiated from the Eighth Five Year Plan (1992-97). The National Backward Classes Finance and Development Corporation (NBCFDC) was set up in 1992 with an authorized share capital of Rs. 200 crore. This was augmented to Rs. 700 crore in the Ninth Five Year Plan (1997-2002). The objective of the NBCFDC is to promote self-employment projects among the OBCs living below the poverty line.

NBCFDC provides financial assistance through State Channelising Agencies (SCAs) nominated by the State Governments/UTs. NBCFDC assists a wide range of income-generating activities which include agricultural and allied activities, artisan and traditional occupations, technical trades, small scale and tiny industry, small business, transport services etc. Entrepreneurs with annual income less than double the poverty line are eligible for concessional finance.

During the Ninth Plan period, programmes such as Pre-Matric and Post-Matric scholarship schemes, construction of hostels and Pre-examination Coaching Centres for OBCs were introduced. The Pre-examination Coaching Scheme for OBCs was merged with the umbrella Coaching and Allied Scheme for Weaker Sections including SCs, OBCs, and Minorities from September 2001.

8.5 De-notified Nomadic and Semi-nomadic Tribes

De-notified nomadic and semi-nomadic tribes and *banjara* communities constitute the most vulnerable and disadvantaged sections of the Indian society. Some of these communities were identified as *Criminal Tribes* during pre-Independence days. Although the Criminal Tribes Act, 1871 was repealed soon after Independence, persons belonging to these communities are still viewed by society as habitual criminals.

Government is keen to undertake schemes as would accelerate the process of integration of the de-notified tribes into the mainstream of society. Unfortunately, these groups still continued to be marginalized and their specific needs even today are neither adequately understood nor catered to. Due to their family's mobility from one place to another children in such tribes remain deprived educationally.

In order to acquire a comprehensive picture of the situation of these communities and to suggest action for their socio-economic development, a National Commission for De-notified Tribes, Nomadic Tribes and Semi-Nomadic Tribes was set up in 2005.

8.6 Minorities

The Constitution of India contains special provisions for the socio-economic development of the SCs, STs and OBCs [Articles 15(4), 16(4) of Part III, Articles 46 of Part IV, and Articles 330-342 of Part XVI of the Indian Constitution]. However, religious and linguistic minorities are excluded from the purview of these special provisions, though cultural and educational rights of the religious and linguistic minorities are regarded as fundamental rights under Articles 29 and 30 of Part III of the Constitution.

While the socio-economic development of the Scheduled Castes (SCs), Scheduled Tribes (STs) and Other Backward Classes (OBCs) formed an important part of the post-Independence development policy, it was presumed that development of the religious and linguistic minorities would be taken care of by the general process of growth and development. However, the socio-economic conditions of some minorities, particularly Muslims, are a cause for concern.

As per the provisions under the National Commission of Minorities (NCM) Act, 1992, five religious communities including Muslims, Christians, Sikhs, Buddhists and Zoroastrians (Parsis) have been notified as Minorities. Among the Minorities, Muslims,, especially Muslim women need special attention since relative to other communities, they have remained socially, educationally and economically backward.

According to 2001 Census, 18.4 percent of India's population belongs to minority communities. Muslims constitute 13.4 percent, Christians 2.3 percent, Sikhs 1.9 percent, Buddhists 0.8 percent and Parsis 0.07 percent of the country's total population. Muslims (nearly 140 million) account for 72.8 percent of the total minority population of 189.5 million.

The distribution of minority population indicates that Muslims are in majority in the Union Territory of Lakshadweep and in the State of Jammu & Kashmir. There are six states where proportion of Muslims in total population is above the national percentage of 13.4 percent: Assam (30.9 percent), West Bengal (25.2 percent), Kerala (24.6 percent), Uttar Pradesh (18.55 percent), Bihar (16.5 percent), and Jharkhand (13.8 percent).

The highest percentages of Christians to total population are found in Nagaland (90 percent), Mizoram (87 percent), and Meghalaya (70.03 percent). There are also substantial numbers of Christians in Kerala, Tamil Nadu, Andhra Pradesh, Jharkhand, Orissa, Maharashtra and Karnataka.

Sikhs constitute 60 percent of the population of Punjab. Buddhists are categorized into traditional and neo-Buddhists. Traditional Buddhists are, by and large, from tribal communities inhabiting hilly areas of Ladhakh, Himachal Pradesh, West Bengal, Sikkim, Assam and the States of Northern Eastern Region. The highest percentage of Buddhists is in Sikkim (28.1 percent) followed by Arunachal Pradesh (13 percent). Parsis number just 69,000 and mostly reside in Maharashtra.

8.6.1 Measures for Socio-economic Development of Minorities: In pursuance of the Constitutional provisions, the Government is committed to the well being of the Minorities. Such measures are not limited to protecting and promoting their language, religion and culture, but in making special efforts for their socio-economic development and mainstreaming. A High Level Committee (Chairman: Gopal

Singh) was set up in 1980 to study the conditions of minorities. The Committee, in its report, concluded that the poor among the Muslims could not avail the opportunities in education, employment and economic activities because of isolation and various historical factors. In view of this, the Prime Minister's 15 Point Programme was launched in 1983 to provide a sense of security to minority communities and ensure their rapid socio-economic development. This Programme was based on a three-pronged approach:

- To tackle the situation arising out of communal riots.
- To ensure adequate representation of the minority communities in employment under the Central and State Governments as well as Public Sector Undertakings.
- To ensure flow of benefits to the minority communities under various development programmes, maintenance and development of religious places, *wakf* properties and redressal of grievances.

In 1989, an autonomous, non-political, non-profit organization, the Maulana Azad Education Foundation (MAEF), was set up to promote education amongst educationally backward Muslims in general and Muslim girls in particular. With a corpus of Rs. 100 crore, it undertook activities like establishing and expanding schools, residential schools, colleges, hostels, purchasing laboratory equipment and furniture, setting up and strengthening vocational and technical training institutes and providing scholarships to meritorious girl students. In the final year of the Tenth Plan the corpus of Rs. 100 crore with the Foundation was doubled.

In 1994, the National Minorities Development and Finance Corporation (NMDFC) was established with an authorized share capital of Rs. 500 crore.

On January 29, 2006, a separate Ministry of Minority Affairs was created. Meanwhile, the Government of India also constituted a High Level Committee (Chairman: Rajinder Sachar) to prepare a report on the social, economic and educational status of the Muslim community. In its Report on

Social, Economic and Educational Status of the Muslim Community of India the Committee observed that Muslims have been left behind the growth and development process. It recommended setting up of an autonomous Assessment Monitoring Authority (AMA), creation of National Data Bank and constitution of an Equal Opportunity Commission (EOC). It also suggested provision of hostel facilities at reasonable cost, setting up and strengthening of state-run Urdu medium schools, linkage of Madarsas to Higher Secondary Board, recognition of the degrees from Madarsas for eligibility in competitive examinations, provision of financial and other support to Madarsas.

8.6.2 Prime Minister's New 15-Point Programme for Minorities: The Prime Minister's New 15-Point programme was launched in 2006 aimed at ensuring the well-being, protection and development of Minorities. While the 15-Point Programme of 1983 centred on communal riots, representation of minorities in services and ensuring flow of benefits to individual beneficiaries, the focus of the New Programme is to make certain that benefits of various schemes/programmes flow equitably to the minorities. For this, it quantifies a certain portion of development projects to be established in the areas with minority concentration. It stipulates that wherever possible, 15 percent of targets and outlays under various schemes should be earmarked for the minorities. All Central Ministries, State Governments and Union Territories have been advised to implement this new Programme. The Ministry of Minority Affairs (MMA) is the nodal Ministry for coordinating and monitoring the implementation of the programme. The elements of the programme are as follows:

(A) Enhancing Opportunities for Education

1. Equitable availability of ICDS Services: A certain percentage of the ICDS projects and Anganwadi Centres to be located in blocks/villages with a substantial population of minority communities; equitable availability of benefits to be ensured

2. Improving access to School Education: A certain percentage of all schools under the Sarva Shiksha Abhiyan, the Kasturba Gandhi Balika Vidyalaya Scheme, and other similar Government schemes will be located in villages/localities having a substantial minority population.
3. Greater resources for teaching Urdu: Recruitment and posting of Urdu language teachers in primary and upper primary schools.
4. Modernizing Madarsa Education: Strengthening the Central Plan Scheme of Area Intensive and Madarsa Modernization Programme to provide basic educational infrastructure in areas of concentration of educationally backward Minorities.
5. Scholarships for meritorious students from minority communities: Formulation of Schemes for pre-matric and post- matric scholarships for students from minority communities.
6. Improving educational infrastructure through the Maulana Azad Education Foundation (MAEF): To expand the activities of MAEF more effectively.

(B) Equitable Share in Economic Activities and Employment

7. Self-Employment and Wage Employment for the poor: A certain percentage of the physical and financial targets under some schemes e.g. Swarnjayanti Gram Swarojgar Yojana (SGSY), Swarn Jayanti Shahari Rozgar Yojana (SJSRY), Sampurna Grameen Rozgar Yojana (SGRY), will be earmarked for beneficiaries belonging to minority communities living below the poverty line in rural areas. Simultaneously, a certain percentage of the allocation will be earmarked for the creation of infrastructure in such villages, which have a substantial population of Minorities.
8. Upgradation of skills through technical training: A certain proportion of all new ITIs will be located in areas predominantly inhabited by minority communities and a proportion of existing ITIs to be upgraded to 'Centres of

Excellence' will be selected on the same basis.

9. Enhanced credit support for economic activities: To strengthen the National Minorities Development & Finance Corporation (NMDFC) by providing it greater equity support to enable it to fully achieve its objectives. An appropriate percentage of the priority sector lending in all categories to be targeted for the minority communities.
10. Recruitment to State and Central Services: In the recruitment of police personnel, Central and State Governments will be advised to give special consideration to Minorities. Composition of selection to have minority representative. Employment opportunities in Railways, nationalized banks and public sector enterprises. Launching of an exclusive scheme to provide coaching to minority candidates.

(C) Improving the Conditions of Living of Minorities

11. Equitable Share in Rural Housing Scheme: Indira Awaas Yojana (IAY) for poor beneficiaries from minority communities in rural areas.
12. Improvement in condition of slums inhabited by minority communities: Ensuring provision of physical amenities and basic service as extended under the schemes of Integrated Housing & Slum Development Programme (IHSDP) and Jawaharlal Nehru National Urban Renewal Mission (JNNURM) equitably to the minority communities and to cities/slums with minority concentrations.

(D) Prevention and Control of Communal Riots

13. Prevention of communal incidents.
14. Prosecution for communal offences.
15. Rehabilitation of victims of communal riots.

8.7 Persons with Disabilities [1]

The Census 2001, enumerated persons with disabilities at 2.13 percent of India's total population. According to Eleventh Five Year Plan (2007-12), "The percentage of disabled people among the total population of any country depends on the definition of *disability* in that particular country as well as the enumeration methodology and its accuracy. In India, the definition of disability used in the Census is very different from that in the Persons with Disabilities Act, 1995. There is an urgent need for both a credible definition and system of data collection relating to persons with disabilities. It can be reasonably assumed that persons with disabilities constitute anywhere between 5 to 6 percent of our total population." [2]

Entry 9 in the State List (List II) in the Seventh Schedule of the Constitution of India directs the State Governments to provide relief and help to the disabled and the unemployable. Article 41 of the Constitution states that the State shall, within the limits of its economic capacity and development, make effective provisions for securing the right to work, to education and to public assistance in cases of unemployment, old age, sickness and disablement.

Besides, there are four legislations specifically directed towards the protection, welfare, rehabilitation and development of people with disabilities: Mental Health Act, 1987; Persons with Disabilities (Equal Opportunities, Protection of Rights and Full Participation) Act, 1995; National Trust for Welfare of Persons with Autism, Cerebral Palsy, Mental Retardation and Multiple Disability Act, 1999 and Rehabilitation Council of India Act, 1992.

In addition to the legal framework, a comprehensive National Policy for Persons with Disabilities was announced in February 2006.

In recent years, there has been a shift from a welfare-based approach for the disabled to rights-based one. As per the provisions of the Persons with Disabilities Act, 1995, 3 percent reservation in employment is being provided to the disabled people. For vocational training, 852 government-run and 105 private-run Industrial Training Institutes (ITIs) provide 3 percent reservation in seats for persons with disabilities. The Swarnjayanti Gram Swarozgar Yojana (SGSY), Indira Awaas

Yojana (IAY), National Rural Employment Guarantee Act (NREGA) and Sampoorna Grameen Rozgar Yojana (SGRY) provide for 3 percent reservation/benefits to the disabled people. The National Handicapped and Finance Development Corporation (NHFDC) provide loans on concessional terms for self-employed persons with disability.

The National Policy for Persons with Disabilities was adopted in 2006. It recognizes that disabled people are valuable human resources for the country. The policy focuses primarily on prevention of disability, early detection and appropriate interventions, physical and economic rehabilitation measures, inclusive education, employment in the public as well as the private sector and self-employment, creation of a barrier-free environment and development of rehabilitation professionals.

Two new schemes, viz. Indira Gandhi National Widow Pension Scheme (IGNWPS) and Indira Gandhi National Disability Pension Scheme (IGNDPS) were launched in 2008-09. The IGNWPS provides pension of Rs. 200 to widows between the age groups of 40-64 years. The IGNDPS aims to provide pension to severely disabled persons.

8.8 Older Persons

India has the second largest population of older (60+) persons in the world. The number of older persons in the population is expected to increase from 71 million in 2001 to 173 million in 2026. The majority (80 percent) of the elderly population in India is in the rural areas, thus making service delivery to them a challenge, and there is a large number of 80+ persons in the country.

As contemplated in the National Policy on Older Persons (NPOP), a National Council for Older Persons (NCOP) has been set up to advise and aid the Government on policies and programmes for older persons and to provide a feedback to the Government on the implementation of the NPOP.

The Maintenance and Welfare of Parents and Senior

Citizens Bill, 2007 which has been presented to the Parliament, stipulates construction of at least one old-age home in each district of the country to accommodate deserving and destitute senior citizens.

This intended Act will make the process for claiming maintenance simpler, speedier and less expensive. Further, the legislation would also ensure adequate medical facilities to older persons and the protection of their life and property.

The programmes/schemes/incentives for older persons include income tax rebate, higher rates of interest in saving schemes, 30 percent concessions in all railway travel and 50 percent discount on basic fare for all domestic flight in economy class in Indian Airlines and Jet Airways.

The Ministry of Social Justice and Empowerment implements an Integrated Programme for Older Persons through voluntary organizations. Under this scheme, voluntary organizations are given 90 percent grant for running Old Age Homes, Day Care Centres and Mobile Medical Care Units. Another scheme for construction of Old Age Home is being implemented through Local Self-help Groups, Panchayati Raj Institutions, voluntary organizations, etc.

8.9 Social Deviants

8.9.1 Juvenile Delinquents: In most cases, social deviants such as juvenile delinquents, alcohol and drug addicts are victims of circumstances and situational compulsions rather than habitual criminals engaged in organized crime. Experts have advocated reform and rehabilitation of these social deviants in a humane rather than a punitive environment, with a view to transforming today's social deviants into tomorrow's responsible citizens.

Under the Programme of Juvenile Justice, the Ministry of Social Justice and Empowerment shares the cost of maintaining mandatory homes for the juveniles with the States and presently assists 30,000 juvenile inmates in over 550 mandatory homes.

8.9.2 Drug Addicts: The problems of substance (drug) and alcohol abuse have existed for a long period, although their nature and extent varies according to the prevailing social and economic conditions. The National Survey on the Extent, Trends and Pattern of Drug Abuse indicated that there are 73.2 million drug users and dependent users in the country. In some parts, especially in North East, drug addiction and the incidence of HIV/AIDS have assumed alarming proportions.

A number of schemes for prevention, treatment and rehabilitation in respect of alcohol and drug abuse are being implemented in partnership with voluntary organizations. Eight Regional Resource and Training Centres (RRTCs) have been established for training to NGOs working for drug abuse prevention and also to undertake advocacy, research and monitoring of drug abuse programmes. Initiatives have been taken up jointly by the Ministry of Social Justice and Empowerment and National Aids Control Organization (NACO) for the integration of HIV/AIDS prevention programmes with substance abuse prevention.

8.10 Beggars

Beggars are found everywhere in the country, especially in the urban centres at religious places, traffic signals etc. They include several categories of persons such as homeless, abandoned, displaced, children, disabled, destitutes, eunuchs etc. Begging is a complex social problem and needs legislative, reformative and rehabilitative interventions. It is often organized and institutionalized as an economic activity.

In 1992-93, a Central Sector Scheme for the prevention of beggary was introduced with the objective of developing facilities for education and vocational training of beggars with a view to training them to engage in productive work.

The States are responsible to take the necessary preventive and rehabilitative steps. Neither is there Central legislation on prevention of begging and rehabilitation of beggars, nor a clear policy on how the problem is to be tackled. There is, therefore, a need to address the problem in a holistic way at the national level. While able-bodied beggars should be given training and help to get employment so that they might give up beggary, there may be many persons who may not be able to work and earn their living because of their physical condition. In such cases the state would have to provide them the basic means of livelihood. This can be done either by maintaining them in beggar homes, or by giving them a pension on which they may subsist.

8.11 Right to Maintenance

Maintenance is a civil right that enables needy persons to receive economic support from those who are liable to protect and maintain their spouse, children, parents etc. By law, parents are bound to maintain minor children, major children their parents, husband his wife and vice versa. The quantum of maintenance varies depending on the economic status of the parties. The various personal laws such as the Hindu Marriage Act, 1955, the Hindu Adoption and Maintenance Act 1955, the Indian Divorce Act 1859, the Parsi Marriage Act, 1954, the Shariat Laws etc. provide for maintenance, also known as alimony or allowance. Civil courts take a long time to dispose off cases. Even if a competent civil court passes a judgement and decree, execution takes months and even years due to cumbersome legal procedures. Even before the maintenance is realised the decree holder may die of starvation.

Realising the above, the right to maintenance has been incorporated in Chapter IX of the Criminal Procedure Code (Cr.P.C.). It is entitled 'order for maintenance of Wives, Children and Parents.' Under Section 125 of the Cr.P.C., 'if any person having sufficient means neglects to maintain (a) his wife, unable to maintain herself, or (b) his legitimate or illegitimate minor child, whether married or not, unable to maintain itself, or (c) his legitimate or illegitimate child (not being married) who has attained majority, where such child is, by reason of any physical or mental abnormality or injury unable to maintain itself, or (d) his father or mother, unable to maintain himself or herself, a magistrate, of the first class, may upon proof of such neglect or refusal, order such person to make a monthly allowance for the maintenance of his wife or such monthly rate not exceeding five hundred rupees on the whole, as the magistrate thinks fit, and to pay the same to such person as the magistrate may from time to time direct.' A ceiling of Rs. 500 per month towards maintenance will not prevent vagrancy though that is the object of the provision. Various women and civil rights organizations and other activists have raised their voice against this ceiling. In West Bengal the amount was raised to Rs. 1,500. Through an amendment to Section 125 of the Cr.P.C, the Government of India enhanced the interim maintenance limit for an estranged wife from Rs. 500 to Rs. 5,000.

Notes

1. Disabilities include orthopaedic, visual, hearing, speech and mental disabilities.
2. Government of India, Planning Commission, *Eleventh Five Year Plan* (2007-12), Vol. I, p. 130.

Part III: Natural Resources

9

Land Resources

The most important natural resource of India is land which is the base for agricultural production. While population grows, the land surface is fixed and only a certain proportion of it is available for cultivation. The non-expandable land resources have to accommodate the competing demands for production of food, fodder, fibre and fuel, minerals, urbanisation, non-agricultural land use etc. for the increasing human and animal population.

In the past, increase in net sown area came about by converting forest area into cultivable area. There is no such scope at present or in near future. The only alternative available is to reclaim the waste land and the land suffering from salinity, alkalinity and water logging. In rcclaiming available wasteland, private sector initiative and expertise should be tapped wherever necessary.

9.1 Use Distribution of India's Geographical Area

After China, India is the most populous country in the world accounting for 16.0 percent of world population. It is the seventh largest country in the world occupying 2.4 percent of total world area. It has a land frontier of 15,200 kilometres and its sea coast runs to the length of 6,100 kilometres. The use distribution of India's geographical area is shown in Table 9.1.

9.2 Declining Per Capita Availability of Land

As against the commercialised nature of agricultural operations in the developed countries, farming in India still remains a source of livelihood for most farmers in India. The main reason for this is the low per capita availability of land. Per capita availability of land (or land-man ratio) declined from 0.92 hectare in 1951 to 0.48 hectare in 1981 and to 0.33 hectare in the year 2000 (Table 9.2). According to Eighth Five Year Plan (1992-97), per capita availability of land is expected to fall further to 0.30 hectares by the year 2007.

Table 9.1: Use Distribution of India's Geographical Area

(Million hectares)

Total geographical area of India Of which	329 (100)
Net area sown	143 (43.5)
Area under forests	75 (22.8)
Uncultivable and fallow lands	100 (30.4)
Others	11 (3.3)

Source: Government of India, Planning Commission, *Seventh Five Year Plan* (1985-90), Vol. 1, para 2.19.

Table 9.2: Declining Per Capita Availability of Land (Land-man Ratio) in India

Year	Total geographical area (million hectares)	Total population (million)	Col.2/Col.3
1	2	3	4
1951	329	361	0.92
1981	329	685	0.48
2000	329	986	0.33
2007 (estimated)	329	1,096	0.30

Sources: Government of India, Planning Commission, *Seventh Five Year Plan* (1985-90), Vol. I, para 2.20; Government of India, Planning Commission, *Eighth Five Year Plan* (1992-97), Vol. I, p. 33.

9.3 Cropping Pattern

Cropping pattern refers to the distribution of cultivated land among different crops grown in a country. Cropping pattern reveals the nature of agricultural operations, e.g. the importance of food crops vis-à-vis cash crops. Cropping pattern is influenced by a host of factors which can be broadly classified into two categories: (a) physical factors and (b) economic factors.

Among the physical factors, the important ones are soil conditions, extent of rainfall and type of climate. The economic factors include relative prices of agricultural commodities, size of the farms, availability of inputs, demand conditions, system of land holding and government policy regarding exports, imports, taxes and subsidies.

There are two main agricultural seasons in India: (a) *kharif* under which crops are planted at the onset of the Southwest monsoon in June-July and harvested in September-October, (b) *rabi* under which crops are planted usually between October and December and harvested between March and May. Major *kharif* crops are rice, jowar, bajra, maize, cotton, sugarcane, soyabean and groundnut. Major *rabi* crops are wheat, barley, gram, linseed, rapeseed and mustard.

India is a large country with diverse climatic, soil and terrain conditions. A wide variety of crops are grown in different parts of the country.

9.3.1 Classification of Agricultural Crops: Due to its rich biological diversity, various types of crops are grown in India. The important among these may be classified as under:

A. Foodgrains: These include rice, wheat, coarse cereals (like maize, gram, *bajra*, *jowar)*, and pulses. These crops constitute the backbone of India's food economy. In India, nearly 75 percent of the cultivated area is occupied by food crops including rice, wheat, millets and pulses. Paddy (rice) is the most important food crop in India followed by wheat. There has been no significant change in the cropping pattern during the post-Independence period. The present cropping pattern is unbalanced as it is heavily tilted in favour of paddy and wheat while area under oilseeds and pulses is less than required.

B. Oilseeds: There are ten major oilseeds produced in India, namely groundnut, castorseed, sesame, nigerseed, soyabean, sunflower, rapeseed, mustard, linseed and safflower. Of these, groundnut, rapeseed, mustard and soyabean occupy commanding position in terms of total production.

C. Fibre Crops: Cotton and jute are the chief crops under this category.

D. Plantation Crops: Sugarcane, tea, coffee, tobacco, rubber, cocoa, cardamom, cashew and coconut. Some of these crops constitute important items of India's exports. India is the largest producer, processor, consumer and exporter of cashew in the world. Coconut is an important tree crop grown extensively in coastal areas providing livelihood to about 10 million people in cultivation, processing and related activities.

E. Horticultural Crops: India, with its wide variability of climate and soil, produces a large range of horticultural crops such as fruits, vegetables, potato, tropical tuber crops, ornamental crops, medicinal and aromatic plants, spices (like black pepper, cardamom, ginger, garlic, turmeric, chillies). The National Horticulture Mission was launched on April 1, 2005. The Mission will ensure end-to-end approach having backward and forward linkages covering research, production, post-harvest management, processing and marketing. Indian agriculture has indeed diversified from foodgrains to a variety of crops but more needs to be done in this regard. In his 2005-06 budget speech, the Finance Minister announced the preparation of a roadmap by the Ministry of Agriculture. The roadmap will focus on fruits, vegetables, flowers, dairy, poultry, fisheries, pulses and oilseeds.

9.4 Land and Water Relationship

It is important to appreciate the inextricably close relationship between land and water management. Water, which is a renewable resource, can in fact be put to good use only if the land on which it falls, and the land to which it is applied, are properly cared for. Land, which is for all purposes a non-renewable and inelastic resource, must be managed in such a manner as to be benefited rather than suffer damage as a result of its contact with water. The key to environmental quality, therefore, lies in scientific land and water management.

9.5 Land Pollution and Land Degradation

Pollution of land results largely from the insanitary disposal of solid wastes. In India open dumping of such wastes of municipal and industrial origin on low lying land is a common phenomenon. This serves as a breeding ground for pests and disease carrying vectors.

Land, a non-renewable resource, is central to all primary production systems. Over the years, India's landmass has suffered from different types of degradations. Floods and droughts are recurrent phenomena in India, severely constraining agriculture. The problem of land degradation gets exacerbated due to large scale land erosion in which fertile top soil is lost.

Intensive agricultural practices that rely heavily on water, chemical fertilisers and pesticides have caused water-logging and salinity in many parts of the country. The expansion of the irrigation system without adequate steps for treatment of the catchment areas has exacerbated this. The quest for increased agricultural productivity has led to intensive cultivation of marginal lands causing their degradation. Land degradation has a direct bearing on the productivity of soil, its vulnerability to rainfall variations, scarcity of drinking water, fodder and fuel wood. Given the inter-linkages of crop production, livestock economy and environment, land degradation has a major impact on the livelihoods of the people, especially in rural areas.

Some of the most degraded lands in the country are the common property resources (CPRs). CPRs are resources on which people have an equal right of use. These resources include community pastures, community forests, wastelands and common dumping and threshing grounds. In spite of concerted efforts to check deforestation and the various afforestation schemes taken up during successive Plan periods, large tracks of forest continue to be classified as degraded.

In addition to the wastelands, other areas such as deserts, drought-prone, flood-prone and tribal areas have been subjected to severe forms of degradation. The capacity of these lands is limited due to environmental factors. Pressures of human and livestock population have further compromised them.

The prevention of land degradation and the augmentation of the carrying capacity of land to provide food, fuel and fodder requirements have, therefore, been a primary concern of the Government. Special Area Development Programmes have been funded to mitigate the harsh living conditions of people through better land management, water harvesting and conservation practices on a watershed basis.

India has paid a good deal of attention to harness its water resources by way of construction of major, medium and minor irrigation projects and the development of ground water resources. Organizations have also been set up in this field, namely Central and State Irrigation Departments, Central Water Commission and the Central Ground Water Board. However, very little attention has been paid to the proper management of our land and soil resources with the result that they have suffered very serious degradation. The losses which the country is bearing on account of the continuing degradation of its land resources are of staggering dimensions and constitute one of the important threats to India's economic progress.

9.6 Development of Wastelands

Land is the most important natural resource upon which all human activity is based. Man's inexorable progress towards development has, however, considerably damaged our land resource base. Land suffers from various kinds of soil erosion, degradation and deforestation. To harness the full potential of the available land resources and prevent its further degradation, wasteland development is of great significance. The problem of degraded land and its management is complex and multi-dimensional and its development requires a scientific, holistic and innovative approach.

To accelerate the pace of development of wastelands/degraded lands and to focus attention in this regard, the Government had set up the National Wastelands Development Board in 1985 under the Ministry of Environment & Forests. Later, a separate Department of Wastelands Development in the Ministry of Rural Development and Poverty Alleviation was created in 1992 and the National Wastelands Development Board was transferred to it. In April 1999, Department of Wastelands Development was renamed as the Department of Land Resources to act as the nodal agency for land resource management. Consequently, all land-based development programmes and the land reforms Division were brought under this Department.

9.6.1 Wastelands Atlas, 2005: Wastelands can be defined as "degraded lands which can be brought under vegetative cover with reasonable efforts and which are currently underutilized, and also the land which is deteriorating for lack of appropriate water & soil management or on account of natural causes." Several agencies have estimated the extent of wastelands in India. However, these figures vary considerably—ranging between 30 million hectares and 175 million hectares, partly because of the varied definitions of wastelands.

Updation of Wasteland Atlas was initiated in 2003 to monitor changes in wastelands. NRSA carried out mapping of wastelands across the country over a period of two years during 2003-05 using one-time IRS data (of the year 2003). The result of this exercise has been brought as "Wastelands Atlas of India-2005". As per the latest estimates arrived through this exercise, the total extent of wastelands in the country stands at 55.27 million hectares as compared to 63.85 million hectares as per Wasteland Atlas 2000.

A study titled "Comprehensive Assessment of Watershed Programmes in India" has been assigned to the International Crops Research Institute for the Semi-Arid Tropics (ICRISAT), Hyderabad to critically assess the impact of various watershed development programmes in India and to identify the positive factors leading to reduction of wastelands by about 8.58 million hectares over a period of 5 years as indicated by Wastelands Atlases brought out in 2000 and 2005.

The main emerging messages from this study are:

- Targeted interventions to benefit the vulnerable groups enhanced the impact, sustainability of the programmes through development of social capital.
- Vast scope exists to enhance the benefits and doubling the productivity of rain-fed areas by upgrading watershed programmes in the country with sustained and increased investments.

9.6.2 Area Development Programmes: The Area Development Programmes namely Drought Prone Areas Programme (DPAP), Desert Development Programme (DDP) and the Integrated Wastelands Development Programme (IWDP) are implemented in a project based approach in a watershed, which is a geo-hydrological unit draining into a common point, for in-situ soil and water conservation, afforestation etc. Presently 972 blocks of 185 Districts in 16 States are covered under Drought Prone Areas Programme (DPAP). Similarly, 235 Blocks of 40 Districts in 7 States are covered under the Desert Development Programme (DDP). The coverage under Integrated Wastelands Development Programme (IWDP) extends generally to Blocks that are not covered in the above programmes.

A. Drought Prone Areas Programme: Drought Prone Areas Programme (DPAP) is the earliest area development programme launched by the Central Government in 1973-74 to tackle the special problems faced by those fragile areas, which are constantly affected by severe drought conditions. These areas are characterized by large human and cattle populations which are continuously putting heavy pressure on the already degraded natural resources for food, fodder and fuel. The major problems are continuous depletion of vegetative cover, increase in soil erosion and fall in ground water levels due to continuous exploitation without any effort to recharge the underground aquifers.

1. Objectives: The basic objective of the programme is to minimize the adverse impacts of drought on the production of crops and livestock and productivity of land, water and human resources thereby ultimately leading to the drought proofing of the affected areas. The programme aims at promoting overall economic development and improving the socio-economic condition of the resource poor and disadvantaged sections inhabiting the programme areas through creation, widening and equitable distribution of the resource base and increased employment opportunities. The objectives of the programme are being addressed in general by taking up development works through watershed approach for land development, water resource development and afforestation/pasture development.

At present the Drought Prone Areas Programme (DPAP) is under implementation in 972 blocks of 185 districts in 16 States. Till March 1999 the funds were shared on 50:50 basis between the Central Government and the State Governments. However, with effect from 1st April 1999, the funding is shared on 75:25 basis between the Centre and State Government. The projects of 500 ha. are sanctioned under the programme. However with effect from 1.4.2000, uniform cost norms @ Rs. 6,000 per hectare have been introduced. These norms are applicable to projects sanctioned during and after 2000-2001.

2. Physical and Financial Progress: Since 1995-96 to 2007-08, 27,439 projects covering an area of 137.195 lakh hectare had been sanctioned and Rs. 2,739.84 crore released. The plan wise sanction of area covered is depicted in the graph below. These projects are at various stages of implementation in different states. Against a budget provision of Rs. 370 crore for DPAP in the year 2007-08, Rs. 285 crore had been released till January 31, 2008. Keeping the huge on-going liability in view, no new projects have been sanctioned during 2007-08. During 2007-08, a total of 121 projects had been completed up to January 31, 2008. Under DPAP, during 2007-08, Mid-Term evaluations by the independent evaluators have been carried out in 923 micro-watersheds. The reports indicated a positive impact on soil and moisture conservation, rise in ground water level, increase in availability of fuel & fodder and enhanced wage-employment.

B. Desert Development Programme: The Desert Development Programme (DDP) was started both in hot desert areas of Rajasthan, Gujarat and Haryana and the cold deserts of Jammu & Kashmir and Himachal Pradesh in 1977-78. From 1995-96, the coverage has been extended to a few more districts in Andhra Pradesh and Karnataka.

A Technical Committee reviewed the programme in 1994-95. The main reason identified by the Committee for below satisfactory results under the programme was that area development was not taken up on watershed basis and the involvement of the local people was virtually non-existent, both in planning and execution of the programme. Besides inadequacy of funds, non-availability of trained personnel and taking up of too many activities, which were neither properly integrated nor necessarily related to the objectives of the programme, were also identified as contributory factors towards reducing the impact of the programme.

Based on the recommendations of the Committee, new Blocks//Districts were included under the programme. Comprehensive Guidelines for Watershed Development commonly applicable to different area development programmes were issued in October 1994 and made applicable with effect from April 1, 1995. Subsequently, based upon the feedback received from the various stakeholders, revised guidelines were circulated in September, 2001. These guidelines are applicable for projects sanctioned during 2000-2001 and thereafter. In 2003 these Guidelines were revised and Hariyali Guidelines have been in vogue since then. The Common Guidelines for Watershed Development Projects, 2008 will come into force from April 1, 2008.

1. Objectives: The programme has been conceived as a long-term measure for restoration of ecological balance by conserving, developing and harnessing land, water, livestock and human resources. It seeks to promote the economic development of the village community and improve the economic conditions of the resource poor and disadvantaged sections of society in the rural areas. The major objectives of the programme are as under:

- To mitigate the adverse effects of desertification and adverse climatic conditions on crops, human and livestock population and combating desertification.
- To restore ecological balance by harnessing, conserving and developing natural resources, i.e. land, water, vegetative cover and raising land productivity.
- To implement development works through the watershed approach, for land development, water resources development and afforestation/pasture development.

The Desert Development Programme (DDP) is under implementation in 235 blocks of 40 districts in 7 States. The DDP is a Centrally Sponsored Programme and funds are directly released to DRDAs/ZPs for implementation of the programme.

With effect from April 1, 1999, the programme is being funded on the basis of 75:25 for the watershed projects sanctioned on or after April 1, 1999. However, projects sanctioned prior to 31.3.99 continued to be funded on the old pattern. Further, up to 1999-2000, the project cost was Rs. 22.5 lakh per project in respect of Hot Arid (non-sandy) areas and Rs. 25 lakh in other areas. However, this has been enhanced to a uniform rate of Rs. 30 lakh per project and this revised rate is applicable for the projects sanctioned on or after April 1, 2000.

The projects sanctioned before 31.3.2000 continued to be implemented on old cost norms.

2. Physical and Financial Performance: Since 1995-96 to 2007-08, 15,746 projects covering an area of 78.73 lakh hectare had been sanctioned and Rs. 2,060.17 crore released up to January 31, 2008. These projects are at various stages of implementation in different states. Against a budget provision of Rs. 260.00 crore for DDP in the year 2007-08, Rs 222.18 crore has been released till January 31, 2008. No new project has been sanctioned in 2007-08 owing to a committed liability of ongoing projects. During 2007-08, 477 projects were completed by January 31, 2008. An area of 2.38 lakh ha. has been covered as a result of completion of these projects. 47 Mid Term Evaluation reports in case of 1,029 projects were received during this year by January 31, 2008. The reports indicated a positive impact on increase in area under cultivation, fodder and fuel availability, strengthening of drinking water resources, reduction in migration and stabilization of sand dunes.

C. Integrated Wastelands Development Programme (IWDP)

1. Background: IWDP, a Centrally Sponsored Programme, has been under implementation since 1989-90. From 1st April 1995, the programme is being implemented through watershed approach under the Common Guidelines for Watershed Development. The development of wastelands and degraded lands under the programme is expected to promote the generation of employment in the rural areas besides enhancing the participation of people at all stages - leading to sustainable development of land and equitable sharing of the benefits. IWDP envisages the development of non-forests wastelands in the country. The basic approach in implementation of this programme has been modified from April 1, 1995 when the Guidelines for Watershed Development through watershed approach came into force. Since then, projects for development of wastelands on micro watershed basis have been sanctioned.

2. Objectives: The programme is aimed at integrated development of wastelands/degraded lands based on village/micro watershed plans. The Programme aims at fulfilment of the following objectives:

- Developing wastelands/degraded lands on watershed basis, keeping in view the capability of land, site conditions and local needs.
- Promoting the overall economic development and improving the socio-economic condition of the poor and disadvantaged sections inhabiting the programme areas.
- Restoring ecological balance by harnessing, conserving and developing natural resources, i.e. land, water vegetative cover.
- Encouraging village community for (a) sustainable community action for the operation and maintenance of assets created and further development of the natural resources in the watershed and (b) simple, easy and affordable technological solutions and institutional arrangements that make use, and build upon, local technical knowledge and available material.
- Employment generation, poverty alleviation, community empowerment and development of human and other economic resources of the village.

The projects under the programme are generally sanctioned in the Blocks not covered by DDP and DPAP. At present, the projects under the Programme are being implemented in 470 districts of the country.

Prior to March 31, 2000, watershed development projects under the programme were sanctioned at a cost norm of Rs.4,000 per hectare. These were funded entirely by the Central Government. The cost norms were revised to Rs. 6,000 per hectare for the projects sanctioned after April 1, 2000. The funding of the projects is shared between the Centre and States in the ratio of Rs. 5,500 per hectare. and Rs. 500 per hectare respectively. However, the old projects sanctioned up to March

31, 2000 continue to be funded entirely by the Central Government.

3. Physical and Financial Progress: 1,877 IWDP projects have been sanctioned since April 1, 1995 to treat a total project area of about 107.22 lakh hectares. The plan wise sanction of area covered is depicted in the graph below. These projects are at various stages of implementation in different states. 170 projects covering an area of 15.48 lakh hectares were completed by January 31, 2008. During 2007-08, 40 projects were completed by January 31, 2008. An area of 3.31 lakh hectare has been treated as a result of completion of these projects in 2007-08. The activities completed in these projects included pasture development over 19,011 hectare horticulture development over 16,105 hectare and afforestation of 26,762 ha besides creation of water harvesting structures and soil and moisture conservation works.

Mid-term evaluation reports were received for 161 projects during this year by January 31, 2008. The reports indicated a positive impact on increase in area under cultivation, increase in fodder availability, strengthening of drinking water resources, rise in ground water table and reduction in migration. The budget provision of Rs. 373.00 crore for non-NE states has been fully utilized under IWDP in the year 2007-08. In NE states against a budget provision of Rs. 112.00 crore, Rs. 70.65 crore has been released till January 31, 2008. Although new projects have not been sanctioned during this year, the releases for ongoing projects have increased by 61 percent in the north east states and by 54 percent in other states during 2007-08 as compared to 2006-07. The financial utilization reports received from the States showed an expenditure of Rs. 328.09 crore during the year up to December 31, 2007.

9.6.3 Integrated Watershed Management Programme: The Ministry of Rural Development set up a technical committee on Drought Prone Areas Programme (DPAP), Desert Development Programme (DDP) and Integrated

Wastelands Development Programme (IWDP) chaired by Shri S. Parthasarathy vide a resolution dated 14.2.2005 to address major issues in watershed programmes and recommend viable strategies and mechanisms for strengthening implementation of these programmes. The committee held wide ranging discussions with State Governments, reputed NGOs and institutions, visited a number of watershed projects and held discussions on project sites with village communities to formulate recommendations. Based on the recommendation of the committee, it is proposed to integrate and consolidate the three area development programmes of Ministry of Rural Development, namely Drought Prone Areas Programme (DPAP), Desert Development Programme (DDP) and Integrated Wastelands Development Programme (IWDP) into a single programme called Integrated Watershed Management Programme (IWMP). This consolidation is for optimum use of resources, sustainable outcomes and integrated planning. The common guidelines for the Watershed Development Projects have been finalized and will be operational with effect from April 1, 2008.

The key features of the Common Guidelines for Watershed Development Projects are as under:

A. Livelihood Orientation: The livelihoods perspective is to be incorporated at the planning stage itself rather than as an add-on after the physical works have been completed. Resource development and usage will be planned to promote farming and allied activities to promote local livelihoods while ensuring resource conservation and regeneration. The new approach would systematically integrate livestock management as a central intervention and encourage dairying and marketing of dairy products.

B. Cluster Approach: At present, the conventional concept of geo-hydrological boundaries of a micro-watershed is being followed in watershed planning. The concept of developing a fixed area of 500 ha under a specific project excludes many important areas within the watershed from treatment. Particularly, the areas situated at the higher reaches and forestlands are ignored while prioritizing the treatment plan through participatory rural appraisal techniques. As a result, the task of full treatment of the watershed remains unaccomplished and whatever treatments are taken up, their sustainability remains threatened. The approach of 500-hectare projects is also not viable for agricultural production and market linkages. The new approach envisages a broader vision of natural hydro-geographical units of average size of 1,000 to 5,000 hectares comprising of clusters of micro-watersheds.

C. Scientific Planning: Currently, the area development programmes suffer from the serious lacuna of the absence of detailed scientific planning. There has hardly been any attempt to harness available technologies or to coordinate with organizations such as National Remote Sensing Agency (NRSA). The new approach will look at the incorporation of scientific planning methodologies. Remote sensing inputs with a judicious mix of Geographical Information System (GIS) and Global Positioning System (GPS) would help in resource characterization, prioritization of areas for treatment, detailed project and regional planning, preparation of DPRs, and monitoring of targets and outcomes.

An MIS with GIS web based application would be used as a tool for planning and monitoring from National level down to district/microwatershed level. The MIS will include GIS layers on disaggregated wasteland data along with demographic details including poverty mapping, tribal areas, drought prone areas, dark zones with acute drinking water scarcity and clearly defined bench marks indicating type of structures created, extent of land treatment, increase in water table and other parameters as outcomes of different schemes being implemented.

D. Coordination and Synergy: Activities undertaken in the Watershed Development Programmes for soil and water conservation pertain to wage employment. Thus, implementation of these activities will be coordinated with NREGS for wage employment purposes for sustainable livelihood opportunities. Shelves of projects related to water conservation, plantation and afforestation, renovation of existing traditional structures of water sources, soil conservation and structures dealing with drought under NREGS at district level will be appropriately linked to Watershed Development Work Plans at Block level for coordination in planning and implementation. Watershed Development Teams (WDT) would be properly trained for identification of resources and scientific analysis for implementation of Watershed Development Programmes in coordination with NREGS activities.

The IWMP will also be closely linked to the related initiatives of other Ministries and Departments such as the National Horticulture Mission, National Bamboo Mission, Artificial Ground Water Recharge, Backward Region Grants Fund etc. for sustainable outcomes.

E. Institutional Framework: The lack of dedicated institutional structures and adequate professional support has been a major weakness in the implementation of the area development programmes. It is, therefore, proposed to bring in suitable institutional mechanisms, which will ensure both professional support and dedicated implementation agencies at the national, state and district level.

At the national level, there will be a dedicated agency with a technical Secretariat which will be called the Central Level Nodal Agency (CLNA). This will be a professional and output-oriented agency with autonomy and functional freedom which will be responsible for managing the watershed programme. At the State level there will be a State Level Nodal Agency (SLNA) with requisite professional support. At the District level, there will be a dedicated team which will be fully involved with the implementation of the programme from start to finish. They will provide technical as well as administrative inputs and will ensure high levels of quality with respect to the deliverables.

The State Level Nodal Agency would be empowered to scrutinize and sanction projects within the State. A representative of the Department of Land Resources, MoRD will be a member of this Committee. The day-to-day management will be done by the State Level Nodal Agency with district level interaction. In line with the considered suggestion of the Parthasarathy Committee, the Department would make a suitable recommendation for enhancement of the cost norms.

Capacity building has been identified as a key area of weakness of watershed programmes so far. Capacity building is a crucial component for achieving the desired result of livelihood enhancement through natural resource management. This is a continuous process that enables functionaries to enhance their knowledge, skills and attitudes, thereby becoming more effective in performing their roles and responsibilities. Each State will have an Annual Training Plan to be approved and monitored by the SLNA. Similarly, each DWMU will prepare a training plan for the district which will incorporate the training plan prepared by each PIA for capacity building of the various functionaries at the watershed level. These plans will be regularly monitored and reviewed at the state and district level.

There will be both a concurrent evaluation as well as a post project evaluation for every project. Each evaluation will include physical, financial and social audit of the work done. Panchayati Raj Institutions (PRIs) at the Gram Panchayat, intermediate panchayat and Zilla Parishad levels would have full responsibility to oversee implementation of the programmes and they would provide all governance and administrative support. The role of NGOs has been recognized for creation of awareness, social mobilization, capacity building and implementation.

9.6.4 Technology Development Extension and Training (TDET) Scheme: This scheme was launched in 1993-94 to promote the development of cost effective and proven technologies for reclamation of various categories of wasteland land. Objectives of the scheme include:

- Development of a database for wastelands,
- Operationalisation of appropriate, cost effective and proven technologies for development of various categories of wastelands, and
- Dissemination of research finding and appropriate technologies for promoting wasteland development.

The scheme is being implemented through ICAR institutes, state agricultural universities, District Rural Development Agencies and government institutions with adequate institutional framework and organizational back up. Successful implementation of the scheme is expected to bridge the gap between existing technologies relevant to the latest situation for development of non-forest wasteland and wider application by organizations and agencies dealing with land based programme.

Under the scheme, 100 percent grant is admissible to implement projects on wastelands owned by government, public sector undertakings, universities, panchayats, etc. In case projects include the development of wastelands of private farmers and corporate bodies, the project cost is to be shared 60:40 between government and beneficiaries.

Till January 2008, 200 projects have been sanctioned under the scheme at an outlay of Rs. 252.59 crore. Of these, 84 have been completed or foreclosed. Important activities under taken include development of a data base on wastelands, promotion and testing of various agro-forestry models in different agro-climatic zones of the country, test effective technologies for increasing the productivity of saline and alkaline soils, promotion of medicinal and herbal plantations of non-forest wastelands, composite technologies for water harvesting, treatment of degraded lands through bio-fertilisers, (vermiculture, mycorrhiza, bio-pesticides) food stock modes techniques and development of technology for jojaoba plantation in arid and semiarid areas through Israeli collaboration. Technical brochures have been brought out on different technologies that could be adopted for development of different categories of problem lands.

Some of the innovative projects that have been taken up under the Scheme are:

- In collaboration with NRSA, Hyderabad, a detailed exercise has been undertaken to digitally map and prioritize watersheds in 3 States on the basis of different thematic layers like land use, soil type, water availability etc. on a pilot basis. This information could be usefully employed to identify watersheds for development as per priority.
- IIT, Delhi has undertaken a pilot project and evolved a low-cost technology to convert domestic and farm waste into bio-fertilizers and successfully used the bio-fertilizer in growing fruit trees in public wastelands in Haryana and Rajasthan.
- Gujarat Institute of Desert Ecology, Bhuj has developed an integrated model for reclamation of saline lands in the Rann of Kutch region that included suitable agro-forestry species, water conservation and land reclamation measurers.
- The Forest Development Agency, Solan, Himachal Pradesh has successfully demonstrated the usefulness of a peoples participatory model in reclaiming forest wastelands through cultivation of medicinal plants and facilitating necessary linkages for marketing and processing the produce so that sustainable livelihoods are provided to the beneficiaries involved.
- The Minor Irrigation Department, Sangli, Maharashtra has completed a pilot project in executing a sub-surface drainage system in waterlogged and saline lands of Dudhgaon village. With this SSD system, the waterlogged areas that have been unused for decades due to severe salinity have successfully been reclaimed and the

beneficiary farmers have reported that these lands have not only been brought under plough but also are yielding substantial returns just within a year of cultivation.

During the financial year 2007-2008, fifteen new projects at a total cost of Rs. 36.58 crore were sanctioned. Funds amounting to Rs. 16.06 crore have been released towards implementation of these projects. Total funds of Rs. 24.89 crore have been released under TDET towards new and ongoing projects up to January 31, 2008.

9.6.5 National Mission on Bio-diesel: The committee set up by the Planning Commission on "Development of Bio-fuel" had submitted its report in April 2003. The main recommendations in the Report include launching of a national Mission on Bio- diesel with special focus on plantation of Jatropha curcas. The proposed National Mission is proposed to be implemented in two phases i.e. Phase I as Demonstration Project and Phase II a self sustaining expansion of Bio-diesel programme. For launching of the demonstration project of the National mission on Bio-diesel, the Ministry of rural Development has been identified as the nodal Ministry.

One of the primary objectives of the National Mission is to make it an effective means of bringing unutilized wastelands into productive use and make it a major pro-poor initiative for generating rural employment and income. Besides, the Mission would lend itself as an effective instrument for meeting national energy/ecological needs. The ultimate output of the Mission would be to reduce the country's dependence on imported petroleum diesel by supplementation of bio-diesel to the extent of 20 percent, by the end of Phase-II of the programme.

The Demonstration Phase under the National Mission on Bio-diesel will be taken up in a "Mission Mode" and will be a Centrally Sponsored Scheme to be implemented by State governments. After detailed discussions with the States and considering the preference shown by the southern States for pongamia plantation also, the scheme, as now proposed, envisages promotion of Jatropha (Ratanjot) and Pongamia (Karanj) plantations on 5 lakh hectares in forest and non-forest areas over a period of 5 years. The plantations would be taken up essentially on degraded forestlands and wastelands belonging to the village communities/panchayats/government as well as on unutilized marginal lands belonging to the marginal and small farmers as a means of providing them supplementary livelihood opportunities.

Since there is no reliable and tested database on various aspects of cultivating bio-diesel plants and costs and returns involved, R&D (applicable to planting and processing, training, awareness building etc) would also be an important and significant component of the Demonstration Phase. As far as launching the Demonstration Phase of the National mission on Bio-Diesel is concerned, the proposal has since been processed through the Expenditure Finance Committee (EFC) at its meeting held on October 9, 2006. Subsequently, the proposal was considered by the CCEA at its meeting on 8th March 2007. The proposal has been referred to the Group of Ministers (GOM) for further examination and recommendations. The first meeting of the GoM was held on 16th May 2007 wherein it was decided that the Ministry of Rural Development, Ministry of Science & Technology and ICAR would make presentations before the GoM before a final view is taken. The next meeting of the GoM for these presentations has yet to be convened.

During 2006-07, a budgetary provision of Rs. 50 crore was made for the Bio-fuels programme. Out of this, an amount of Rs. 49 crore was released to 15 identified States for the purpose of raising Jatropha/Pongamia saplings in nurseries so that these saplings would be readily available for plantation as soon as the Demonstration phase would be launched with the approval of the CCEA.

9.7 Conclusion

An ever-increasing population has placed enormous

demands on land resources of India which has only 2.4 percent of the world's geographical area but supports over 16 percent of the world's population. It has 0.5 percent of the world's grazing area but has over 18 percent of world's cattle population. These pressures have led to drastic changes in the proportion of land utilised for agricultural activities, urbanisation and industrial development.

It is necessary to ascertain the extent to which land now lying waste can become available for cultivation. Increasing population also means withdrawal of areas now under farms for building houses. Development of communications such as roads, railways, and airways may take up fertile land. Owing to rapid urbanisation and growth of large cities land is needed for parks and open spaces. Irrigation dams may submerge fertile areas. Industrial plants and other establishments also require substantial areas. In all these developments wherever fertile land can be saved efforts should be made to do so. This indicates the need for a comprehensive inventory of land and for greater refinement in land classification and continuous attention to land use.

10

Water Resources

India with 2.4 percent of the world's total area has 16 percent of the world's population; but has only 4 percent of the total available fresh water. This clearly indicates the need for water resources development, conservation and their optimum use.

10.1 Constitutional Provisions

In the Constitution of India, water and power development is a State activity subject to Central control. Water supplies, irrigation and canals, drainage and embankments, water storage and water power belong to the States vide Entry 17 in State List (List II) in the Seventh Schedule of the Constitution of India. But these are subject to the provisions of Entry 56 in Union List (List I) in the same Schedule which deals with the regulation and development of inter-State rivers and river valleys. Since electricity belongs to Concurrent List (List III) [Entry 38], the Centre's concurrent jurisdiction on water power is automatic.

10.2 Rivers of India

In India, rivers have had a powerful influence on national and local life. Successful agriculture in most parts of the country is not possible without the use of river waters. The large land resources of India cannot be put to productive use without a simultaneous development and use of water resources. In fact, an integrated development of the land and water resources is of fundamental importance to the country's economy.

From times immemorial, life and civilization in India have been dependent largely on rivers. The earliest civilizations developed along the banks of Indus and Ganga and their tributaries. In the Deccan, except for the narrow strip along the western coast, large parts of the population have depended for their existence on river waters.

Irrigation (artificial application of water to crops), is an old art in India. It began with agriculture itself. References to the practice of irrigation in India have been traced to many centuries prior to the commencement of the Christian era. The large numbers of tanks, which are found in the Deccan, have been in existence for ages. Cauvery delta canals date back to the 2nd century and Yamuna canals were constructed originally about the 14th century. Apart from rivers, underground water constitutes an important source of water supply for domestic and agricultural purposes.

The rivers of India may be broadly divided into two groups: (a) The snow-fed rivers of northern India and (b) the rivers of central and southern India. The Himalayas give rise to three important river systems of northern India: Indus, Ganga and Brahmaputra. The chief rivers of central and southern India are Mahanadi, Godavari, Krishna and Cauvery flowing eastward into the Bay of Bengal and Narmada and Tapti flowing westward into the Arabian Sea. Chambal, Betwa and Sone drain the northern edge of the Peninsula and flow into the Ganga system.

The rivers of northern India, rising in the Himalayas, are snow-fed and flow all the year round though the supplies available in winter are low. The rivers rise with the melting of snow in spring and with the arrival of monsoons they swell further and carry enormous floods during the rainy season, the supplies falling again from October onwards. The rivers of central and southern India have no snow-fields at their heads and their supplies depend entirely on rainfall. Since this rainfall is confined to a small part of the year, the rivers carry large supplies in these months and the dry weather flow sometimes dwindles down to almost a trickle.

There are numerous other rivers and rivulets in which

waters are available for utilization, mostly on an intermittent basis during the rainy season. On quite a large number of these, small irrigation reservoirs have already been built but many more can be constructed and there is an increasing activity all over the country to utilize the waters of these small streams.

10.3 Rainfall in India

India is endowed with substantial water resources. The country's average annual rainfall is about 1194 mm. The outstanding feature of the rainfall in India is its unequal distribution during the year and its variation from year to year in respect of quantity, incidence and duration.

Rainfall in India, as in all tropical countries, is confined mainly to the southwest monsoon months of June to September. The rainfall is not even and has spatial and temporal variation causing droughts in some parts of the country and floods in others. The all-India annual average rainfall is 1,194 mm but it varies from 100 mm (about five rain days) in the western deserts to 11,000 mm (about 15 rain days) in the north-eastern region. Irrigation has, therefore, since time immemorial, been recognized as a vital input for agriculture, contributing not only directly by meeting the evapo-transpiration needs of plants, but also indirectly by recharging ground water.

10.4 Underground Water

Water resources may be divided broadly into surface water and underground water. Their development has to be viewed in relation to the need to increase the productivity of land through irrigation, flood control, drainage and other means and also to domestic and industrial requirements.

Rivers and their tributaries, canals, lakes, reservoirs, tanks and ponds constitute sources of surface water.

Substantial water supplies for irrigation, industrial and municipal uses are available from under-ground waters. Wells have been constructed in all parts of India for domestic water supply and for irrigation of land and they are in use from times immemorial. However, large-scale irrigation from this source is possible only with the help of tube wells operated by power pumps. No inventory of the ground water resources for the country as a whole has as yet been prepared. The information available indicates that ground water is generally available in all parts of the country.

10.5 Water Resources Potential

The water resources potential of the country has been assessed from time to time by different agencies. The different estimates are shown in Table 10.1. It may be seen that since 1954, the estimates have stabilized and are within the proximity of the currently accepted estimate of 1869 billion cubic metre (BCM) which includes replenishable groundwater which gets charged on annual basis.

Table 10.1: Estimates of Water Resources in India

Estimating agency	Estimate in BCM*
First Irrigation Commission (1902-03)	1443
Dr. A.N. Khosla (1949)	1673
Central Water and Power Commission (1954-66)	1881
National Commission on Agriculture	1850
Central Water Commission (1988)	1880
Central Water Commission (1993)	1869

*BCM = Billion Cubic Metre

Source: Government of India, Planning Commission, *Eleventh Five Year Plan* (2007-12), Vol., III, p. 44.

According to Eleventh Five Year Plan (2007-12), "Within the limitations of physiographic conditions, socio- political environment, legal and constitutional constraints and the technology available at hand, the *utilizable water resources* of the country have been assessed at 1,123 Billion Cubic Metre

(BCM), of which 690 BCM is from surface water and 433 BCM from ground water sources. Harnessing of 690 BCM of utilizable surface water is possible only if matching storages are built. Trans-basin transfer of water, if taken up to the full extent as proposed under the National Perspective Plan, would further increase the utilizable quantity by approximately 220 BCM. The irrigation potential of the country has been estimated to be 139.9 million hectare (m.ha.) without inter-basin sharing of water, and 175 m.ha. with inter-basin sharing.

While the total water resources availability in the country remains constant, the per capita availability of water has been steadily declining since 1951 due to population growth. The twin indicators of water scarcity are per capita availability and storage. A per capita availability of less than 1,700 cubic metres (m^3) is termed a water stressed condition while if it falls below 1,000 cubic meters, it is termed as water scarcity condition. While on an average we may be nearing the water stressed condition, on an individual river basin-wise situation, 9 out of our 20 river basins with 200 million population are already facing a water scarcity condition. Even after constructing 4,525 large and small dams, the per capita storage in the country is 213 m^3 as against 6,103 m^3 in Russia, 4,733 m^3 in Australia, 1,964 m^3 in USA and 1,111 m^3 of China. It may touch 400 m^3 in India only after the completion of all the ongoing and proposed dams." [1]

10.6 Utilization of Water

The major use of water is for irrigation and hydropower generation, but water is also used for public water supply, industrial and navigation purposes. Water supply for irrigation can be obtained both from surface and underground resources.

The major uses of water in industry are for cooling, processing and boiler feed. Industrial needs of water are increasing rapidly. Hence the need to pay attention to methods of conservation and re-use of water in industries has become urgent. Most of the water used for industrial purposes is renewable in the sense that it becomes available for re-use if properly reconditioned.

The massive development of irrigation in India after Independence has been recognized as one of the major factors which have contributed to the spectacular rise in the production of food and fibre.

10.7 Water Pollution

There is now a wealth of documented evidence of the adverse effects of water pollution from all over the country. These range from the transmittal of water-borne diseases like cholera, jaundice, typhoid and dysentery to fish kills and loss of agricultural productivity through the use of polluted water. From the Dal Lake in the North, to the Periyar and Chaliyar rivers in the South, from the Damodar and Hooghly in the East to the Thana Creek in the West, the picture of water pollution is uniformly gloomy. Even our large perennial rivers like the Ganga are today heavily polluted.

Investigations by the Central and State Boards for the Prevention and Control of Water Pollution show that the major sources of pollution of our natural water courses including coastal waters is the discharge of community wastes from human settlements. Most of the community and industrial waste waters go straight into water courses rendering them unfit for most uses, least of all as drinking water sources.

One of the important problems associated with industrialisation and urbanisation is the pollution of available water supplies, especially rivers, by industrial effluents and trade waste. This leads, amongst others, to mortality of fish and contamination of drinking water. Proper disposal of these wastes is difficult and costly. There is need for coordinated surveys and experimental work. These should cover analysis of effluents, data on extent of pollution caused by them, development of methods for their treatment and preparation of standards to which they should conform, before they can be discharged into rivers.

10.8 Climate Change and Uncertainty in Water Availability

The threat of climate change is now considered an established fact. General Circulation Models (GCM) have simulated the behaviour of atmosphere and painted "what if" scenarios for various levels of Green House Gases emissions. Using these models the weather experts have predicted the following:

- Global warming will intensify the hydrologic cycle.
- More intense rainfall will occur in fewer spells.
- Floods and droughts both will become more intense.
- Floods will be more frequent.
- Rainfall will shift towards winter.
- There may be a significant reduction in the mass of glaciers, resulting in increased flows in the initial few decades but substantially reduced flows thereafter.

Ministry of Water Resources has already initiated some studies in co-operation with research institutions and reputed academic institutions to assess the impact of climate change on water resources.

The hydrologists are yet to translate what climate change means for the water availability, its distribution in time and space, and changes in demand. An increase in mean temperatures would increase the energy flux for evapo-transpiration. The increased potential evapo-transpiration in the forests could trigger major changes in the environment, and in the farms it would result in an increased crop water requirement. The changes in seasonal temperatures could change the crop seasons. Enough data is now available to paint "what if" scenarios for different possibilities, and to formulate some tentative plans to respond to these possibilities.

In the post climate change scenario, systems that are more resilient will fare better than systems that are less so. Engineering infrastructure that enable the water managers to store and transfer water with greater certainty can reduce the impact of uncertainty. Climate change considerations need to be factored in as we plan water resources infrastructure.

10.9 Future Requirements of Water

The requirement of water for various sectors has been assessed by the National Commission on Integrated Water Resources Development (NCIWRD) in the year 2000. This requirement is based on the assumption that the irrigation efficiency will increase to 60 percent from the present level of 35 to 40 percent. The Standing Committee of MoWR also assesses it periodically. These are shown in Table 10.2.

Table 10.2: Projections of Water Requirements of Various Sectors of the Indian Economy

Sector	Water Demand in km^3 (or BCM*)					
	Standing Sub-Committee of MoWR**			NCIWRD***		
	2010	2025	2050	2010	2025	2050
Irrigation	688	910	1072	557	611	807
Drinking Water	56	73	102	43	62	111
Industry	12	23	63	37	67	81
Energy	5	15	130	19	33	70
Others	52	72	80	54	70	111
Total	813	1093	1447	710	843	1180

*Billion Cubic Metre; **Ministry of Water Resources; *** National Commission on Integrated Water Resources Development.

Source: Government of India, Planning Commission, *Eleventh Five Year Plan* (2007-12), Vol., III, p. 46.

10.10 Water Crisis Scenario

Sustainable development and efficient management of water is an increasingly complex challenge in India. Increasing population, growing urbanization and rapid industrialisation combined with the need for raising agricultural production generates competing claims for water. The growing perception of an impending water crisis in the country was highlighted by the Eleventh Five Year Plan (2007-12) by bringing out the following facts:

- "There is hardly any city which gets 24 hours supply of drinking water.
- Many rural habitations which had been covered under the drinking water programme are now being reported as having slipped back with target dates for completion continuously pushed back. There are pockets where arsenic, nitrate and fluoride in drinking water are posing a serious health hazard.
- In many parts, the ground water table declines due to over exploitation imposing an increasing financial burden on farmers who need to deepen their wells and replace their pump sets and on State Governments whose subsidy burden for electricity supplies rises.
- Many major and medium irrigation projects seem to remain under execution forever as they slip from one plan to the other with enormous cost and time overruns.
- Due to lack of maintenance the capacity of the older systems seems to be going down.
- The gross irrigated area does not seem to be rising in a manner that it should given the investment in irrigation. The difference between potential created and area actually irrigated remains large. Unless we bridge the gap, significant increase in agricultural production will be difficult to realise.
- Floods are a recurring problem in many parts of the country. Degradation of catchment areas and loss of flood plains to urban development and agriculture have accentuated the intensity of floods.
- Water quality in our rivers and lakes are far from satisfactory. Water in most parts of rivers is not fit for bathing, let alone drinking. Untreated or partially treated sewage from towns and cities is being dumped into river.
- Untreated or inadequately treated industrial effluents pollute water bodies as also contaminate ground water.
- At the same time water conflicts are increasing. Apart

from the traditional conflicts about water rights between upper and lower riparians in a river, conflicts about quality of water, people's right for rain water harvesting in a watershed against downstream users, industrial use of ground water and its impact on water tables and between urban and rural users have emerged." [2]

10.11 Conclusion

The colossal damage done by the denudation of the Himalayan and other watersheds to our water resources also needs to be properly appreciated. Since the run-off of rainwater from denuded areas is far greater than from well-wooded slopes, a great deal of the water which would otherwise have been retained as sub-soil and ground water is today being lost as surface run-off often causing further erosion and floods in the process. The seriousness of such losses can hardly be over-estimated.

Due to growing population, the per capita availability of water is steadily going down and many areas of the country are already facing water stress. This, coupled with urbanisation and industrialisation, has raised concerns about the deteriorating quality of surface and ground water. Any strategy for integrated development of water resources and its management will necessarily have to go beyond the technical issues to include economic, social and administrative issues.

Notes

1. Government of India, Planning Commission, Eleventh Five Year Plan (2007-12), Vol., III, p. 44.
2. Ibid., p. 43.

11

Forest Resources

11.1 Importance of Forests

Forests play a vital role in social, cultural, historical, economic and industrial development of any country and in maintaining its ecological balance. They are the resource base for sustenance of its population and a storehouse of biodiversity. Other vocations of land use, such as agriculture and animal husbandry, are dependent on forests and forestlands. Forests not only maintain and improve the moisture regime and provide clean air but also produce humus and maintain soil fertility.

The importance of forests can be understood by recognizing them as the primary producers and protectors of several natural resources. As long as the economic benefits in terms of climate control, pollution abatement, and wildlife maintenance are not satisfactorily calculated, timber and pulp are regarded the chief economic products of forests. Forests are also vital as watersheds. Because of the thick humus layer, loose soil and the soil-retaining powers of tree-roots, forests are vitally important for maintaining and regulating water flows and sub-soil water regimes. Almost all water ultimately comes from forestlands, forest-rivers and lakes and from forest-derived water tables. In addition, forests are habitats for diverse species; they sustain the majority of diversity in nature. The wild counterparts of our food plants and livestock, the genetic importance of which is being increasingly realized, occur in the forests and grasslands.

They also harbour our wild medicinal plants. They provide recreation and aesthetic refreshment for people, and irreplaceable supplies of oxygen and soil nutrients. Forests clean the environment by muffling noises, buffering strong winds and trapping dust and gases. They also moderate extremes of temperature. The most important benefit that the human race has been deriving from these ecosystems is the security of life-support systems. Viable populations of fauna and flora by their interdependent collective activities, ensure that the quality of natural systems is kept at levels that maintain their life-giving quality for all life forms. Deforestation has become a major environmental concern, as it can destabilize the earth's temperature, humidity, and carbon dioxide levels.

11.2 Constitutional Provisions Regarding Forests

As part of the natural environment and life-support system, forests have engaged the attention of all sections of society. The Constitution of India has given due recognition to forest and wildlife and the tribal communities dependent on forests. Thus, Part IV of the Constitution of India contains Directive Principles of State Policy. Article 48A of the Constitution falling under Part IV states, "The State shall endeavour to protect and improve the environment and to safeguard the forests and wildlife of the country".

Similarly, Part IVA of the Constitution, inserted by the Constitution (Forty-second Amendment) Act, 1976, contains Fundamental Duties of every citizen of India. Article 51A (g) of the Constitution falling under Part IVA states, "It shall be the duty of every citizen of India to protect and improve the natural environment including forests, lakes, rivers and wildlife, and to have compassion for living creatures".

11.3 Important Legislations Pertaining to Forests

11.3.1 Wild Life (Protection) Act, 1972: This is an Act to provide for the protection of wild animals, birds and plants and for matters connected therewith or ancillary or incidental thereto with a view to ensuring the ecological and environmental security of the country. The new provisions of the Act following the amendment of 2002, pertain to establishing the Zoo Authority of India to oversee management of all zoos in the country, protection of rare and endangered species of plants and animals and providing individual with the power to file complaints against offenders.

11.3.2 Forest (Conservation) Act, 1980: This Act was enacted to check indiscriminate diversion of forestland. Under this legislation, approval of the Central Government is required before any forestland (noted as such in Government records) is diverted for non-forestry purposes. Moreover, the transfer is allowed only with the provision that compensatory plantations/afforestation in an equivalent area of non-forestland, or double the area in degraded forestlands, are raised.

In 1988, the Act was amended to make existing provisions more stringent. Some procedural difficulties were, however, experienced in implementing the Act. In order to streamline disposal of applications under the Act, the process of decision-making has been decentralized and procedures and requirements have been rationalized. Revised and comprehensive rules and guidelines under the Act, were issued in 1992.

This Act is, by far, the most important tool the Government of India has to regulate and control the change in the land use of recorded forestland.

11.3.3 Environment (Protection) Act, 1986: This Act provides for the protection and improvement of environment and for matters connected therewith. India participated at the United Nations Conference on the Human Environment held at Stockholm in June 1972 and decided to take appropriate steps for the protection and improvement of environment and the prevention of hazards to human life and health, other living creatures, plants and property. The Act has 4 Chapters and 26 Sections.

11.3.4 Biological Diversity Act, 2002: The Act has a reference to the United Nations Convention on Biological Diversity at Rio de Janeiro in 1992, which reaffirmed the sovereign rights of the States over their biological resources. The Act provides for the conservation of biological diversity, sustainable use of its components and fair and equitable sharing of the benefits arising out of the use of biological resources, knowledge and for connected matters. It has 12 Chapters and 65 Sections.

11.4 Present Status of Forests in India

The existing information on forest/tree cover based on the satellite data of 2002 indicates a green cover of 23.68 percent. The present extent of forest lands in the country is 77.47 million hectare. Per capita forest area is only 0.064 hectare against the world average of 0.64 hectare.

Humans, especially those living in and around forests, were earlier using natural resource just for sustenance and not for commercial purposes. With modern civilization being consumption-oriented, our natural resources and particularly forests, had to bear the brunt of indiscriminate use. Poverty, hunger, illiteracy and unmanageable population are some of the possible reasons of the apathy of developing countries towards conservation of their natural resources.

With increasing human and development activities, forests have been severely fragmented and at many places degraded, causing threat of local extinction to many wild species of plants and animals. By and large, people in India are not aware that our national stakes in biodiversity wealth are of the order of more than 80,000 known species of animals and 45,000 species of plants, of which 15,000 are known to be of medicinal value.

The present status of forests is none too satisfactory at best and deplorable at worst. Sustainability of forest ecosystem is an essential component of the environmental conservation efforts and any degradation of forests will have an adverse impact on various systems such as water resources, agriculture, biodiversity, environment, climate and human health, besides upon the subsistence living of tribal and other communities living in and around forest areas. Therefore, the functions with respect to conservation of soil, water and biodiversity are vital for the welfare of present and future generations. About 41 percent of forest cover of the country has already been degraded and dense forests are losing their crown density and productivity continuously. A large number of India's livestock population graze in forests, causing serious damage to regeneration and productivity. The use of forests beyond its carrying capacity and encroachments, upon forestlands are the main cause of the continuous degradation of forests.

11.5 Protected Areas

In order that we do not lose sight of the importance of our national natural heritage and destroy it unwittingly, the Indian Board for Wildlife was constituted in 1952 to advise the Government on measures to be adopted for the conservation of our wildlife resources. Over the past five decades there have been stories of success as well as of failures in achieving the targets set by the Board from time to time. In order to protect critical ecosystems and also to preserve the genetic resources of un-quantifiable commercial as well as non-commercial values, 95 national parks and over 500 wildlife sanctuaries, and two conservation reserves have been created in India, over the years, with the prime objective of preserving them as samples of interdependent ecological gene-pool combinations and a gene-bank capital. These are all under tremendous stress caused by human interventions. Almost 40 percent of these protected areas are subject to effects of traditional livestock grazing, fodder extraction; timber extraction, non-timber forest produce collection and more than 45 percent have public thoroughfares dissecting them into smaller parts. Almost all have human habitations in or around them and a conflict of interest pervades the interface areas between the gene-pool reserves and the exploiters of the forest resources. These pressures are increasing with the rapid rise in the population of the country.

11.6 Reasons for Unsatisfactory State of Forests

11.6.1 Demographic Changes: From about 30 crore in the late 1940s, when India gained independence, the human population now stands over one billion, which implies a 3.5 times increase of human to land and human to forests ratios. This reality has induced large-scale land use changes reducing the extent of natural areas of all types, and has also caused degradation of the residual area from the overuse.

11.6.2 Mega-Development: Major development projects of all hues have affected forests and wildlife in two ways. One was by diverting both natural areas as well as village commons, the latter with little compensation or alternatives to villagers. Left with no alternatives, rural population mount further pressures on the residual natural areas leading to accelerated degradation. Another was by the diversion and export of local resources, e.g. water, without meeting the genuine demand of the communities.

11.6.3 Rural Development Imbalances: Rural development inputs in natural-area dominated landscapes have been and continue to be much lower as compared to those in other areas. Not only is this true, but such inputs also do not accord with the basic premise that rural ecosystems in these regions depend directly upon the well-being of natural ecosystems. This has led to a vicious cycle of community impoverishment, fuelling degradation of natural areas.

11.6.4 Market Pressures: Market pressures have led to aberrations in practices of collection and removal of both timber and non-timber forest produce, even where state trading has 'eliminated' the contractor system. Village communities due to lack of viable livelihood alternatives are forced into excessive and even abusive exploitation, leading to decline in productivity of the resource as well as attrition in the productivity parameters. Degradation of natural and rural ecosystems and the concomitant impoverishment of rural communities in the 'natural landscapes and seascapes' have been the inevitable consequences of such combined adverse causes. Even where steadfast effort has held the fort thus far, the scene is one of an 'island syndrome', such as in places like Kanha, Kalakaad-Mundanthurai, Great Himalayan National Park and Periyar, where visionary managers took to 'eco-development' and participatory forestry in permissible use zones as a combined strategy to provide supplemental livelihoods and meet the demand of bio-resources.

11.6.5 Lack of Political Will: Conservation leadership and direction in India have traditionally flowed from the "top". Though there have been individuals and communities who have made significant contribution to conservation and the religious sentiments, ethics and vegetarian food habits of the majority populace have also helped, there has been no systematized "green" movement in India. Thus, the political will for conservation has been linked with the convictions and commitment—or the lack of it—of the rulers. It would not be incorrect to say that in the previous two decades this interest in, and thus, commitment to environmental conservation, has been lacking in the country's leadership, whatever may be the 'lip-service' given to its importance. With coalition governance likely to continue as the order of the day, there appears to be little likelihood of any up-gradation in the priority accorded to nature and the environment. There is no denying also that enforcement has also been weakened by political expediency.

11.6.6 Lax Implementation: Legislation and policy already in place can significantly improve the situation, if effectively implemented. But not only is the already lax implementation likely to become more lax, but there is already a move afoot to both change the policies and then the laws to suit populist political objectives under the guise of equity, sustainability, progress and poverty alleviation. All the while a facade is being maintained of the importance accorded to forest and the environment. This paradox of the prevalent situation, which may get even more aggravated in the future for political reasons is, perhaps, the single greatest threat to forests, wildlife, wilderness and the environment.

11.6.7 Encroachment and Degradation: The Forest (Conservation) Act, 1980 (FC Act) became operative on 25 October 1980. This can be stated as one of the most important Central legislations, which has been responsible for halting the process of deforestation owing to the diversion of forestlands for non-forestry purposes. The FC Act ensures that no diversion of forestland is possible without the prior approval of the Government of India. The National Forest Policy, 1988, also stipulates that there would be no regularisation of existing encroachments.

In 1990, the Government of India issued guidelines to deal with cases on which commitments have been made by State Governments before October 25, 1980. All such cases were to be reviewed by a joint team of Revenue, Forest and Tribal Welfare Departments. It was also decided that all post-1980 encroachments would not be regularised.

It is extremely important to appreciate the fact that the ever-growing demand for regularisation of encroachments is one of the most important reasons for decimation of forests. Encroachments on forestland are an ongoing process. Most of the States adopt a rather passive attitude towards containing this problem, and have been inactive towards evicting the post-1980 encroachments. Thus, by and large, it would not be an overstatement to surmise that States are fostering encroachment on forestland, perhaps to avoid any adverse political response.

11.6.8 Other Reasons: While some of the major threats to India's forests and wildlife have been outlined above, some other threats are listed below:

- Insufficient and inappropriate manpower, inadequately equipped.
- Inadequate financial resources.
- Diversion of habitats for development projects, especially for dams, power plants and roads.
- Damage from mining.

- Habitat degradation caused by overuse and abuse by man and livestock.
- Degradation and diversion of water bodies and wetlands.
- Fire, man-caused and repeated a number of times each year, causing damage to nests of ground-laying birds, death to reptiles, soil compaction, damage to plant regeneration and impoverishment of water regions. Fire in an evergreen forest permanently changes the biome to semi-evergreen.
- Exponential growth of weeds and exotics, particularly *Eupatorium odoratum*, *Mikania scandens*, *Lantana camara*, *Strobilanthus* and others.
- Grazing, carrying with it concomitant fire and the danger of bovine disease contagion.
- The Protected Areas (PAs) are very small and usually ecologically incomplete biomes and biotopes not encompassing the food and seasonal movement requirements of most species of birds and large mammals. To compound matters, the linkages with habitats is being lost and the PAs have become islands surrounded by seas of humanity, most of which are not favourably disposed towards the PAs.
- Man-animal conflict, especially in respect of the elephant, tiger, leopard, nilgai, wild boar and blackbuck. The planting of favourable food plants close to herbivore populations has further aggravated the conflict.
- Adverse impact of tourism, and the tendency of the Government to give preference to tourism against the conservation imperatives.
- Tardy fund flow to field units from States despite Central assistance.
- Field staff vacancies.
- Need for Management Plans in Protected Areas.
- The presence of a large part of the nation's biodiversity outside the PA system, in reserves and protected forests etc where the Working Plans are largely based on the

needs of production forestry.

- Lack of inventory of the biodiversity of the country.

11.7 Forest Policy of the Government

The National Commission on Agriculture (NCA) in 1976 ushered in a major shift in the forestry sector, when it pronounced the need of a new forest policy to address the production of industrial wood for forest based industry, defence and communication and the present and future demand for protective and re-creative functions of forests.

The policy that was enunciated in 1988 and is in effect on date, is a comprehensive document with directives on afforestation, forestry and farm forestry, management of forests, rights and concessions, diversion of forestland, wildlife conservation, tribal communities, discouragement of shifting cultivation, management of forest fires and grazing, forest based industries, forest extension, forest education, forestry research, personnel management, forest survey and database, and legal and financial support. The evolving policies supported by various Acts and Rules and the administrative set-up checked to some extent the downhill trend in forest resources. Among the various steps taken, two, viz. creation of protected areas and joint forest management, are noteworthy.

Acting upon the recommendation of the National Commission on Agriculture, Government of India, through a resolution dated December 7, 1988 formulated a new forest policy with the following basic objectives:

- Maintenance of environmental stability through preservation and, where necessary, restoration of the ecological balance that has been adversely disturbed by serious depletion of the forests of the country.
- Conserving the natural heritage of the country by preserving the remaining natural forests with the vast variety of flora and fauna, which represent the remarkable biological diversity and genetic resources of the country.
- Checking soil erosion and denudation in the catchment

areas of rivers, lakes, and reservoirs in the interest of soil and water conservation, for mitigating floods and droughts and for the retardation of siltation of reservoirs.

- Checking the extension of sand dunes in the desert areas of Rajasthan and along the coastal tracts.
- Increasing the sustainability of the forest/tree cover in the country through massive afforestation and social forestry programmes, especially on all denuded, degraded and unproductive lands.
- Meeting the requirements of fuel wood, fodder, minor forest produce and small timber of the rural and tribal populations.
- Increasing the productivity of forests to meet essential national needs.
- Encouraging efficient utilization of forest produce and maximising substitution of wood.
- Creating a massive people's movement with the involvement of women for achieving these objectives and to minimise pressure on existing forests.

This was a clear improvement over the Forest Policy in 1952, as for the first time "environmental stability" was considered as the prime object of the Forest Policy and direct economic benefits were subordinated to this principal aim. While initiating this policy, it was acknowledged in the "Preamble" that despite the 1952 Policy, forests in the country have suffered serious depletion.

11.8 Joint Forest Management

Joint Forest Management (JFM) or Participatory Forest Management, which has taken firm roots in the country, is now the central policy of forestry sector in all the 28 States. Initiated with the circular of the Ministry of Environment and Forests on June 1 1990 on people's involvement in forest conservation and management, the JFM regime has evolved gradually and at present 1,06,482 committees (22 million participants) are functioning in 28 states covering 22.02

million hectares of forests. This participatory regime is seen as a potential strength of forest management for the forest fringes. The challenge now is to effectively empower the local communities with appropriate rights and responsibilities, and ensure that substantial benefits from forest conservation accrue to them. The movement has picked up because of institutional funding under the Ministry of Environment and Forests (MoEF), National Afforestation Programme (NAP) and externally-aided forestry sector projects.

11.8.1 Joint Forest Management Rules/Guidelines: As per the provisions of National Forest Policy, 1988, Government of India, on June 1, 1990, outlined and conveyed to State Governments a framework for creating massive people's movement through the involvement of village committees for the protection, regeneration and development of degraded forestlands situated in the vicinity of villages. This gave birth to JFM. Guidelines were issued in 2000 and 2002 for further strengthening JFM. Guidelines in brief are:

1. Joint Forest Management Committees (JFMCs) have been registered under different names in various States but many of them do not have legal support. A uniform name i.e. JFMC should be adopted and registration should be done under the Societies Registration Act, 1860 to provide them with legal power.
2. A Memorandum of Understanding (MoU) with clearly defined roles and responsibilities for different work and/or areas to be separately assigned and signed between the State Governments and the Committees.
3. All adults of the villages should be eligible to become members of the JFMC.
4. Considering the immense potential and genuine need for women's participation in JFM, at least 50 percent members of the JFM general body should be women. For the general body meeting, the presence of at least 50 percent women members should be a prerequisite for holding the general body meeting. At least 33 percent of the membership in

the JFM Executive Committee/Management Committee should be filled from amongst the women members. The quorum for holding meeting of such an Executive/Management Committee should be one-third of women executive members or a minimum of one whichever is more. One of the posts of office bearer i.e. President/Vice-President/Secretary should be filled by a woman member of the Committee.

5. Joint Forest Management programme should cover both the degraded as well as good forests (except the Protected Area Network) with a crown density above 40 percent. JFM activities should concentrate on NTFP management i.e. regeneration, development and sustainable harvesting of NTFP which can be given free or concessional rates, as per the existing practice in degraded areas under JFM. The benefit sharing mechanism will also be different for the good forest areas. JFM Committees will be eligible for benefit sharing for timber only if they have satisfactorily protected the good forests for a minimum period of the previous 10 years and the sharing percentage should be kept limited to a maximum of 20 percent of the revenue from the final harvest. The extent of good forest areas to be allowed will depend upon the number of village household and should be restricted to a maximum limit of 100 ha and generally limited to 2 km from the village boundary. For degraded forests as far as possible JFM should be first concentrated on areas up to 5 km from the village boundary.
6. New Working Plans should provide for a JFM overlapping working circle with prescriptions keeping in mind the health of the forest and the needs of the forest dependent community. Micro-plans should be prepared at the local level after detailed participatory rural appraisal exercise and should reflect the consumption and livelihood needs of the local communities as well as sustainability of resource.
7. Forums or working groups at various levels need to be

established for conflict resolution.

8. Community groups in many States who have been traditionally protecting and assisting in the regeneration of forests, need to be identified, recognized and registered as JFMCs.
9. For long-term sustainability of resources, it is essential that not less than 25 percent of the revenue earned from final harvest should form the share of village community and deposited in the village development fund for meeting the conservation and development needs of the forests. A matching contribution may be made by the Forest Department from its share of such sales.
10. Concurrent monitoring of progress and performance should be undertaken at Division and State levels.

11.9 Agro-forestry

11.9.1 Definition and Significance: Agro-forestry means practice of agriculture and forestry on the same piece of land. It has been defined as a sustainable management system for land that increases overall production, combines agricultural crops and animals simultaneously. It also connotes a land use system that integrates trees, crops and animals in a way that is scientifically sound, ecologically desirable, practically feasible and socially acceptable to the farmers.

Another widely used definition given by the International Centre for Research in Agro-forestry (ICRAF) Nairobi, Kenya reads:

"Agro-forestry is a collective name for all land use systems and practices where woody perennials are deliberately grown on the same land management unit as agricultural crops or animals in some form of spatial arrangement or temporal sequence".

It is an age-old practice that went into disuse in modern agriculture context. AF is capable of meeting the present challenges of resource conservation and improvement of environmental quality. In low rainfall areas, AFP increases rainfall utilization by extending the growing season. AFS provides insurance against risks caused by weather aberrations, controlling erosion hazards and ensuring sustainable production of the land. In AF, maintenance of a sufficient ground cover during the period of erosive rains has a high potential to reduce erosion. The effectiveness in conserving water is proportional to the speed of decomposition of the litter.

Effects of the tree-crop mixture on the water balance are cumulative. If water is conserved, the water saved can be carried forward through dry periods in lower soil horizons. Some traditional AFS have built in dynamism for restoration of soil fertility, amelioration of soil and providing sustained yield. They should be utilized for developing AF technologies in different agro-climatic regions. The mass erosion areas (landslide, torrents, mine spoils, ravines etc.) could be rehabilitated through bio-(AF)-engineering measures. The interventions significantly reduce sediment load; improve vegetation cover, dry weather flow, water quality; besides improving the soil fertility. Integrated development of watersheds including AF interventions reduced runoff or moderated flooding of downstream reaches and improved in situ moisture conservation for increased biomass production.

The reasons for higher production under agro-forestry system include:

- Greater efficiency of tree species for photosynthesis;
- Improved soil structure and fertility with increasing effects on crop yield;
- Reduce losses from soil erosion and more closed cycling of organic matter and nutrients;
- Creating better micro climatic conditions for the growth of agricultural crops The tangible and intangible benefits of agro-forestry are mentioned below:

- ♦ To meet the demand of fuel, fodder and timber for the increasing population.
- ♦ To reduce the biotic pressure on existing forests.

- To obtain maximum output in terms of yield from the same piece of land.
- To develop wasteland/ degraded lands by planting suitable tree species with agricultural crops.

11.9.2 Area Available: National Forestry Action Plan (NFAP), 1999 estimated about 25.4 million hectare out of 55 million hectare wasteland available for tree plantations. Yet, even this area can hardly be counted as available given prolific urbanization and increasing price of land. Only about 12 million hectare of wastelands may be available for tree plantations. The only hope is the 142 m. ha agriculture land, which may be used in agro-forestry models for increasing tree cover.

Earlier studies have shown that about 5 percent of total agricultural lands are generally available for tree plantations with the available tree species under agro-forestry models. So about 7 m. ha agriculture land may be made available for tree cover.

11.9.3 Significance of Agro-forestry: It is only too obvious that government owned forests cannot meet the current requirement of the country, let alone in the future. Even our forests at the optimum level of conservation and productivity would find this task not possible. At the present level of degradation caused by ever-increasing demographic pressures, with 60 percent of the country's livestock being grazed on forestlands and 175 million tonnes of fodder being annually harvested from them (NFAP, 1999) the task is well-nigh impossible. Approximately Rs. 2000 crore worth of timber is being imported annually.

With forests under increasing pressure, agro-forestry is the only segment that can record growth in production – in timber, fuel wood, industrial wood, fodder and grass, medicinal plants and the rest. The current situation and future prospects must alter the role of forests and forestry, and with it the forest personnel would also have to change their recruitment, training, attitudes and mindset. The country's needs of timber, fuel wood, fodder, industrial wood and medicinal plants must be met with from private lands and community lands. This can only happen if the farmers get remunerative returns and no hassles in harvesting, transport and market access.

Agro-forestry has been a sleeping giant. Agriculture Departments, research centres and universities have been pre-occupied with agricultural crops and in giving impetus to the green revolution. The forest department has been only concerned with forests. The former are now giving greater attention to agro-forestry, but much greater impetus is required. This focus must filter down to the district and tahsil/block levels and the State agriculture departments supported by research institutions and universities must treat agro-forestry as an important agricultural crop and provide guidance and support to the farmers. The forest departments, on their parts, must produce seedlings, at least in the initial stage and not only cooperate in providing technical inputs, but also by removing barriers to the harvesting and marketing of agro-forestry products. Import of timber must also be regulated to keep the price of timber remunerative for the agro-forestry farmer, who is making a long-term investment and is making a novel venture in preference to traditional crops.

A disconcerting feature has been a drop in farm grown wood prices. In Yamuna Nagar, the biggest market of poplar wood, the average price between 1987 to 1997 for poplars with over 24" girth, was about Rs. 500 per quintal. By November 2002, the same commodity was fetching only Rs. 225 per quintal. Elsewhere too the prices have plummeted.

Another field, which needs to be urgently attended to, is plant multiplication and quality plantation. Forest Departments have traditionally been growing seedlings in nurseries. There is no assurance about the seed quality and variation among seedlings does occur.

With the advancement of biotechnology, techniques like tissue culture and cloning must be adopted by the forest departments. If such facilities cannot be created by the State

Governments, there should be linkages with private laboratories and institutions. The Department of Biotechnology have identified TERI, the National Chemical Laboratory and the Jainarayan University of Jodhpur as National Facilities for raising tissue culture for multiplication of trees and bamboo. The various forest departments should establish working partnerships with such institutes for tissue culture purposes if they cannot propagate it themselves. The research bodies under the FDs should identify quality seed and material for multiplication, which will be done by approved institutions and registered private growers. Tissue culture plants have an added advantage of being able to produce disease-free plants.

Of the total area under agriculture of approximately 142 million ha, about an equivalent of about 14 million hectare (about 10 percent of agriculture area) could be brought under tree cover through agro-forestry and farm forestry. To this may be added the area under horticulture. There is, thus, a great potential to extend and maintain tree cover under agro-forestry and farm forestry.

Agro-forestry offers a number of advantages. Timber and fuel wood produced under agro-forestry meet the local demands in rural areas and thus the problems and expenditure related to transport is avoided. Productivity of agro-forestry plantations is much higher than that of natural forests or plantations in forest areas. Production cost of timber or pulpwood and normally even their transportation in agro-forestry plantations are much lower than the same in case of forest department's plantations. Transportation costs to industries and users are also much less. Thus, the investment required per cubic meter of wood produced is much lower in case of agro-forestry plantations as compared to plantations raised on forestland. Government resources, both financial and human, needed for agro-forestry will be small. Agro-forestry also helps in poverty alleviation in rural areas.

Production and processing of wood produced under agro-forestry is estimated to generate substantial employment in rural areas, major part of which will be in processing of timber such as sawing, joinery, furniture making, etc. Government spending on such employment generation will hardly be any. Agro-forestry thus offers great potential of providing off-farm employment, which is the need of the day to take surplus labour off agriculture.

The National Forest Policy, 1988 provides that diversion of good and productive agricultural lands to forestry should be discouraged in view of the need for increased food production. The rich farmers can provide investments required for tree growing more easily than by poor farmers. It is observed that relatively wealthier farmers could benefit more than poorer farmers because of inequitable patterns of land ownership and the difficulties in marketing. In some areas, however, small farmers also took to tree growing.

On the whole, agro-forestry has picked up and about 50 percent of the planting done after 1980 is reported to be under agro-forestry. The profitability of agro-forestry under reasonable conditions is quite high . The experience of Andhra Pradesh shows that through the use of improved planting material, yield of Eucalyptus could be improved from 7 to 20 m/ha/yr. Expansion of agro-forestry will require extension support; supply of genetically improved good quality planting stock, marketing support, and above all, removal of restrictions on harvesting and sale of trees and timber. The MoEF has the mandate to bring one third of geographical area of the country under forest and tree cover. The SFDs have only 23 percent of geographical area under their control and hence to achieve the target, afforestation is required to be done outside the designated forestlands. The land where planting could be done include panchayat land, revenue land, land with other departments, institutions, private land and agriculture farms. Since more than 46.6 percent of land is under agriculture, farmers can grow trees simultaneously with agricultural crops.

However, the farmers would grow commercially important

species only if they would get remunerative price for their produce and are free to fell and transport wherever they plant. Non-availability of quality planting stock of commercially important species, inadequate extension services on the benefits of planting tree species, and restrictions on felling and transport imposed by the States under different forestry related enactments, lack of market linkages, etc., are some of the constraints which discourage bringing more area under farm forestry.

11.10 Social Forestry

11.10.1Introduction: Social forestry was first recognized as an important component of forestry for meeting rural needs in the interim report of the National Commission on Agriculture (NCA), 1972. The objectives of social forestry adopted by the NCA were to fulfil the basic and economic needs of the community.

The scope of social forestry defined by the NCA included farm forestry, community woodlots and reforestation in degraded lands. By mid-1980, the concept of social forestry was firmly established as forestry 'for the people, with the people and by the people'.

11.10.2 Farm Forestry: The tree planting programme called farm forestry was kicked off in the late 1970s with a view to fulfil the subsistence needs of rural households for fodder and fuel. The NCA noted that any programme of planting trees on farms should serve the following general objectives:

- To supplement the production of fuel wood and small timber to meet increasing requirements.
- To release cow dung for use as manure.
- To increase the production of leaf fodder.
- To create a diverse eco-system by having trees interspersed with cultivation to create wind breaks.

11.10.3 Community Woodlots: The community woodlots, which were conceptualized to be plantations of fuel wood species on community village lands, had an intended objective of increasing a villager's access to fuel wood, fruits and fodder. This component was assumed to have the greatest potential for addressing the fuel wood problem. The steps recommended by the NCA were that mixed forestry in village where wastelands should be acceptable to the people, and only quick growing species and those whose products of immediate concern should be taken up for planting, with optimum input and technology.

11.10.4 Rehabilitation of Degraded Forests: As a third component, the interim report of the NCA suggested reforestation of degraded forests to achieve the following objectives:

- To grow short rotation fuel and timber species for meeting the requirements.
- To organize fuel wood supplies at reasonable rates, which will prevent pilferage from neighbouring commercial forests.
- To tie up degraded forest areas with the nearby rural and semi-urban centres for their requirements of fuel wood.
- To provide employment.
- To rehabilitate the degraded forests in the process.

11.11 Forestry Institutions in India

The forest and wildlife resources of the States/Union Territories cannot be administered and managed efficiently in isolation by the State Forest Departments (SFDs) without the support of various training and research institutes. For this purpose, there exist many institutions whose role, mandate, weaknesses and requirements are described below.

11.11.1 Indira Gandhi National Forest Academy, Dehradun: The erstwhile Indian Forest College, Dehradun, established in 1938 to train officers of the superior forest service in India, was upgraded as the Indira Gandhi National Forest Academy (IGNFA) in May 1987, to function as a staff college for the Indian Forest Service (IFS). The Academy is directly under the administrative control of the MoEF. It is headed by a Director assisted by an Additional Director and other staff. The academic faculty includes two Professors, twelve Associate Professors, two Assistant Professors and a Sports Officer. The IFS officers are appointed as the Director, Additional Director and to faculty positions, by the MoEF under the Central Staffing Scheme (CSS) for IFS officers, for fixed tenures. Assistant Professors and the Sports Officer are recruited through the Union Public Service Commission, or on a deputation basis. The other administrative staff constitutes the permanent staff. The Academy also invites guest faculty as having expertise in various fields. It is funded by the MoEF through an annual budget of about Rs. 5.00 crore under the Plan and Rs. 3.00 crore under non-plan budget heads.

The objectives of the Academy is to prepare a cadre of competent forest officers to manage India's forest resources and serve as an apex institution for capacity building among forestry personnel. To address these needs, the Academy conducts the following training courses:

- Forestry induction training for IFS probationers.
- Professional skill upgradation course for SFS officers inducted into the IFS.
- Advanced Forest Management (AFM) courses for the IFS officers in their 10th, 17th and 21st years of service
- Organizing workshops and seminars on various emerging issues in forestry, wildlife and environment.
- Theme-based short-term refresher training courses

11.11.2 Directorate of Forest Education, Dehradun: After reorganization of the Forest Research Institute and Colleges and the creation of an Indian Council of Forestry Research and Education (ICFRE) under the MoEF in the year 1987, the Directorate was de-linked from the Forest Research Institute and Colleges. It now functions under the direct administrative control of the MoEF and is funded through regular budgetary provisions. The average annual budget under the Plan is Rs. 01.50 crore and Rs. 2.00 crore under non-plan.

The Directorate is responsible for the following:

- Conducting induction training for the direct recruits to the State Forest Service (SFS) and in the Eastern Forest Rangers College, Kurseong, for Forest Range Officers (FROs) and exercising technical control over the induction training for the FROs being organized by the colleges under the State Governments.
- Conducting in-service training for SFS officers and FROs, and organizing courses for the frontline staff, (Deputy FROs, Foresters and Forest Guards), in the form of short term refresher and theme-based courses.

At present there are three SFS colleges at Burnihat, Coimbatore and Dehradun and one Forest Rangers College, namely, the Eastern Forest Rangers College, Kurseong, under the control of the Directorate. Besides, the technical control over the State-run Ranger colleges vests with the Directorate. The IFS officers are appointed as Director, Forest Education (DFE), principals of colleges and lecturers by the MoEF under the CSS for the IFS officers on central deputation basis for fixed tenures. Some of the faculty positions are filled from among the SFS officers and FROs and other permanent faculty posts for fixed tenures and on a permanent basis. The Directorate also invites guest faculty for imparting lectures to trainees on specific topics.

11.11.3 Indian Council of Forestry Research and Education, Dehradun: The Indian Council of Forestry Research and Education (ICFRE) was constituted in December 1986 and has eight research institutes and three advanced research centres. It was subsequently granted autonomy during June 1991. The institutes are located at Dehradun, Shimla, Ranchi, Jorhat, Jodhpur, Bangalore and Coimbatore and the research centres at Allahabad, Chhindwara and Hyderabad. MoEF has also approved establishment of a new Advanced Research Centre for Bamboos and Rattans at Aizawl, Mizoram under the Regional Forest Research Institute (RFRI), Jorhat. The objectives of the council are to undertake, aid, promote and coordinate forestry education, research and its applications; develop and maintain a national library and information centre for forestry research and allied sciences; act as a clearing-house for research and general information, and develop forestry extension programmes and propagate the same and to provide consultancy services in the field of forestry research, education and training and allied sciences.

The activities of the Council are governed by the ICFRE Society and a Board of Governors (BOG), which oversees planning, administration and financing of the Council. The DG, ICFRE is the chief executive of the Council. The scientific, technical and administrative personnel of the Council include a permanent cadre of scientists, technical staff and the IFS officers/SFS officers appointed for fixed tenures. The recruitment is made on the recommendations of the various selection committees constituted for the purpose.

The vision of the Council is to assist in efforts to increase the forest cover and enhance forest productivity through operationalising the National Forestry Action Programme (NFAP) and the National Forestry Research Plan (NFRP). The NFRP launched in May 2000, has plan component of five years and a vision of 20 years. There are 588 prioritized research projects for the current action plan and the cost implications are to the tune of about Rs. 234 crore.

The FRI, Dehradun has been granted the status of a 'deemed university' in December 1991. The university at present conducts three postgraduate degree and three diploma courses, apart from awarding doctorate degrees. The main source of funding of the Council is through grants-in-aid by the MoEF. The levels of annual grants-in-aid are on an average of about Rs. 35 crore under plan and Rs. 12 crore under non-plan. In addition, the Council generates its own resources through undertaking projects from user agencies, including a few externally aided projects.

11.11.4 Indian Institute of Forest Management, Bhopal: The Indian Institute of Forest Management (IIFM), was established as an autonomous institution in 1982 under the MoEF. The objectives of the Institute are to provide training in management and related subjects to persons and personnel of forest related industries with a view to equip them to practice the profession of forest management, prepare outstanding talented persons for careers leading to management responsibilities in forestry and forest-related systems, to provide up-to-date information on forest management and to carry out research in matters concerning management and in allied techniques and methods conducive to the development of forestry. Activities of the Institute are governed by the IIFM Society and a Board of Governors (BOG) which oversees planning, administration and financing of the Institute. The Institute is headed by a Director on deputation for a fixed tenure. The personnel of the Institute include administrative staff, a permanent faculty and IFS officers on deputation.

The level of annual grant-in-aid from the MoEF is approximately Rs. 04.00 crore under Plan and Rs. 80 lakh under non-plan. The Institute has established two corpus funds, one SIDA corpus fund for payment of stipends to candidates undergoing post-graduate programme in forestry management and the other with the revenue generated through various sources, to be utilized for self-sustenance of the Institute once an adequate corpus in built. Major activities include organizing courses on post-graduate programmes in forestry management, courses in natural resource management, programmes in general management, sectoral management and functional management; research projects of interdisciplinary nature and consultancies of multi-disciplinary nature

11.11.5 Indian Plywood Industries Research and Training Institute, Bangalore: The Indian Plywood Manufacturers' Research Association (IPMRA) was formed in 1962 as a co-operative research laboratory under the umbrella of the CSIR, for undertaking applied research on plywood. It was re-designated as Indian Plywood Industries Research Institute (IPIRTI) in 1970. Its administrative control was transferred to the Ministry of Industries in 1978. Recognizing its greater role in conservation of a natural resource, its administrative control was further transferred to the MoEF during 1990. The activities of the Institute are governed by the IPIRTI Society and there is a Board of Governors which oversees its planning, administration and financing. The Institute is headed by a Director on deputation for a fixed tenure. The other personnel of the Institute include permanent administrative, technical and scientific staff. The level of annual grant-in-aid under plan is Rs. 02.50 crore and under non-plan is Rs. 01.00 crore approximately.

The Institute has been established with the objective to undertake research on all aspects of production of sawn timber, manufacturing of plywood and other allied engineered products.

11.11.6 Wildlife Institute of India, Dehradun: The Wildlife Institute of India (WII) was set up at Dehradun in 1982 and was accorded autonomy in April 1986. It has a mandate to produce a cadre of trained wildlife managers and field biologists who could collect scientific information on wildlife and PAs for their effective management, and to train personnel at various levels for nature conservation. It advises governments on matters of conservation and management of wildlife resources and PAs. In more than 20 years of its existence it has trained 756 wildlife managers. Sixty-eight students have done their post graduation in wildlife sciences.

The activities of the Institute are governed by the WII Society and there is a Board of Governors which oversees planning, administration, and financing. The Institute is headed by a Director. The faculty includes both wildlife scientists and IFS officers on deputation. The Institute is funded through grants-in-aid by the MoEF and it also generates its own finances through consultancy services, organizing training and undertaking research projects. The level of annual support by the MoEF is about Rs. 10.00 crore under plan and Rs. 1.00 crore under non-plan. WII's research projects being conducted in the field are primary sources of scientific information.

11.11.7 Forest Survey of India, Dehradun: The Forest Survey of India (FSI) was created in June 1981 with the objective of monitoring, periodically, the changing situation of land and forest resources and present the data for national planning, for conservation and management of forests and the environment. After a critical review of its activities, the FSI was re-organized during 1986. The revised objectives of FSI are the following:

- Prepare a comprehensive State of Forest Report (SFR) including a National Forest Vegetation Map (NFVM) once every two years.
- Collect, store and retrieve necessary forestry and forestry related data for national and State level planning.
- Design methodologies for forest surveys and undertake their subsequent updating.
- Undertake work with regard to preparation of forest inventories in selected States/Union Territories until the establishment of their own resource survey units.
- Impart training in modern forest survey techniques to Foresters at various levels.
- Advise the States/Union Territories on the design and development of basic and regional national forest inventory systems.
- Support and oversee related techniques and inventory work undertaken by the SFDs.

The FSI is headed by a Director with headquarters at Dehradun. It has four zonal offices, each headed by an Additional Director, located at Shimla, Kolkata, Nagpur and Bangalore. The IFS officers are appointed on deputation. One Deputy Director (Statistics) is drawn from the Indian Statistical Service on deputation. Other administrative and technical staff is appointed on permanent as well as on a deputation basis. Major functions of each zonal office are to organize fieldwork to collect inventory data, interpretation of aerial photographs and to conduct wood consumption studies.

The FSI is directly under the control of the MoEF and funded through regular budgetary provisions.

11.12 Forest Administration in India

11.12.1 Indian Forest Service: Forest administration in India is more than a century old. It was established towards the middle of the 19th century with the need to exploit forests for the construction of railways and other requirements. A Forest Department under the Government of India (GOI) to deal with all matters related to forests in the Provinces, was created in November 1864 and Dietrich Brandis was appointed as the first Inspector General of Forests (IGF). The IGF was not vested with any power of control over forest management under the Provincial governments.

Initially, appointments to the forest service were made from amongst the police, army or other branches of public services. The Indian Forest Service (IFS) was created and the first batch of IFS officers was deputed for training to France and Germany in 1867. Training was continued in Europe up to 1886 and thereafter it was arranged in the United Kingdom. From 1926 to 1932, IFS probationers were trained at Dehradun. With the Indianisation of the IFS in 1922, 40 percent of the vacancies were reserved for Indians. In a period of 65 years, 860 IFS probationers were trained giving a yearly average of nine officers; abnormal recruitment of 178 officers in five years (1921-25) took place to meet post-war requirements.

Recruitment to IFS was discontinued in 1930 and the last batch completed training in 1932. The IFS was constituted again in 1966. Its recruitment is done by the Central government, but each State has a separate cadre. Joint cadres also exist in respect of Union Territories and some of the States.

11.13 Forest Cover Target of the Eleventh Five Year Plan

The monitorable target of the Eleventh Five Year Plan is

to increase the forest cover by 5 percent of the total geographical area. This would require an additional cover of about 16 million hectare.

12

Mineral Resources

12.1 Mineral Wealth of India

Mining activity provides large employment, much of it in backward areas. It also provides, together with agriculture, the raw materials required by industry. In fact, mining provides the sinews for all industrial growth by way of inputs for energy and metal based industries. Since minerals are essentially *wasting assets*, their use requires to be regulated in the interest of conservation.

Mineral resources are non-renewable and therefore call for more vigorous and sustained efforts for the discovery and exploration of mineral deposits, scientifically planned demand management, and replacement by substitutes. Mineral exploration activities are risky ventures with long gestation period and need huge investment.

Prior to Independence, mineral rights in the permanent settlement areas vested with the zamindars. In the rest of British India and the princely states, mineral rights vested with the Provincial Governments and the princely states.

During the Second World War various regulatory steps were taken in consultation with the Provinces/States, mainly in respect of minerals required for the war effort. After the war, the interim Government convened a Mineral Policy Conference in January 1947, in recognition of the importance of the development of mining. Later, after Independence, the Central Government enacted the Mines and Minerals (Regulation and Development) Act in 1948 followed by the framing of Mineral Concession Rules (MC Rules) in April 1949, for regulating the grant of prospecting licences and mining leases for minerals other than petroleum and natural gas. The Indian Mines Act was passed in March 1952 to deal with mine safety and associated regulations.

Amongst natural resources, minerals form a special category as they are wasting assets. Once they are taken out of the ground and utilised, they are lost for ever. They should, therefore, be treated on a different footing from replenishable natural resources. Minerals figure in the export trade of India and contribute to the earning of foreign exchange. They are exported, however, largely in the raw state.

Coal, iron ore, manganese ore, mica, limonite and kyanite are produced in quantities of real importance to industry and other sectors of economy. Of these, mica, manganese ore, kyanite and limonite are wholly or largely exported. Private sector participation in coal mines has been allowed in recent years to fill the gap between coal demand and production.

Mineral wealth of India, though by no means inexhaustible, comprises an adequate range of useful products that are necessary for the industrial development of the country. An appraisal of the reserves shows that while in respect of minerals essential for basic industries—coal and iron—the reserves are ample, the country is deficient in a fairly long list of vital minerals like ores of copper, tin, lead, zinc, nickel, cobalt and in sulphur and most important of all, petroleum. The position with regard to aluminium ore, refractories, abrasives, limestone etc. may be considered as fairly adequate while in respect of titanium and thorium ores and of mica, the country has considerable reserves.

As minerals form the basis of modern industry in peace and in war, it is necessary to have a rational policy as regards their working and utilisation. The keynote of this policy should be conservation and economic working. Excepting the requirements of sulphur, petroleum and copper and other non-ferrous metals, India has the basic mineral and power resources needed for the industrial expansion envisaged.

Accelerated growth rate of Indian economy needs rapid development of the mining sector, on which most of the basic industries depend. Efforts for locating minerals since

Independence have enhanced reserves for various minerals like mica, barites, chromite (metallurgical), coal (thermal), lignite, bauxite (metallurgical), manganese ore and iron ore, and have placed the country among top ten producers of these minerals. However, in respect of fertilizer minerals, diamond, gold, nickel, copper, lead, zinc, platinum group of metals and rare metals there has hardly been any discovery despite an extremely favourable geological environment.

With the surge in demand for metals in response to strong economic growth, it has become necessary to mount a well-planned, comprehensive and time-bound programme for regional and detailed exploration for locating and delineating the country's hidden mineral deposits, which are likely to be considerable.

Geological Survey of India, Indian Bureau of Mines, State Directorates of Mines and Geology, State Mining Corporations, Central Public Sector Undertakings and private and joint venture exploration and mining companies are the key players in the mineral sector.

12.2 Profiling of Important Minerals

12.2.1 Coal: Coal is India's most important mineral asset and is the main source of commercial energy. The overall coal resources are highly concentrated. About 80 per cent of the present supply comes from a group of mines in a 200-mile section of Bihar and West Bengal, thereby making it necessary for coal to be hauled over long distances for consumption in Southern and Western India.

The Coal Mines Conservation and Safety Act, 1952 provides for the adoption and enforcement of methods of conservation in regard to coal.

Private sector participation in coal mines has been allowed in recent years to fill the gap between coal demand and production. It makes, therefore, imperative to bring in necessary legislative changes to the existing legal framework to facilitate private sector participation in coal production and distribution. Action has already been initiated to achieve this objective. Efforts would need to be made to further streamline the administrative procedures to expedite the necessary clearances and required legislative changes.

The role of private sector at present is limited to the extent of allocating captive mines for power generation, steel plants and for cement making. Private participation should be encouraged in coal mining in the years to come. Regulatory mechanism will have to be created to ensure proper and systematic development and exploitation of coal mines, and appropriate pricing of different grades of coal (including fixing of royalty) so that the consumers benefit and greater competition is encouraged. A proper evaluation of recoverable reserves is also important for the purpose of fixing of royalty, the basis of which should not be the quantity of coal actually mined but the recoverable reserves.

12.2.2 Petroleum and Natural Gas: Next to coal, petroleum and natural gas are major sources of commercial energy. So far India has not developed any considerable domestic petroleum supplies. The country is heavily dependent on imports of crude oil and petroleum products and this dependence will increase in the years to come. As a result, there is substantial foreign exchange outgo. Raising of domestic oil production, setting up of refineries, laying pipeline for transportation of gas as well as oil products will raise the requirement for investible resources.

The indigenous crude oil production will have to be augmented by acceleration of exploration efforts in deep off-shore, unexplored/less explored off-shore as well as on-shore areas, improving reservoir management and enhanced oil recovery (EOR). A New Exploration Licensing Policy (NELP) with certain fiscal and financial incentives has been announced recently to boost investment in exploration. This should help in accretion of the hydrocarbon reserves. The average recovery factor in India is low by international standards. An improvement in the recovery factor would give additional amount of oil without corresponding accretion of reserves. In the wake of the ongoing liberalisation programme, the petroleum industry (both upstream and the downstream) has been thrown open to private sector participation (both Indian and foreign). The response, particularly in the downstream sector, has been encouraging.

A large amount of gas was being flared till the late 1980s. However, in recent years flaring has declined. Gas utilisation would improve further with the commissioning of gas compression and evacuation facilities as well as augmentation of existing pipeline network.

In order to meet the increasing demand for oil products, additional infrastructure, viz. port handling facilities for crude oil and petroleum products, pipelines, tankers, rail wagons etc. will have to be established and this will involve large financial requirements. Joint ventures among public sector undertakings as well as between the public and private sector undertakings could go a long way to finance these activities.

The prices of oil products continue to be largely administered. In view of the greater need for raising the resources for expansion of oil sector as well as large-scale private sector participation, it is important that the present administered pricing regime (APR) is dismantled at the earliest. The initial steps in this direction have already been taken and these need to be carried through to the logical conclusion. Since the country is a net importer of crude oil as well as petroleum products, border prices should be the guiding principle in fixing the prices of crude oil as well as petroleum products in the economy.

Recent Initiatives in Oil and Gas: Lately, the Government has taken a number of steps to control and regulate the volatility in petroleum prices and augment production of oil and natural gas. Some of these measures are listed below.

1. Petroleum and Natural Gas Regulatory Act, 2006 was notified on April 3, 2006 to regulate specific activities relating to petroleum, petroleum products and natural gas

consequent to deregulation of the petroleum sector.

2. Taking into account the oil security of India, Government has decided to set up strategic crude oil storage facility of 5 million tonnes at various locations in the country.
3. Sale of 5 percent ethanol blended petrol in various parts of the country was allowed, subject to commercial viability, from November 1, 2006.
4. Sixth Round of New Exploration Licensing Policy (NELP) was launched on February 23, 2006 by offering 55 exploration blocks covering an area of 3.52 lakh square kilometres.
5. Coal Bed Methane (CBM) has emerged as another alternative viable source of gas. The third round of CBM-II policy was launched, and 10 CBM blocks were awarded.
6. On December 20, 2006 Government notified the Policy for Development of Natural Gas Pipelines and City or Local Natural Gas Distribution Networks, which, inter alia, seeks to promote competition and arm's length business.
7. ONGC Videsh Limited (OVL) has presence in 15 countries and has set a target to acquire 20 million tonnes per annum of oil and oil equivalent gas production by 2020.

12.2.3 Iron Ore: Iron ore resources identified so far and estimated on the UNFC basis as on April 1, 2005 are about 14,630 million tonnes of haematite ore and about 10,619 million tones of magnetite ores. Unlike haematite, almost the entire magnetite resource is still to be converted to reserves. Even the small proportion, which has been converted so far by NMDC is in the Western Ghats biodiversity area and is presently not available for extraction because of the ban imposed by the Supreme Court for reasons of environmental protection.

Due to the increase in the demand and production of steel worldwide and particularly in China, there was considerable buoyancy in the production and exports of iron ore in recent years.

12.2.4 Manganese Ore: All India total resources of manganese ore as on April 1, 2005 are 380 million tonnes. Out of these, 37.29 percent are in reserve category and balance 62.71 percent in remaining resource category. Of the total resources, the blast furnace grade constituted 130.2 million tonnes, medium grade 31.63 million tones and ferro-manganese grade 25.3 million tonnes.

12.2.5 Chromite: The all India total resources of chromite are 232.12 million tonnes as on April 1, 2005, of which 28.48 percent are in the reserve category and 71.52 percent are remaining resources. Bulk of the resources i.e. 93.38 percent are located in Orissa. Out of the 161 million tonnes of resources in leasehold, 33.67 percent are in public sector, and 66.33 percent in private sector. Chromite deposits associated with Iron Ore Group are the most important. Among them two belts namely Sukinda Ultramafic Belt and Nausahi Ultramafic Belt of Orissa contain about 97 percent of total Indian resources of chromite.

12.2.6 Bauxite: The all India total resources of Bauxite as on April 1, 2005 are 3,306 million tonnes. Out of these, 915 million tonnes are under reserve category and the balance 2,392 million tones under remaining resource category. Out of the lease hold resources of 1079 million MT, 41.94 percent are in public sector and 49.06 percent in private sector. Out of the total resources, 54.35 percent are in captive and 45.65 percent in non-captive sector. Out of the public sector resources of 453 million tonnes, 300 million tonnes are in captive area.

12.2.7 Copper Ore: The all India total resources of copper ore as on April 1, 2005 are 1,394 million tonnes, with a metal content of 11.41 million tonnes. Out of these, 369.5 million tonnes of ore with a metal content of 4.4 million tonnes is under reserve category and the balance in remaining resource category.

Hindustan Copper Ltd., a CPSE, is the only undertaking mining copper ore in the country. Most of the copper deposits under mining have been explored in detail. Exploration activities have also led to discovery of small deposits in Western, Eastern, Southern and Central Precambrian shield areas of the country. It is necessary to intensify exploration activities for copper and for this HCL could enter into joint ventures with specialized companies abroad that have the technology to undertake exploration activity using the latest techniques.

12.2.8 Non- ferrous Metals:

A. Aluminum: Panchpatmali bauxite mine of NALCO in Orissa accounts for about 40 percent of the country's production. It is a world class fully mechanized mine with existing capacity of 4.8 million tonnes per annum. There are six alumina refineries owned by five aluminium companies in the country, namely NALCO, HINDALCO, INDAL, BALCO and MALCO.

B. Copper: India has substantial capacity in the production of primary copper metal but is significantly dependent on the import of copper metal-in-concentrates (MIC). Although India is dependent on imports of copper concentrate, its smelting capacity in the metal grew almost threefold and production by about 60 percent during the Tenth Five Year Plan period.

C. Lead and Zinc: The all India total resources of Lead-zinc ore are 522 million tonnes with 7.2 million tonnes of lead metal and 24.25 million tonnes of zinc metal. Out of the total resources, 126 million tonnes with 2.6 million tonnes of lead metal and 11.0 million tones of zinc metal are under reserve category. Out of the total resources, 352.82 million tonnes with 3.7 million tonnes of lead metal and 8.99 million tonnes of zinc metal are in freehold sector. In the leasehold, the total resources are 169.7 million tonnes with 3.5 million tonnes of lead metal and 15.26 million tonnes of zinc metal.

After privatization, HZL expanded its zinc mining and used the mineral from its captive Rampura Agucha mines to expand smelting.

12.3 Mines and Minerals (Development and Regulation) Act, 1957

Mines and Minerals (Regulation and Development) Act, 1948 which was subsequently amended and elaborated in 1957, and the rules framed thereunder brought a measure of uniformity in regard to leasing of mineral properties and for ensuring systematic development of the mineral resources of the country.

In keeping with the spirit of economic liberalisation, the Government has taken a series of initiatives under the overall framework of the National Mineral Policy, 1993 for the growth of the mineral sector. It amended the Mines and Minerals (Regulation and Development) Act, 1957 in 1994 and 1999 and renamed it as the Mines and Minerals (Development and Regulation) Act (MMDR Act). The amendments were aimed at attracting private investment including foreign direct investment (FDI) into the sector.

12.4 Offshore Areas Mineral (Development and Regulation) Act, 2002

The Act notified on January 31, 2003 provides for the development and regulation of mineral resources in the territorial waters, continental shelf, and the exclusive economic zone of India. The legislation would enable streamlining of mineral exploration and development in the offshore areas and ensure systematic and scientific exploitation of mineral reserves (except petroleum, natural gas and hydrocarbon resources) for attracting private investment in the offshore mineral sector.

In 2000, the ceiling of 74 percent on FDI in exploration and mining of diamonds and precious stones was removed though it continued to require approval of Foreign Investment Promotion Board (FIPB). In 2006, this restriction too was removed and all FDI in the mining sector, including FDI above 74 percent in mining of diamonds and precious stones, is now on the automatic route.

However, the actual flows have been minimal in the absence of policies conducive to FDI for prospecting. Attracting FDI into exploration and prospecting will require a revision of the current mining regime and adoption of a multi-disciplinary approach, embracing the legal framework, technology, sustainability, infrastructure and procedural streamlining.

12.5 High Level Committee on National Mineral Policy, 2006

For a comprehensive review of the National Mineral Policy and for suggesting possible amendments to the Mines and Minerals (Development and Regulation) Act, 1957, the Planning Commission constituted a High Level Committee under the Chairmanship of Sh. Anwarul Hoda, Member (Industry), Planning Commission. The High Level Committee submitted its Report to the Government on July 19, 2006. The Committee recommended a number of changes in the National Mineral Policy and in the relevant laws and rules to bring them in line with international best practices. For augmenting State revenues from the mineral sector, the Committee recommended that the method of fixation of royalty should move decisively toward ad valorem rates, away from the tonnage system currently prevailing for a number of economically important minerals.

Main recommendations of the Committee were as under:

1. Mining involves broadly three stages, reconnaissance, prospecting and mining proper. The transition from Reconnaissance Permit (RP) to Prospecting License (PL) to Mining Leases (ML) should be seamless, by giving the right to the RP holder to get a PL and to the PL holder to get a ML.
2. Provisions in the Act and the Rules that enable the Centre and the States to abridge and even cancel the concession should be amended so that concessionaires have security of tenure.

3. RPs should be non-exclusive with an open sky policy to maximise investment in exploration.
4. Prospecting companies should have a right to transfer the PL with the accompanying right to be granted a ML. Easy transferability of concessions would result in unbundling of exploration from exploitation activity and stimulate investment in exploration.
5. Where a State Government has not passed an order within the prescribed time frame the Central Government may pass an appropriate order, after giving an opportunity to the State Government of being heard.
6. Mining companies should develop the social infrastructure in the villages in the area where the mine is situated. One option suggested by the Committee is that mining companies should spend three per cent of the turnover on the social infrastructure in the villages.
7. The method of fixing Royalty rates should be ad valorem rates so as to substantially augment State revenues.
8. Where a mineral-rich State receives multiple applications, it should be entitled to give preference to the applicant who offers to set up an industry based on the mineral. However, where no applicants have made a proposal for setting up an industry, these should not be held up in the expectation that in future such an applicant might turn up.
9. In the best interest of the country the mining policy should provide space for both stand-alone and captive mines.
10. The regime of quantitative restrictions and canalization of iron ore exports should be replaced by an export duty (only on high grade lumps with Fe content of 65 per cent and above) and elimination of restrictions on fines and lower grade fines.

12.6 Why is Mining Sector Investment Shy?

The main reason for the lack of private sector investment in exploration and mining activity is that there is no assurance that the reconnaissance permit (RP) holder will get the prospecting licence (PL) and the PL holder will get the mining lease (ML). Further, even after an entrepreneur gets the ML, several discretionary provisions in the statutes pose a threat to the ML holder's security of tenure.

Even though the Regulations contain time limits for the State Government in disposing of applications they may defer indefinitely a decision on an application for RP/PL/ML in the hope that applications would come in future from value-adders.

Procedural delays in the disposal of applications occur for a number of reasons. One of them is that a great deal of time is taken for the verification of mineral titles. The availability of a spatially represented, easily accessible registry of all pending and granted exploration titles is a key part of a modern regulatory system.

Several State Government undertakings are involved in mining activity and since the State is also a regulator the State's involvement in mining, in competition with private mining companies can become a disincentive for private sector investment.

While deficiencies in arterial roadways, railways and port infrastructure need to be addressed by the Central Government, equally crucial for the development of mining is infrastructure that links mines to the arterial routes. While the Central Government is providing funds for arterial routes, there is a need for funds for linking infrastructure as well.

12.7 Mineral Development and Environmental Protection

Mineral development faces opposition in the country on two accounts. First, there is scepticism about mining operations being done in a manner that does not have an adverse impact on the environment. Second, there is a feeling among project-affected persons that they have not received enough compensation. More importantly, there are unfulfilled expectations from mining companies for providing development services in return for the social licence to operate the mines.

There are two statutes viz. the Forest (Conservation) Act, 1980 and the Environment (Protection) Act, 1986, which lay down the law that must be followed in the development of mines. A criticism that has been made is that the two statutes have a preoccupation with two concerns, namely compensation for diversion of forest land to non-forest use in various forms (including compensatory afforestation) and the need for environment impact studies prior to the grant of environmental clearances. The best practice internationally goes much beyond these concerns. Worldwide, mining interventions are becoming increasingly sophisticated and the objective is 'to ensure that the critical natural capital is maintained, that ecosystems are enhanced where possible, and that mineral wealth contributes to net environmental continuity.

As for relief and rehabilitation, various mineral rich States already have in position policies and executive orders that lay down the entitlements of the project affected persons. But the practice in the country falls short of that prevailing internationally in mining sector interventions. The international best practices include 2 percent to 3 percent of the turnover of mining companies being expended on social infrastructure in the region, a direct financial stake in the mining venture to indigenous communities (e.g. tribals) in the form of equity and all this is in addition to fair compensation to project-affected persons by way of cash, housing and jobs.

Mining companies in India now under statutory obligations, routinely undertake welfare measures for the development of entire local communities. However, these are unorganized ad hoc initiatives that are voluntary in nature and for which there is no accountability to outside agencies. It is necessary to have a formalized framework so that standards are laid down and adherence to the standards ensured.

In order to enhance the contribution of mining to the enrichment of the environment and improve the well-being of the indigenous communities beyond what the current law and policy provides, the High Level Committee on the Mineral Policy has recommended that a framework should be prepared and adapted to the Indian mining context on the basis of the Sustainable Development Framework (SDF) developed by the International Council of Mining and Metals (ICMM) and the International Union for the Conservation of Nature and Natural Resources (IUCN).

Once such a framework has been prepared under which, all mining lease holders would be required to adhere to it as a condition of their lease. The Government would establish a mechanism for monitoring such adherence in a participative mode along with NGOs and PAPs.

12.8 Tenth Five Year Plan (2002-07) on Mineral Sector Policy

Mid-Term Appraisal of the Tenth Plan released by the Government in June 2005 observed as follows, "There is tremendous scope for attracting investments, both domestic and FDI, and associated new technology in mineral exploration and mining. However investments and injection of new technology in this sector are held up by excessively complicated procedures with considerable duplication at the State and National level. Most mineral resources occur in forest areas and clearance from forest and environmental angle compound the problem. Weaknesses in infrastructures (power, roads and rail in particular) are another big constraint. The current policies suffer from a bias against issue of large mining leases consistent with development of mines with application of new technology. The procedure regarding environmental and forest clearances is also non-transparent and highly dilatory. A high level committee needs to be set up for reviewing the National Mineral Policy and to suggest measures including possible amendments to the Mines and Minerals Development and Regulation Act and also in other Acts or procedures to attract adequate investment in this sector." [1]

12.9 Mineral Sector Objectives of Eleventh Five Year Plan (2007-12)

The following are the main objectives of the Eleventh Five Year Plan in the mining sector:

1. "Intensification of exploration for low volume high value minerals like gold, diamond, base metals and platinum group of minerals and efforts towards augmentation of the existing resources in respect of ferrous and non-ferrous minerals and industrial minerals.
2. Improvement of the National Mineral Inventory particularly for those minerals in which reserves are low such as base metals, nickel, tin, graphite, noble metals, precious stones and rock phosphate.
3. Restructuring and modernization of the Geological Survey of India in the areas of instrumentation for both ground and airborne surveys, and acquisition of State of–the-art laboratory facilities with high precision capabilities. Establishment of a comprehensive portal giving meta data in respect of regional exploration work done by GSI and the scope for investment based on such work.
4. Modernisation of the Indian Bureau of Mines and the State Directorates for establishment of a national registry (Cadastre) and a Mineral Atlas. The database would comprise both physical and resource inventory and include a Tenement Registry with details of green field areas, brown field areas and relinquished areas including areas identified by the GSI as not worth pursuing. The data would be maintained online giving instant information to prospective investors on what is available for reconnaissance, prospecting and mining.
5. Acceleration of the process of adoption of United Nations Framework Classification (UNFC) system of classification of mineral resources so as to present reserves /resources of minerals on an internationally uniform system and help in attracting more private investment into the sector.
6. Development of minerals in the North Eastern Region with

the State s of this region playing a major role and the Central government agencies facilitating their initiatives with specific interventions.

7. Strengthening Research and Development activities in all aspects of mining." [2]

12.9.1 Eleventh Plan Strategy: Outlining its strategy for mineral development, the Plan Document noted, "Giving the technology and resource limitations of Geological Survey of India (GSI), it would be necessary to encourage private sector initiative as the main driver of investment in exploration even as the GSI is strengthened to access the latest technologies such as deep imaging and electro magnetic probing.

In line with the current economic policy, in future the core functions of the State in mining will be facilitation of exploration and mining activities of investors and entrepreneurs, provision of infrastructure, regulation and tax collection. Where it is deemed necessary for the State to continue in mining activities, there shall be arm's length between State agencies that explore and mine and those that regulate. Transparency would be maintained in the allocation of ore bodies for mining.

An environment conducive for private sector investment will be promoted by streamlining licensing procedures, granting security of tenure to RP/PL/ML holders, minimizing procedural delays and improving transport infrastructure.

It would be ensured that mining is done in a sustainable manner, without any adverse effect on the environment, by effective enforcement of the laws and by developing a Sustainable Development Framework, specially tailored to the context of India's mining environment, to be adhered to voluntarily by the mining firms.

New relief &rehabilitation norms (to be adhered to on a voluntary basis) will be developed building on the existing packages announced by the States for compensation to the project affected persons as well as for the benefit that must accrue to the communities living in the villages around the mining area." [3]

12.10 Indian Mineral Scenario, 2009-2010

Based on the overall trend so far the index of mineral production (base 1993-94=100) for the year 2009-10 is estimated to be 189.90 as compared to 175.96 for 2008-09 showing a positive growth of 7.92%. The total value of mineral production (excluding atomic minerals) during 2009-10 is estimated at Rs.1,27,921.42 crores. During 2009-10, provisional value for fuel minerals account for Rs. 79,602.69 crores or 62.23%, metallic minerals, Rs. 27571.16 crores or 21.55% of the total value and non-metallic minerals including minor minerals Rs. 20747.56 crores or 16.22% of the total value.

The number of mines which reported mineral production (excluding minor minerals, petroleum (crude), natural gas and atomic minerals) in India was 2729 in 2009-10. Out of 2729 reporting mines, 404 were located in Andhra Pradesh followed by Gujarat (398), Jharkhand (284), Madhya Pradesh (250), Rajasthan (236), Orissa (220), Karnataka (209), Maharashtra (145), Tamil Nadu (138), Chhattisgarh (126) and West Bengal (111). These 11 states together accounted for 92.38 % of total number of mines in the country in 2009-10.

During 2008-09, the Public Sector continued to play a dominant role in mineral production accounting for 72% or Rs. 76,651 crores in the total value and concentrate. By and large, almost the entire production of Lignite, Gold (primary and secondary of indigenous origin) and Gypsum was from Public Sector. In 2008-09, the Public Sector accounted for sizeable 92% production of coal, 86% of petroleum (crude), 76% of Natural gas (utilized), 80% Tin concentrate, 97% of Barytes, 83% of Kyanite, 76% of Sillemanite and 60% of Magnesite.

The value of metallic minerals in 2008-09 at Rs. 31533.97 crores increased by about 7.49% over the previous year.

12.11 Conclusion

Though in the recent past a considerable amount of work

has been done in the study of mineral resources and in assessing reserves in quantitative and qualitative terms in particular areas, in the context of rapid industrial development of the country and the consequent increasing demand for mineral raw materials, exploration for and investigation of mineral deposits requires to be pursued with greater vigour in order to know more fully the minerals available and eventually their quality and quantity.

Apart from the urgent necessity of more intensive exploration for minerals, there is need for enforcement of measures for conservation. Measures for conservation in relation to minerals will mean mainly avoidance of waste in mining and processing and in a large sense the substitution of scarce materials by those which are abundantly available in the country.

Potential of the mineral sector in the country remains largely unrealized in the absence of exploration activities on the scale needed. The public sector bodies are hamstrung by the lack of financial resources and the private sector does not find the legal framework and the procedures to be conducive for enterprise. There are other challenges as well, particularly those relating to the transport infrastructure, the protection of the environment, rehabilitation of the people displaced by the mining activity and increasing the revenue for the State governments from mining activity.

Notes

1. Government of India, Planning Commission, Mid-Term Appraisal of the Tenth Five Year Plan, June 2005, p. 19.
2. Government of India, Planning Commission, Eleventh Five Year Plan (2007-12), Vol. III, pp. 209-10.
3. Ibid., pp. 210-11.

13

Natural Ecosystems

13.1 India's Rich Ecosystems Heritage

India has an unparalleled range of natural ecosystems because of her wide latitudinal range, varied physiognomic features, diverse climatic regimes, long coastlines and tropical islands. Human societies with a long-standing conservation ethos anchored in the cultural and religious traditions of several millennia have used this natural bounty. This use has gradually given rise to rich secondary ecosystems, which have their own unique assemblages of floral and faunal communities and are the notable abodes of large agglomerations of spectacular animals and birds.

Water and fertile soil are the two most important prerequisites of India's food security. Both are irrevocably linked with forest and watershed conservation. The gravity and consequences of India's water scarcity are as yet not fully realized and hence it has not yet been universally acknowledged that the greatest product of forests—both qualitative as well as quantitative—is water. Natural vegetation, both forests and grasslands, are the prime conservers of soil and the providers of nutrients and humus. The functional lifespan of most of hydro-projects has been drastically reduced due to exponential siltation, caused by overuse and abuse of forests and rangelands.

Grasslands are the only breeding grounds of a number of avian species, whose nesting time is the monsoon. Due to the presence of crops in the fields, the monsoon is the period most affected by free-ranging livestock, who have nowhere else to go. This is the time when the grass grows. If grass is over-grazed at this time, it not only prevents fodder production and seed formation, but nests of ground-living birds are also trampled. No grasslands, however resilient, can bear the overuse and abuse that they are subjected to presently.

13.2 Animal and Plant Diversity

India is endowed with an immense variety of natural living resources in its rich animal and plant heritage, which sustains millions of its people. While the maintenance of the country's basic biological productivity through proper land and water management is of vital ecological concern, the preservation of its genetic diversity and conservation of its species and ecosystems for sustainable utilization is of crucial importance for the future survival and development of our people.

Due to disappearing species and ecosystems under the relentless pressures of an exploding population and unplanned development of natural environments, the habitats of species are being rapidly lost or modified. In India, five species of mammals and birds are known to have become extinct in the recent past while 103 such species are listed as endangered under the Wildlife (Protection) Act, 1972.

At the present inadequate level of scientific knowledge, it is difficult to know how many species of flora and fauna are threatened, endangered or extinct, but the number must be considerable in view of the very rapid shrinkage of all natural forests and other ecosystems throughout the country in recent years. With the introduction of scientific plant and animal breeding in recent decades, the inestimable value of a number of wild and unutilised relatives of domesticated plants and animals had been recognised. India abounds in such wild and semi-wild relatives whose value is still unknown and they remain untapped resources. The rich variety of citrus—the species to which oranges, limes and lemons belong—in the hills of north-east India, is an example of one such resource. Other species, which are not directly exploited by man, have contributed to his success in evolving high-yielding varieties by serving as model experimental organisms. It is, therefore, evident that the diversity of biological organisms is a vital resource which needs to be carefully protected in natural ecosystems.

The natural ecosystems represent hope for finding the basic material for restoring the health of completely devastated landscapes such as much of the Himalayan hill slopes. The forests under management have been treated from the very narrow viewpoint of production of commercial timber and pulpwood so that they have been rapidly converted into stands of teak, pine or eucalyptus with no thought given for even the maintenance of species producing valuable minor forest produce such as oilseeds. Wildlife conservation efforts have so far been primarily directed to the maintenance of areas with one or more spectacular animals such as the tiger or the rhino.

13.3 Marine Ecosystems

There is inadequate knowledge and understanding of the country's valuable marine ecosystems, and total absence of protective measures has led to wanton exploitation and destruction of these resources.

The coral reefs, rich in limestone, have been thoughtlessly plundered for the manufacture of cement in the Gulf of Mannar (Tamil Nadu) and in the Pirotan Islands (Gujarat), thus exposing the coastal areas to sea erosion. These rare and unique ecosystems need urgent protection as *marine reserves*.

Similarly, India's coastal mangroves constitute extraordinarily rich ecosystems which contain many unique species adapted to the unusual habitat and are also key nursery areas for many species of fish which need protection. These mangroves, which form a vital protection against cyclone damage, have already been lost from most of coastal areas, and now deserve full protection where they still exist.

Some of the Island ecosystems of the Andaman and Nicobar and Lakshdweep groups are very rich and delicately balanced but vulnerable to intrusions. These islands need to be scientifically surveyed and protected in appropriate reserves under technical management.

13.4 Biosphere Reserves

There is a compelling conservation need to set aside sufficient representative examples of biotic provinces to extend protection to entire community of species in viable terrestrial and marine ecosystems to be designed as *biosphere reserves*. The concept of such Reserves was evolved under UNESCO's Man and Biosphere (MAB) Programme with the following objectives:

1. To save for the present and future human use the diversity and integrity of biotic communities of plants and animals within natural ecosystems, and to safeguard the genetic diversity of species on which their continuing evolution depends.
2. To provide areas for ecological and environmental research, including baseline studies, both within and adjacent to those reserves.
3. To provide facilities for education and training. The biosphere reserves should comprise not only completely natural ecosystems but also semi-natural established land-use practices. Among such reserves, areas that have outstanding potential for restoration to natural conditions, should also be included. Biosphere reserves are not meant to substitute established national parks and sanctuaries but may often coincide partly with national parks and sanctuaries.

Preservation of the biological diversity of India would require a detailed survey and classification of the conservation and ecosystem types to ensure the conservation of as many representative examples of each as possible. In view of the virtual disappearance of many genuinely natural ecosystems in the country, those that remain in such natural or near-natural condition need to be identified for full protection as biosphere reserves with the greatest urgency. Other man-modified ecosystems, which retain their natural diversity should also be protected.

Bibliography

Bibliography

Ahuluwalia, S.S. (1998), *Employment Promotion in the Urban Informal Sector,* edited by Ramanujan et al, New Age International (P) Ltd., Delhi.

Bahuguna, Sunderlal, Vandana Shiva and M.N. Buch, *Environment Crisis and Sustainable Development*, Natraj Publishers, Dehradun, 1992.

Basu, Durga Das, *Introduction to the Constitution of India* (New Delhi: Prentice-Hall of India Private Ltd.).

Centre for Science and Environment (CSE), Proceedings of the Seminar on Traditional Water Harvesting System in India, October 9-11, New Delhi, 1990.

D'Monte, Darryl, *Ecology vs. the Economy in India*, New Leader, May 1982.

Dandekar, V.M. and N. Rath, Poverty in India, *Economic and Political Weekly*, January 1971.

Daniel M. Dworkin, *Environmental Sciences in Developing Countries*, USA, 1974.

Dasgupta, Biplab, The Environment Debate: Some Issues and Trends, *Economic and Political Weekly*, Annual 1978.

Deaton, A. and Jean Dreze, 'Poverty and Inequality in India: A Re-examination', *Economic and Political Weekly*, September 7, 2002.

Desai, Bharat, *Water Pollution in India: Law and Enforcement*, Lancers, New Delhi, 1990.

Dogra, Bharat, Environment Protection: Myths and Reality, *The Financial Express*, New Delhi, July 27, 1991.

Fernandes, Paul, Subernarekha Multipurpose Project: Towards Evolving a Strategy for the Management of Displaced Families, XLRI, Jamshedpur, 1985.

Frank, Andre Gunder and Marta Fuentes, Nine Theses on Social Movements, *Economic and Political Weekly*, August 29, 1987

Gadgil, Madhav and Ramchandra Guha, *This Fissured Land:*

An Ecological History of India, Oxford University Press, New Delhi, 1992.

Gautham Naviakha, "Urban Pollution: Driving Workers to Desperation" *Economic and Political Weekly* 35 (51) Dec. 16-22, 2000.

Government of India, *Budget Papers* (various years).

—— *Economic Survey* (various years).

—— Ministry of Labour, *Report of the National Commission on Labour* (Chairman: Ravindra Verma), 2002.

—— Planning Commission, Various Plan Documents.

Guha, Ramchandra, 'Ideological Trends in Indian Environmentalism', *Economic and Political Weekly*, vol.23, no.49, December 3, 1988.

Hammer Marks Jr and Hammer Jr Mark J, *Water and Waste Technology* Fourth Ed, Prentice Hall of India PVT Ltd, New Delhi 2002.

International Labour Office (1998), *Contract Labour*, Report to the 86th Session of the International Labour Conference, ILO, Geneva.

International Labour Organization (ILO) Convention No. 130 and Recommendation No. 69 contain guidelines for the provision of medical care under social security.

International Monetary Fund, *World Economic Outlook* (various issues).

Jadhav H.V., *Environmental Pollution* Himalaya Publishing house IST Ed 1995, Bombay.

Jerry A. Nathanson, *Basic Environmental Technology*, Fourth Edition, Prentice Hall of India PVT Ltd, New Delhi, 2002.

Khoshoo, T.N., Ecology Must Blend with Economy, *The Times of India*, New Delhi, January 4, 1992.

Kohli, Atul, The State and Poverty in India: The Politics of Reform, Cambridge University Press, Cambridge, 1987.

Kothari Commission on Educational Reforms, 1966.

Krishna Kannan, *Fundamental of Environmental Pollution*, S. Chand and Co New Delhi, 1997.

Kumar and Kakrani, *Water Environment and Pollution*, Agro

bios India, Jodhpur, 2000.

Mathur, A.N. (1992), *Employment Security and Industrial Restructuring in India: Separating Facts from Folklore - The Exit Policy Controversy,* Indian Institute of Management, Calcutta.

Naidu, D.P.A. (1999), *Contract Labour in South Asia,* Bureau for Workers Activities, International Labour Organisation, ILO, Geneva.

Punekar, S.D., Deodhar, S.B. and Sankaran, Saraswathi (1999) *Labour Welfare, Trade Unionism and Industrial Relations*, Himalaya Publishing House, New Delhi.

Singh, Shekhar, Some Aspects of the Ecological Crisis in India, *Social Scientist*, 1985.

Sodhi, J.S., Emerging Trends in Industrial Relations and Human Resource Management in Indian Industry, *Indian Journal of Industrial Relations*, Vol.30, No.1, July 1994.

United Nations, *Millennium Development Goals and the United Nations Role* (2003).

——*World Economic and Social Survey* (various years).

World Bank, Economic Development in India: Achievements and Challenges, 1996, World Bank Country Study.

——*World Development Report* (various years).

——*Gender and Poverty in India: A World Bank Country Study,* 1991.

——*India: Sustaining Reform, Reducing Poverty*, A World Bank Development Policy Review, Oxford University Press, 2003.

Index

Index

Index

Index